JOSSEY-BASS TEACHER

J ossey-Bass Teacher provides educators with practical knowledge and tools to create a positive and lifelong impact on student learning. We offer classroom-tested and research-based teaching resources for a variety of grade levels and subject areas. Whether you are an aspiring, new, or veteran teacher, we want to help you make every teaching day your best.

From ready-to-use classroom activities to the latest teaching framework, our value-packed books provide insightful, practical, and comprehensive materials on the topics that matter most to K–12 teachers. We hope to become your trusted source for the best ideas from the most experienced and respected experts in the field.

PowerPoint for Teachers

DYNAMIC PRESENTATIONS AND INTERACTIVE CLASSROOM PROJECTS (GRADES K–12)

Ellen Finkelstein
Pavel Samsonov

JOSSEY-BASS
A Wiley Imprint
www.josseybass.com

Published by Jossey-Bass
A Wiley Imprint
989 Market Street, San Francisco, CA 94103-1741 www.josseybass.com

Jossey-Bass books and products are available through most bookstores. To contact Jossey-Bass directly call our Customer Care Department within the U.S. at 800-956-7739, outside the U.S. at 317-572-3986, or fax 317-572-4002.

Jossey-Bass also publishes its books in a variety of electronic formats. Some content that appears in print may not be available in electronic books.

ISBN: 978–0–7879–9717–5

Printed in the United States of America
FIRST EDITION
PB Printing   10 9 8 7 6 5 4 3 2 1

ABOUT THIS BOOK

We wrote *PowerPoint for Teachers: Dynamic Presentations and Interactive Classroom Projects* because we saw that most information available on PowerPoint was designed for business users and believed that the business model wasn't appropriate for teachers. We also knew that teachers needed a simple way to create interactive, lively projects that would spur students to learn in an enjoyable way. Although PowerPoint was a very capable program, many teachers didn't know how to make use of its full possibilities. Besides, we knew that PowerPoint was the most common and user-friendly program available in every school in the nation. We wanted to write a book that would give teachers the tools they needed to use PowerPoint to improve their teaching outcomes.

In this book, you'll find a basic tutorial on PowerPoint for those of you who are beginners, in which you'll create a lesson on the water cycle. Then you'll find lots of specific techniques to create quizzes, games, clickable maps, menu-based resources, and even graded tests. We also discuss best practices, multimedia, research, and many online resources. You'll get age-appropriate ideas for Power-Point projects as well as ideas for teaching PowerPoint to your students. We think that *PowerPoint for Teachers* is a complete resource for all the ways you can use PowerPoint in the classroom.

THE AUTHORS

Ellen Finkelstein has written several computer books on PowerPoint (*How to Do Everything with PowerPoint 2007* and previous editions), AutoCAD, and Flash. She writes numerous articles on AutoCAD and PowerPoint, and maintains a Web site of

118247

AutoCAD and PowerPoint tips, techniques, and tutorials at www.ellenfinkelstein. com, where you can sign up for her free monthly PowerPoint Tips Newsletter or read her PowerPoint Tips Blog. She also teaches undergraduate and graduate business courses in Human Resources Management and eBusiness.

Dr. Pavel Samsonov teaches instructional technology to pre-service and in-service teachers at the University of Louisiana at Lafayette. PowerPoint in education is one of the foci of his teaching and research.

ACKNOWLEDGMENTS

My utmost appreciation goes to my co-author, Pavel Samsonov, for his creativity, intelligence, and energy. He has so many great ideas! He was also a pleasure to work with throughout the project.

Thanks to Myron B. Gershenson, who suggested in 2005 that I write a book on PowerPoint especially for educators. My great appreciation goes to David M. Marcovitz, author of *Powerful PowerPoint for Educators*, for permission to use some VBA code from his book, as well as for the thorough review he provided of Chapter 9. Chapter 9 would not have been possible without him.

Thanks to Patrick Crispen, who sent me his presentation, "How Do I Use PowerPoint to Teach" that included not only good advice but loads of scholarly references. This presentation made it clear that there was significant content to cover in a book on PowerPoint for teachers. Bob Matthews submitted two excellent presentations that he uses to teach and test high school math. Also Michiel Van Deenen sent us an awesome, but very difficult, test on PowerPoint, created, of course, in PowerPoint.

Ken Daley, a professor at Maharishi University of Management, offered me the opportunity to teach a two-day seminar on PowerPoint to the student teachers in his class. This seminar allowed me to see firsthand what worked and what didn't, and improved my understanding of how the PowerPoint techniques in this book could be helpful to teachers.

I want to thank my family for supporting me while I was writing this book. My husband, Evan, and my children, Yeshayah and Eliyah, were helpful and understanding.

— *Ellen Finkelstein*

I want to thank my research director Dr. Yvonna Lincoln of Texas A&M University for her great inspiration in my research.

I would also like to thank my wife, Pamela Gajan Samsonov, for her encouragements and ideas for the book from the perspective of a school teacher and librarian.

Special thanks to Ellen Finkelstein, who provided me with leadership, great ideas, and professional guidance in writing this book. Without Ellen I could never have written my part!

— Pavel Samsonov

Margie McAneny was our able and supportive acquisitions editor. Julia Palmer helped organize our submissions. Geetesh Bajaj did a great job as technical editor, providing many useful suggestions, as did copyeditor Sandra Beriss.

— Ellen Finkelstein and Pavel Samsonov

To MMY who has taught me how to use inner intelligence to drive outer accomplishment.

— Ellen Finkelstein

To Lesha, Masha, Oleg, Vladimir, and Grant.

— Pavel Samsonov

CONTENTS

Introduction   1
Is This Book for You?   2
Structure of the Book   2
Conventions   4
   Icons   4
   Fonts, Symbols, and More   5
Companion Web Site   5
Enjoy!   5

PART ONE Why PowerPoint?

ONE Supporting All Aspects of Learning   9
PowerPoint for All the Ways You Teach   9
   PowerPoint and the Constructivist Approach   10
   An Amazingly Versatile Tool   10
   Bet You Didn't Know . . .   11
Support for Your Instruction   11
   Value of Repetition   12
   A Picture Paints a Thousand Words   13
   Linear versus Nonlinear   15
   Teaching with Games   17
   Assessing Retention and Understanding   17
   Encouraging Problem-Based Learning   17

From Pre-K Through Ph.D.   18
    Fun in the Early Years   18
    Beginning to Think in the Lower Grades   19
    Expanding the Mind in Middle and High School 19
    Expressing Knowledge in College   20
When Not to Use PowerPoint   20
Summary   21

TWO Creating Your First Presentation   23

A Presentation to Support a Lesson on the Water Cycle   23
    Creating Your Lesson Plan   24
    Outlining Your Talk   24
    Gathering Media   24
Starting a New Presentation   26
    Creating a Title Slide   28
    Adding a Slide   28
    Choosing a Layout   30
    Adding Notes   31
    Inserting a Slide with a Specified Layout   32
Saving Your Project   33
Adding Text   36
Entering an Outline in PowerPoint   37
Moving Around a Presentation   41
Adding Images   42
    Inserting Image Files   43
    Inserting Clip Art   44
    Editing Images   45
Adding Shapes   50
    Inserting Shapes   50
    Using the Slide Master   52
    Editing and Formatting Shapes   55
    Using Charts and Diagrams   62
Adding a Background   62

Moving a Slide   69
   Using Slide Sorter View   69
   Dragging a Slide to a New Position   70
   Copying and Pasting a Slide   71
   Deleting a Slide   71
Adding Animation   71
   Adding Text Animation   72
   Adding Object Animation   73
   Adding Slide Transitions   75
Presenting the Slide Show   76
   Entering Slide Show View   77
   Navigating Through Slides   78
   Saving Your Project as a PowerPoint Show 79
Summary   79

THREE Multimedia and Learning with PowerPoint   81

What Is Multimedia?   81
Using Multimedia Effectively   82
Using Images   84
   Creating Graphs   86
   Creating Diagrams   89
Adding Sounds, Music, and Narration   92
   Adding a Sound or Music File   92
   Adding Background Music   95
   Adding Narration   97
Using Video   99
Multimedia Resources   100
Summary   101

FOUR Understanding Best Practices   103

Backgrounds   103
Age-Appropriateness   105
Special Effects   106
   Color Schemes   106

Animation Effects   107

Sounds   108

Bullets Are Boring   109

Using Text Wisely   112

The Importance of Context   113

Your Presentation   114

Viewed as a Class   115

Viewed Individually   115

Maximizing Learning   116

Helping Students Take Better Notes   116

Printing Handouts and Notes   118

Providing Electronic Access   119

The Importance of You   120

Summary   121

PART TWO Creating Great Projects Using PowerPoint

FIVE Interactive Reviews   125

Choosing the Important Points   125

Writing the Questions   126

Writing Multiple-Choice Answers   126

Interactivity   128

Adding the "Try Again!" Response   128

Creating a Link to the "Try Again!" Response   129

Creating a Back Link   132

Adding the "Good Job!" Response   139

Creating a Forward Link   139

Options for More Fun   141

Summary   142

SIX Interactive Maps   143

Creating a Geography Review   143

Selecting an Appropriate Picture   143

Copying and Pasting the Slide   144

Creating Question and Negative Feedback Slides   145
Drawing a Hot (Clickable) Spot   146
Linking the Hot Spot to Positive Feedback   147
Creating a Hot Spot for the Wrong Area   149
Adding Audio or Narration   150
Tips for More Fun   150
Summary   151

SEVEN Menu-Based Projects   153

Why Nonlinear?   153
Creating Sections   154
Adding a Menu Slide   156
Adding Hyperlinks   159
Linking from the Sections to the Menu   160
Creating Navigation from Slide to Slide   161
Linking from the Menu Slide to the Sections   163
Creating Hyperlinks to the Web   164
Testing All the Links   166
Summary   166

EIGHT Class Games   167

Memorization Games   167
Creating a Slide with Complete Text   168
Creating a Slide with Less Text   168
Spelling Games   173
Who Wants to Be a Millionaire? PowerPoint Version   176
Jeopardy PowerPoint Version   179
More Games   181
Summary   182

NINE Graded Tests   183

PowerPoint and Programming   183
Benefits of VBA   184
Making It Easy   185

Creating a Multiple-Choice Test   186
   Creating a Cover Slide   186
   Creating the First Question Slide   188
   Finishing the Presentation   189
Adding the Code   190
   Opening the VBA Window   190
   Checking Security Settings   190
   Pasting in the Code   192
   Understanding the Code   193
   Starting Over   207
Assigning Macros to the Buttons   207
Testing the Test   209
Adding More   209
   Creating a Quiz with More Than Two Answer Choices   209
   Adding More Questions   210
Summary   212

PART THREE Projects and Resources

TEN PowerPoint Projects for Pre-Kindergarten to Grade 1   215

Fun in the Early Years   215
Language Arts   215
Math   216
   Collecting Images for a Math Project   218
   Animating the Objects   219
   Using AutoShapes to Teach Math   223
Science   225
Social Studies   227
An Interdisciplinary Approach   227
Summary   228

ELEVEN PowerPoint Projects for Grades 2 to 5   229

Language Arts   229
Math   230

Teaching Fractions   230

Teaching Money and Percent Concepts   237

Showing Metric System Concepts   238

Science   241

Life Cycle Projects   242

Animals and Their Habitats   244

The Water Cycle Revisited   244

Parts of a Cell   244

The Solar System   245

Using Your Own Pictures and Video   247

Social Studies   247

Summary   248

TWELVE PowerPoint Projects for Grades 6 to 12   249

Library   249

Book Talks   250

Book Reference System   251

Literature   251

History and Geography   252

Civics   254

Science   254

Math   258

Art and Music   262

Interdisciplinary Projects   263

Summary   263

THIRTEEN Online Resources for Teachers Using PowerPoint   265

PowerPoint and Education Resources   266

Games   268

Downloadable Presentations   270

Articles   271

Tips and Tutorials   272

Guidelines and Rubrics   275

Summary   276

PART FOUR Teaching PowerPoint to Students

FOURTEEN Teaching PowerPoint in Elementary School   279

PowerPoint and Kids   279
   Physical Arrangement of Computers   280
   Learning PowerPoint, Working on Projects   281
   More Pictures, Fewer Words   281
   Animation Is Fun!   282
   What They Can and Can't Do   282
   Small Fingers, Large Imaginations   282
   Start Simply   283
Summary   285

FIFTEEN Teaching PowerPoint in Middle and High School   287

Project-Based and Problem-Based Activities   288
Teaching Presentation Skills   289
Organizing Content   290
Introducing Design Principles   290
   Consistency versus Variety   290
   Layout Options   291
   Color   291
   Animation   291
   Nonlinear versus Linear Approaches   292
   Interactivity   293
Collaborating with Peers   293
Encouraging Creativity and Interest in Computer Science   293
Summary   294

SIXTEEN Teaching and Using PowerPoint at the College Level   295

Arts and Humanities   296
Social Sciences   298
Math   300
   Displaying Equations   300
   Geometry   302

Science   305
Business   306
Teaching PowerPoint   307
Summary   310

REFERENCES   311
APPENDIX A Research on Multimedia and Learning   313
APPENDIX B What's on the Companion Web Site   319
INDEX   321

This book came into being because of our frustration with current books and articles on PowerPoint. Although many excellent books are available, none do a good job of helping teachers make best use of PowerPoint in the educational setting. And almost all the articles we've read on how to create good presentations in Power-Point were from the business point of view. As one of the authors wrote in an article on PowerPoint principles for education, "Experts speak of creating presentations that entertain and motivate the audience and with the premise that listeners can only absorb a small amount of information in one sitting. But if you're a teacher your goals are different. Yes, you want motivated students, but the goal is for students to learn. Ultimately they will be tested on the course's content. Your job is not to entertain, but to teach. You want to grab your students intellectually, not necessarily emotionally" (Finkelstein, 2005). We started to feel that the advice just wasn't appropriate for people using PowerPoint in an educational setting. For example, experts wrote that presentations should motivate and convince. But shouldn't they educate?

As experienced educators and PowerPoint users, we decided to join forces to write this book on PowerPoint techniques that are especially suited to teachers.

And so *PowerPoint for Teachers: Dynamic Presentations and Interactive Classroom Projects* was born.

This book is an easy and comprehensive manual, with detailed step-by-step instructions to teach you how to develop your own fantastic educational projects.

IS THIS BOOK FOR YOU?

We wrote this book to be useful to both PowerPoint beginners and those who have used PowerPoint for a while. Even if you have never used PowerPoint, you can learn it in this book. If you're more of an expert, you'll find Chapter 2 to be an easy tutorial, but you'll still enjoy creating the water cycle project we describe there.

This book is useful for both beginners and experts because its emphasis is on using PowerPoint in the classroom. Even experts can use good project ideas!

If you have already used PowerPoint in your teaching, chances are that you developed a traditional project: a presentation with some facts, figures, bullets, and maybe pictures. Although we explain how to use PowerPoint in the traditional sense as an accompaniment to a lesson, our emphasis is on interactive projects; we want to take you beyond the one-way presentation. We show you how to create these projects using hyperlinks, clickable hot spots, fun games, and other involving and exciting activities.

Finally, we also discuss other topics—such as best practices, how to teach PowerPoint to your students, and multimedia research—that will be valuable to all teachers.

STRUCTURE OF THE BOOK

PowerPoint for Teachers is structured to start readers at the beginning and quickly get them up and running so that they can learn how to create quizzes, games, and more.

Part I is titled "Why PowerPoint?" and serves as an introduction. It contains the following chapters:

- Chapter 1, "Supporting All Aspects of Learning," explains how you can use PowerPoint to support, reinforce, and enhance teaching and learning with reviews, games, quizzes, and other activities.
- Chapter 2, "Creating Your First Presentation," offers a tutorial on PowerPoint for beginners and a first project for everyone—a presentation to support a lesson on the water cycle.

- Chapter 3, "Multimedia and Learning with PowerPoint," introduces you to PowerPoint's multimedia features.

- Chapter 4, "Understanding Best Practices," explains the do's and don'ts for best results.

Part II, "Creating Great Projects Using PowerPoint," includes five chapters, each covering an important interactive technique:

- Chapter 5, "Interactive Reviews," explains how to create a simple quiz or review, with positive and negative reinforcement.

- Chapter 6, "Interactive Maps," sets out the steps you need to take to create a clickable map with hot spots.

- Chapter 7, "Menu-Based Projects," explains how to design a menu-based presentation with internal and external links.

- Chapter 8, "Class Games," provides instructions for creating several popular games in PowerPoint.

- Chapter 9, "Graded Tests," describes an advanced method for creating a graded test using existing VBA code.

Part III, "Projects and Resources," offers ideas for specific projects at various age levels as well as online resources that you can use:

- Chapter 10, "PowerPoint Projects for Pre-Kindergarten to Grade 1," lists projects appropriate for the youngest students.

- Chapter 11, "PowerPoint Projects for Grades 2 to 5," describes projects for lower-school students.

- Chapter 12, "PowerPoint Projects for Grades 6 to 12," includes projects appropriate for middle and high school students.

- Chapter 13, "Online Resources for Teachers Using PowerPoint," provides an extensive list of these resources.

Part IV, "Teaching PowerPoint to Students," offers guidelines for teaching students of various ages. It also contains our one chapter on using and teaching PowerPoint at the college level.

- Chapter 14, "Teaching PowerPoint in Elementary School," discusses how to teach PowerPoint to lower-school children, usually in grades 4 to 6, including ideas for projects the students can do while they're learning and a sample lesson plan.

• Chapter 15, "Teaching PowerPoint in Middle and High School," offers ideas for projects the students can do while they're learning.

• Chapter 16, "Teaching and Using PowerPoint at the College Level," discusses the use of PowerPoint in various majors and offers project ideas. The chapter also has an outline of topics you need to cover if you're teaching PowerPoint to college students.

Appendix A, "Research on Multimedia and Learning," provides an overview and bibliography of research on multimedia and learning. Appendix B, "What's on the Companion Web Site," lists supplementary PowerPoint presentations and other resources that are on the book's companion Web site.

CONVENTIONS

By "conventions" we mean the following symbols and typographical features that we use in this book to help you understand what we're saying.

Icons

We've used icons in the margin to call out certain material:

 Content that looks like this is a note. We use notes to reference other parts of the book and let you know when you need to take special notice of some information.

 This is a tip. Tips help you perform tasks more easily or quickly.

 This is a warning. We don't have too many of these, but sometimes you need to be careful to avoid losing your work, or some other minor catastrophe. In these cases, we let you know how to avoid the problem.

Fonts, Symbols, and More

Sometimes we use special fonts:

- We use *italics* when we're defining a word.

- We use **boldface** when you need to type something.

- The ➤ symbol is an arrow that we use to indicate choosing options on a menu. For example, to save a file you would choose File ➤ Save. That means you click File and then you click Save.

- When we give you instructions that are specific to various versions of Power-Point, we put it in a "How to Do It" box. Look for your version of PowerPoint and follow the appropriate instructions. You'll also find a few Spotlight side-bars, which discuss interesting points of note.

COMPANION WEB SITE

We're pleased to offer additional resources on the companion Web site at www.ellenfinkelstein.com/powerpointforteachers.html. There you'll find presentations that we've shown you in this book, such as the water cycle presentation from Chapter 2. We've also collected a few presentations from teachers and student teachers, a list of multimedia resources, and some multimedia files. We'll continue to update this site periodically.

ENJOY!

We invite you to learn how enjoyable PowerPoint can be as you create projects that will be both fun and educational for your students. We hope that you find this book useful. We'd love to hear your feedback at ellen@ellenfinkelstein.com or psamsonov@louisiana.edu.

PART ONE

Why PowerPoint?

Chapter 1: Supporting All Aspects of Learning

Chapter 2: Creating Your First Presentation

Chapter 3: Multimedia and Learning with PowerPoint

Chapter 4: Understanding Best Practices

Part I introduces you to the world of PowerPoint for teachers. We explain why PowerPoint can be so useful to assist you in the teaching process and enumerate some of the ways you can use it. We offer a tutorial on PowerPoint while also guiding you through the process of creating a presentation to support a lesson on the water cycle. Then we delve into using multimedia (audio and video) with PowerPoint. Finally, we discuss best practices for using PowerPoint to aid (rather than hinder) the educational process.

Supporting All Aspects of Learning

Microsoft Office PowerPoint is a versatile and easy-to-use tool that can support learning in its many phases. As a teacher, you can add PowerPoint to your arsenal of educational technologies and enhance the classroom experience in many ways.

This chapter explains how you can use PowerPoint to support, reinforce, and enhance teaching and learning through reviews, games, quizzes, and other activities created in the software. It also explains how and where you can use Power-Point to create interactive projects. You will find the detailed instructions in the following chapters. They're not hard at all!

POWERPOINT FOR ALL THE WAYS YOU TEACH

Incorporating PowerPoint in your teaching will make your teaching more effective and fun. PowerPoint is an incredibly flexible and versatile tool, but a lot of its potential is not immediately apparent. Not all teachers realize how exciting and visually appealing PowerPoint projects can be. They may know little or nothing about the interactivity that PowerPoint can add to their presentations. The following are some important points you may need to know.

PowerPoint and the Constructivist Approach

Do you want to teach effectively? Do you want your students to appreciate your computer skills? Do you want them to be actively involved in learning through exciting and fun activities? Of course you do.

PowerPoint is the answer. You may have heard, read, and implemented what is called the *constructivist approach* to learning and teaching. The Chinese proverb "I hear and I forget; I see and I remember; I do and I understand" encapsulates the spirit of constructivism. A typical PowerPoint presentation is based on the usual process—"hearing and forgetting, seeing and remembering," but leaves out the "doing and understanding" part. That's because the traditional Power-Point presentation relies on seeing and hearing; its interactive potential is rarely revealed. Objectivist (nonconstructivist) methods imply that knowledge is transmitted from the teacher to the learner, that teaching is teacher-directed, systematic, and structured (Roblyer and Edwards, 2000), and this is how PowerPoint is often used: as a linear, one-way presentation created by the teacher to inform the students on a selected subject without any interactivity.

The applications and projects described in this book support the constructivist approach, which suggests that students construct their knowledge through active participation in project-based and problem-based activities, through interaction with the teacher and their peers. You will learn how to create interactive and engaging PowerPoint projects using simple and easy techniques.

An Amazingly Versatile Tool

You can do much more with PowerPoint than simply create bulleted lists. For instance, you can insert pictures and then edit them—making them smaller or larger, darker or lighter, or using them as backgrounds for your projects. You can incorporate sound (music, your narration, and other audio files) and you can show video clips, animated pictures, and much more. PowerPoint is a powerful multimedia tool incorporating imagery, sound, and text in one project, using very simple techniques. In addition, PowerPoint includes powerful animation capabilities that let you visually communicate processes, cycles, evolution—anything that changes. Animation also commands the attention of students during the learning process.

Even better for teachers, PowerPoint enables you to create problem- and project-based activities with your students participating in games, interactive activities, and quizzes. No other software lets you create custom-made quizzes, games, and engaging lessons so easily.

Bet You Didn't Know...

Did you know that you can teach a class to memorize a poem in ten to fifteen minutes using PowerPoint? Or that you can create a nice menu slide with thumbnail images? *Did you know that you can develop or teach your students how to develop a multiple-choice quiz in PowerPoint?* Here are some projects you can create in PowerPoint:

- *A quiz or review.* Students choose from multiple-choice questions and get positive feedback for the right answer and negative feedback for a wrong answer that also takes them back to the question so they can try again. You will find the instructions in Chapter 5.

- *An interactive map.* Students click an area of a slide to answer a question (such as "Where is France?"). They get positive feedback for the right answer and negative feedback for the wrong answer that also takes them back to the question so they can try again. The details are described in Chapter 6.

- *A clickable menu with hyperlinks to many other resources.* Students use menu buttons to choose what they want to learn more about. The buttons link to other slides, other presentations, or the Internet. See Chapter 7 for details.

- *A class question-and-answer game.* Students answer questions individually or on teams and get points for the right answers. You will learn how to create such games in Chapter 8.

- *A graded test.* Students answer multiple-choice questions and view a slide at the end that tells them how many they got right. Chapter 9 provides step-by-step explanations on how to write a graded test in PowerPoint.

    Figure 1.1 shows an example of one PowerPoint interactive project.

SUPPORT FOR YOUR INSTRUCTION

You don't have to have special programs to support your teaching with technology. PowerPoint can help you do that, and very effectively, and almost every school already has PowerPoint.

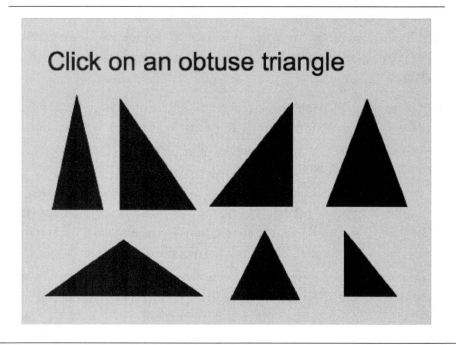

Figure 1.1
In this example of an interactive project in PowerPoint, students click on one of the triangles and get immediate feedback telling them whether their answer is right or wrong.

Value of Repetition

Many teachers use PowerPoint in their lessons—some frequently, some occasionally. Normally, they create a simple presentation, with some facts and figures. Perhaps they add pictures taken from the Microsoft Office Clip Art gallery or downloaded from elsewhere on the Internet. But what if this presentation included a review at the end? Not just a set of questions, but a multiple-choice activity? Wouldn't that liven things up?

Repetitio mater studiorum est ("Repetition is the mother of learning"), according to the Latin saying. But simple repetition is boring.... Instead, why not do the repetition in the form of an amusing overview, with funny feedback and reward points? The slides shown in Figures 1.2, 1.3, and 1.4 offer examples.

Chapter 5 will walk you through the process of creating a review in PowerPoint.

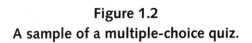

Figure 1.2
A sample of a multiple-choice quiz.

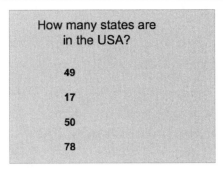

Figure 1.3
An example of negative feedback.

A Picture Paints a Thousand Words

How many times have you heard this? Yet, how many times have you seen a dull PowerPoint presentation with text-cluttered slides and maybe one or two familiar pictures from the Clip Art gallery? Many studies suggest that viewers quickly get tired when shown text-based information, even if it has been well-organized by the presenter. Pictures capture viewers' attention; they support and enhance a PowerPoint project. In this book you will learn how to work with pictures, make

Figure 1.4
Some positive feedback.

Figure 1.5
You can easily use pictures in a PowerPoint project to foster student interest.

them support your project, edit them, and make backgrounds from them. You will also learn how to achieve the most appropriate balance of pictures and text. (We will talk about this in Chapters 2 to 4.)

Figure 1.5 shows a picture on a slide taken from the Clip Art gallery. You can use images like this to encourage student input, or just to display while you're covering a topic.

Read more about the use of pictures in PowerPoint in Chapters 2 and 3.

Linear versus Nonlinear

The word *linear* comes from the word *linearis,* which means *created by lines* or *straight.* Even some textbooks on PowerPoint say that it is designed to create linear presentations. Of course, there is nothing wrong with linearity. A PowerPoint presentation on a recent field trip can provide the viewers with a documented account of the trip from the departure to the return back home, from point A to point Z—that is, from the first slide (A) to the last slide (Z), as shown in Figure 1.6.

However, many projects call for nonlinearity. For example, in a project on classification of animals, you can first present the classes of animals as a menu and then talk about each class, returning to the menu.

Figure 1.7 gives the idea of how slides are organized in a nonlinear project.

The menu slide offers several routes: you can start with mammals, and go from slide A on mammals to the slide Z on mammals, which will lead you back to the main menu. Likewise, slide A on insects will lead you to slides B, C, and so on, and then also bring you back to the menu. Actually, you can make a link from any slide to the menu, as we explain in Chapter 7. For lack of space, the chart does not show the same principle for reptiles and amphibians or fish.

If you choose a "take the quiz" route, a slide showing Question 1 will offer a multiple-choice question. Any wrong choice will lead you (or the student) to the "Try Again" slide, which returns the user to Question 1. The right choice is linked to a "Good Job" slide, which forwards the user to the next question, and so on, until the end of the quiz.

Thus, instead of a linear PowerPoint presentation, you have a nonlinear, more sophisticated presentation. This organization provides students with a better understanding of the idea of classification and categories. Navigation through such

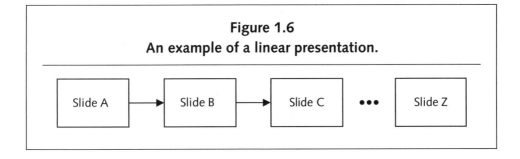

Figure 1.6
An example of a linear presentation.

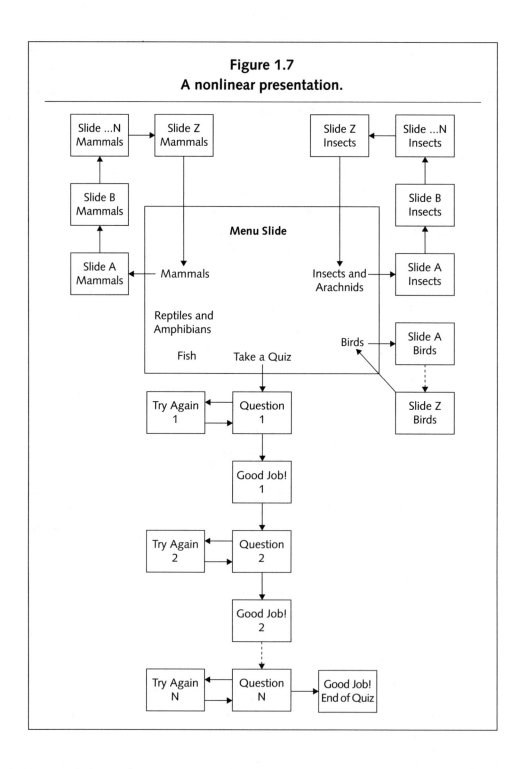

Figure 1.7
A nonlinear presentation.

a PowerPoint show is easier and more in line with the logical structure of classification. A linear PowerPoint presentation can be compared with playing a VHS tape, whereas a nonlinear PowerPoint project is more like playing a DVD that allows a more effective navigation.

To learn how to create a nonlinear PowerPoint presentation see Chapter 7.

Teaching with Games

Such activities as quizzes or short reviews with "true-false" choices can be performed in class in the form of games. You can have competing teams! If you decide to develop your technique of writing quizzes in PowerPoint, you can even give graded tests with points. Multiple-choice quizzes can be further developed into games similar to the TV show *Jeopardy*. For more fun, add music, applause, and other audio effects in your feedback. Clickable maps provide a good opportunity to learn geography, biology, geometry, and other subjects in a fun and exciting way. You will find detailed instructions on how to create such projects in Chapter 8 of this book.

Assessing Retention and Understanding

You can use quizzes and clickable maps for reviews to enhance retention and understanding. The technique for developing these activities is not at all difficult. Ungraded reviews are very easy to create, and you can customize the questions and answers for specific groups or even individual students.

If you're an advanced user, you will find instructions in this book on developing more sophisticated graded tests with calculated final scores as tools of assessment. But don't be afraid! These instructions do not require any knowledge of computer languages; anyone who follows these instructions can create an effective graded test! See Chapter 9.

Encouraging Problem-Based Learning

Quizzes and clickable maps and pictures are big steps in the direction of project- and problem-based activities. However, you can go much further. Creating a fun and interactive PowerPoint project for your students is wonderful, but getting them to create their own projects is even better. People learn by doing, and when students develop their own projects in PowerPoint on a specific topic, make no mistake, they will learn this topic in detail!

How many times have you seen student projects on display in the school's cafeteria or gym, with pictures carved and pasted on cardboard with some hand-written notes underneath? Why not teach your students how to develop the same projects in PowerPoint, with pictures, sound, and interactivity? You can be sure that your students will be more excited and willing to work, and you will not believe the amazing projects they can come up with!

Chapters 14, 15, and 16 of this book discuss how to teach PowerPoint to students. After they have seen the interactive projects that you have created, they will be eager to create their own.

FROM PRE-K THROUGH PH.D.

Because of its tremendous potential to combine sound, image, and animation, PowerPoint can be used effectively with students in virtually all grade levels. The specific way you use this program will, of course, depend on the students' age and other factors.

Fun in the Early Years

So when can you start using PowerPoint with your students? The earlier, the better. Once prekindergarten and kindergarten students learn how to control the mouse, they can view PowerPoint presentations and participate in interactive projects: matching colors, identifying shapes, determining patterns. They don't even have to know how to read to get feedback: a smiley face or a picture of a candy plus a sound file saying something like "Good job!" constitutes great positive reinforcement. You can even narrate the instructions, such as "Click the triangle."

PowerPoint provides you with a flexible tool to enhance your teaching methodology with both smaller and larger projects. In many cases special educational software may not be suitable or available, but you can rely on PowerPoint-based activities to make your teaching more effective. It's hard to overestimate the advantage of developing computer skills with pre-K students.

At the rate that computers are becoming available for education, students will soon be using computer technology as a learning tool from kindergarten through high school. As the number of laptop computer campuses (universities that provide every student with a laptop computer) increases, chances are that when today's kindergarten students reach college they will have a laptop as a basic necessity and a regular tool, as ubiquitous as the ballpoint pen. Chapter 10 provides some project ideas for pre-K to first-grade children.

Beginning to Think in the Lower Grades

One very experienced and acclaimed teacher said: "Poor teachers teach subjects, good teachers teach life." According to vast research, problem-solving skills should be developed as early as primary school. Problem- and project-based education should start from the first grade. Computer technology in general and Power-Point in particular play key roles in problem-based activities and in developing projects that cross curricular boundaries. As they approach the end of elementary school, students can already use basic PowerPoint tools and make it a regular medium for their projects and assignments.

You can enhance almost any topic that you teach with a PowerPoint project or presentation. Math problems and quizzes are easy to design. Science topics are ideal, because you can so easily add images and animation that portray processes, as shown in the water cycle project in Chapter 2. You can bring history and geography alive with paintings of earlier times and clickable maps. A PowerPoint presentation is a great way to display grammatical concepts on a big screen. Even art and music are appropriate subjects for a slide show.

Of course, we don't suggest that students read books in PowerPoint! However, you can use PowerPoint for remedial work and for students with special needs. In many cases, it will be more effective than anything else! It is you who must decide when it is appropriate. The beauty of PowerPoint is that you can reuse your projects as many times as you want!

For ideas on PowerPoint projects for grades 2 to 5, see Chapter 11.

Expanding the Mind in Middle and High School

Problem-based learning, and projects that cross curricula to involve more than one subject, are a modern school's priority. Again, computers are a great tool for this, with PowerPoint being the easiest and most effective software.

Imagine a water project for middle school students involving the following:

- The physical and chemical properties of water
- The importance of water for the human organism and society

- Water pollution

- The historical significance of water for early civilizations

- The amount of water on the earth (a great project to explain math concepts)

You can describe and present these many aspects of water and more in a PowerPoint presentation with pictures, sound, and interactivity.

You can assign and perform group projects, individual projects, projects for school exhibitions, and charts and graphs for display.

By working on such projects, your students will develop teamwork and computer skills—skills they will need in college and beyond. Read Chapter 12 to get great ideas for PowerPoint projects for middle and high school students.

Expressing Knowledge in College

PowerPoint has already become a popular tool for college presentations. Many students present their projects using PowerPoint, but, as mentioned earlier, such presentations mostly involve text, figures, and some pictures from the Clip Art gallery. Not all professors assign their students projects to develop in PowerPoint, but they all welcome such endeavors. Preparing a PowerPoint presentation for economics or sociology classes has become almost a requirement; presenting with PowerPoint in classes on pedagogy or psychology should be more common.

Both college professors and students can add some interactivity and fun to such projects. Why not capture the class's attention with a dynamic interactive activity accompanied by sound and, maybe, music? By college, students are ready to create much more complex presentations, including those with menus and nonlinear structures.

We believe that by the time students reach college, teachers should expect not only well-organized content (an introduction, development, and a conclusion) but well-developed and thought-out concepts. In addition, college is a good time for students to work on public speaking and presentation skills. Chapter 16 offers suggestions on using and teaching PowerPoint at the college level.

WHEN NOT TO USE POWERPOINT

It is the teacher—not PowerPoint or any other technology—who makes the difference. PowerPoint is only a tool; it can be used in a creative and effective way, but it is the teacher who uses this tool. Fruit is good for human health, but most people cannot live on fruit alone; everything is good in moderation. Any tool becomes blunted when used too frequently, and PowerPoint is no exception. Sometimes the computer, or PowerPoint, is not the solution. When you can teach a better lesson without PowerPoint than with it, don't use it! Here are some important tips:

- Do not use PowerPoint when you have a poor or undeveloped project just to make this project more appealing.
- Do not use PowerPoint if your presentation is very short and does not provide much information.
- Do not let a presentation interfere with your rapport with your students. Even during a presentation, there are times to turn off the projector and have a person-to-person discussion.

Again, it is you who presents. PowerPoint is only a supporting tool for your classroom presentation. Use it to create a favorable environment for your project and to enhance the information with visuals, sound, and special effects.

SUMMARY

This chapter explained how PowerPoint can make your teaching style more effective. PowerPoint has special appeal if you are a constructivist: it is a versatile tool for teaching and learning and a great device for project-based learning.

We explained that PowerPoint can incorporate pictures, sounds, and animation. PowerPoint projects can be linear or nonlinear, thus offering you greater flexibility in your teaching.

We explained that PowerPoint's interactive potential allows you to teach with games, devise projects to address retention and understanding, and encourage problem-based learning.

We explained that you can effectively apply PowerPoint at all school levels. We also noted that there are times when it is better not to use PowerPoint than to use it.

Creating Your First Presentation

I n this chapter, you will learn to create a presentation on the water cycle that is suitable for fifth through eighth graders. This presentation is simple and presents only basic information; you can supplement it with any additional content you want.

This chapter is also a tutorial on PowerPoint for beginners. Therefore, while learning to use PowerPoint as an accompaniment to a lesson, you will also learn to use PowerPoint as a tool.

You can use what you learn in this chapter to create a presentation on any topic, simple or advanced. The simplest way to use PowerPoint is to accompany your lesson, with the PowerPoint slides acting as visual aids to enhance what you say. Teachers use PowerPoint this way from about fifth grade through college.

A PRESENTATION TO SUPPORT A LESSON ON THE WATER CYCLE

When you decide that you want to use PowerPoint to supplement your lesson plan, you need to do some planning first. How will PowerPoint help the students learn? What resources do you need? Where will the PowerPoint presentation fit in—at the beginning to introduce the topic, throughout the lesson plan to develop concepts, or at the end as a review? Once you've answered these questions, you can start creating the presentation.

Creating Your Lesson Plan

Of course, the first step is to create your lesson plan. The PowerPoint presentation should support the lesson plan, rather than vice versa. The lesson plan preparation doesn't change just because you're using PowerPoint.

As you work, pencil (or type) in places where a visual (or sound) aid would be helpful. For a lesson on the water cycle, you might note that you want a photo of a river, a water cycle diagram, a sound file of thunder and rain, a video of rain, animation of the water cycle, and so on.

Outlining Your Talk

Type up an outline of what you'll say during the time that you'll be using Power-Point. As you work, insert a box for each slide that you want to use. In the box, place a description of the slide's content.

Consider how you can depict ideas visually, instead of with words. Often a diagram is more useful than bulleted text. You can even use a photograph to evoke ideas from the students.

The boxes become a *storyboard*, which is a layout used for a visual medium such as a movie or a slide show. The boxes guide you when you create your slides in PowerPoint. Figure 2.1 shows part of a sample outline with a storyboard that you might create for a lesson on the water cycle.

As you'll see in Part II of this book, you can use PowerPoint for extension activities and reviews or assessments. Therefore, you can include slides for these parts of your lesson plan as well, although we won't discuss them in this chapter.

Gathering Media

When you have completed your lesson plan and storyboard, start gathering images and other multimedia files, such as sound files and animation. You can find files in many locations. Here are some sources:

- *Microsoft Office Clip Art gallery.* Although clip art usually means line art, the Microsoft Clip Art gallery includes photographs as well. Microsoft Office offers a large selection of images that you can use. We explain how to insert clip art images later in this chapter.

- *Microsoft Clip Art and Media homepage.* You can find thousands more images by going to Microsoft's online clip art center. In the Clip Art task pane, click the Clip Art on Office Online link.

Figure 2.1

With a little planning, you can make the process of creating your talk and the PowerPoint presentation easier.

Steps

We've been talking about water and why it's so important. Today, we'll talk about the water cycle. Where do you think water comes from?

Possible answers: oceans, rain (and snow), rivers, springs

How does the water get in each place?

Take answers and then focus on rain. Where does the rain come from? Students should volunteer that rain comes from clouds.

Slide 1: Where does the rain come from? picture of rain; sound of thunderclap

How does the water get up in the clouds?

 If you don't have that link, go to http://office.microsoft.com/en-us/clipart/default.aspx. (This is the U.S. site.)

- *The Internet.* The Internet is full of clip art and photos. Many such pieces are copyrighted, and not all are free. However, many sites offer access to their huge collections for a very reasonable fee. Just search for clip art or photos.

- *Your own photos.* If you have a digital camera, go out and take pictures! You can easily insert them into PowerPoint.

 The companion Web site—www.ellenfinkelstein.com/powerpointforteachers.html—offers some specific resources for finding multimedia content, including clip art and photos, on the Web.

Later in this chapter we will explain how to insert the images into PowerPoint.

STARTING A NEW PRESENTATION

Once you have your lesson plan done and have collected your images, you're ready to create your PowerPoint presentation. The first step is to fire up PowerPoint. If you have a shortcut/alias on your desktop, just double-click it. Otherwise, follow these instructions:

HOW TO DO IT

- *Windows:* Start ➤ All Programs ➤ Microsoft Office ➤ Microsoft Office PowerPoint 2000/2002/2003/2007.

- *Mac:* Double-click Macintosh HD ➤ Applications ➤ Microsoft Office ➤ Microsoft PowerPoint. In Mac OS X or later, you can also click the PowerPoint icon on the dock.

What do you see when you open PowerPoint? It depends on your version. In most cases, you want to get straight to work, so you want to see the first slide of your presentation on the screen.

HOW TO DO IT

- *Windows 2000:* In the PowerPoint dialog box, choose the Blank Presentation option and click OK.

- *Windows 2002/2003/2007:* You immediately open to a blank slide with the title slide layout.

- *Mac 2001/X/2004:* The Project Gallery dialog box opens. Choose the PowerPoint presentation icon and click OK. Then the New Slide dialog box appears, showing various layouts of slides. For your first slide, choose Title Slide and click OK.

In all versions of PowerPoint, your screen should now look similar to that shown in Figure 2.2. The image on the top shows PowerPoint 2007 in Windows; the one on the bottom shows PowerPoint 2004 on the Mac. (PowerPoint 2007

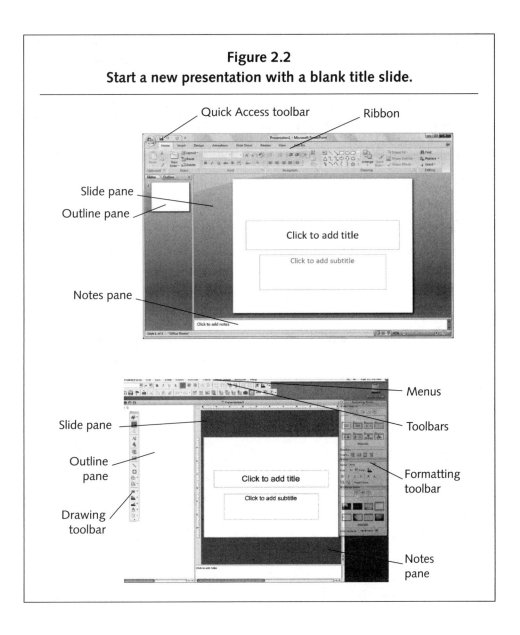

Figure 2.2
Start a new presentation with a blank title slide.

uses a unique interface; all other versions are fairly similar.) This is called *Normal view*, and you do most of your work here.

Normal view has three panes:

• *Slide pane.* The slide is front and center. You can directly edit the slide here.

- *Outline/Slides tabs.* In Windows, the left pane has two tabs, one that shows the text of your slides (Outline tab) and one that shows thumbnails of your slides (Slides tab). On the Mac, you see only the outline text.

- *Notes pane.* This is a place to write teacher notes (what you will say out loud), or any notes to yourself about procedures, set up, and so on.

Here are some other features to remember about the PowerPoint screen:

- *Menus.* You can find most commands on one of the menus.

- *Toolbars.* The toolbars offer a quick way to issue commands to PowerPoint. There are many more toolbars that you don't see at first (except in PowerPoint 2007). To see the list, choose View ➤ Toolbars. Choose any toolbar to display it.

- *Ribbon.* In PowerPoint 2007 only, you have one big, tabbed toolbar. There is also the Quick Access toolbar at the upper-left corner for commands that you use often.

- *Drawing toolbar.* This toolbar offers many tools for adding graphics. In Windows it's usually at the bottom of your screen, but on the Mac it's usually along the left side of your screen. (You can also use the Formatting palette on the Mac.) In PowerPoint 2007, you add graphics from the Insert tab of the ribbon.

Creating a Title Slide

One reason why PowerPoint is so easy to use is that it guides you as you work. When you see the title slide, you know just what to do—click in the two boxes to add a title and a subtitle for your presentation. Just click and start typing.

For our lesson on the water cycle, we want the title to be **The Water Cycle**. Click in the title box and type those words. Then click in the subtitle box and type **Or, where does the rain come from?** Your slide should look similar to the one shown in Figure 2.3.

Adding a Slide

You're now ready to add the next slide. We want to create a slide with a title and a picture. PowerPoint comes with various layouts to help you position objects on a slide. One way to add this slide is to use the default layout and then change the layout to the one you want.

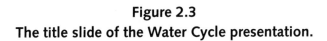

Figure 2.3
The title slide of the Water Cycle presentation.

The Water Cycle

Or, where does the rain come from?

Follow the steps to insert a slide using the default layout:

HOW TO DO IT

- *Windows 2000:* Choose Insert ➢ New Slide. You can also choose Common Tasks ➢ New Slide at the right end of the toolbar or press Ctrl+M. The New Slide dialog box opens with a selection of layouts. Accept the default and click OK.

- *Windows 2002/2003:* Choose Insert ➢ New Slide. You can also choose New Slide at the right end of the toolbar or press Ctrl+M.

- *Windows 2007:* On the Home tab, click the New Slide button.

- *Mac 2001/X/2004:* Choose Insert ➢ New Slide.

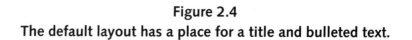

Figure 2.4
The default layout has a place for a title and bulleted text.

Click to add title

• Click to add text

Note that the new slide defaults to a layout that has a place for a title and a place to add text, as shown in Figure 2.4. You can also see the new slide listed in the Outline tab.

For our lesson, in order to capture the interest of the students, we want to start differently. We'd like to add a picture. To do this, we need to change the layout.

Choosing a Layout

Layouts make creating a slide very easy. Of course, you can move objects around anywhere you want, so you're not stuck with PowerPoint's idea of a layout. Right now, we want to change the layout of the new slide you added to make room for a picture. We also want a title at the top. Follow these steps:

You should now see a blank slide that looks like Figure 2.5. (The various versions of PowerPoint may look slightly different. In PowerPoint 2000, you'll see just the title placeholder.) The central part of this slide is called a *content placeholder*; it lets you add a table, chart (graph), clip art, image file (picture), diagram, or movie. We're going to add an image file.

For now, you'll just add the title. Later in this chapter, we'll explain how to add images, and you'll come back to this slide.

Click in the slide title area and type **Where can you find water?** Don't press Enter, but click outside the box to deselect it.

Adding Notes

Because this slide will just have a title and a picture, you may want to add some notes to yourself on this slide. The answers to the question won't be on the slide itself. The idea is to get your students to think of the answers for themselves, but you want to make sure that they come up with all the possible answers.

Click in the Notes pane, where it says Click to Add Notes. Type the following:

> **Water is found throughout the world. It is underground, and in soil, marshes, swamps, ponds, streams, rivers, lakes, glaciers,**

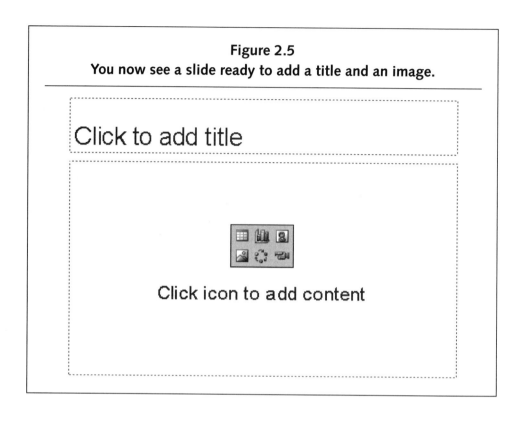

Figure 2.5
You now see a slide ready to add a title and an image.

Click to add title

Click icon to add content

oceans, clouds, and precipitation. Ask, "Which of the following contains the largest amount of water on Earth?" Possible choices are groundwater; lakes and rivers; oceans, seas, and bays; ice caps, glaciers; and permanent snow. The correct answer is oceans, seas, and bays. Then ask, "What is the largest source of drinking water on Earth?" Although ice caps, glaciers, and permanent snow may seem like the correct choice (because the largest amount of *fresh* water is in solid form), the correct answer is groundwater, because most drinking water is obtained from underground.

As you type, the text scrolls up. When you're done, use the Notes pane's scrollbar to see the beginning.

Inserting a Slide with a Specified Layout

You're ready for the next slide. Again, we want to add a slide with a title and an image. In the previous section, you inserted the slide and then changed its layout.

This time, you'll learn how to specify the slide layout while inserting the slide. Follow these steps:

HOW TO DO IT

- *Windows 2000:* Choose Insert ➤ New Slide. You can also choose Common Tasks ➤ New Slide at the right end of the toolbar or press Ctrl+M. The New Slide dialog box opens with a selection of layouts. Click the Title layout and click OK.

- *Windows 2002/2003:* With the Slide Layout task pane displayed, click the down arrow to the right of the Title and Content layout. Choose Insert New Slide.

- *Windows 2007:* On the Home tab, in the Slides group, click the down arrow at the bottom of the New Slide button and choose Title and Content.

- *Mac 2001/X/2004:* Use the Formatting palette. (If it's not displayed, choose View ➤ Formatting Palette.) From the Add Objects section at the top of the Formatting palette, click the Title and Content layout.

To add the title, click in the slide title area and type **Where does the rain come from?** In the Notes area, type **Possible answers: clouds, the ocean, rivers.**

Of course, the students will answer "clouds," but you'll then ask them how the water gets in the clouds to encourage them to think of other sources for rain.

SAVING YOUR PROJECT

You've created three slides already, so it's time to save. Click the Save button on the Standard toolbar. In PowerPoint 2007, click the Save button on the Quick Access toolbar. The Save As dialog box opens, as shown in Figure 2.6 (a & b). Figure 2.6 (a) shows the Windows version; Figure 2.6 (b) shows the Mac version.

First, use the Save In drop-down list to navigate to a location for your file. In the File Name text box, you can see the default name already entered for you. PowerPoint

Figure 2.6 (a) [Windows]
The first time you save a file, the Save As dialog box opens, so you can name the file and give it a location.

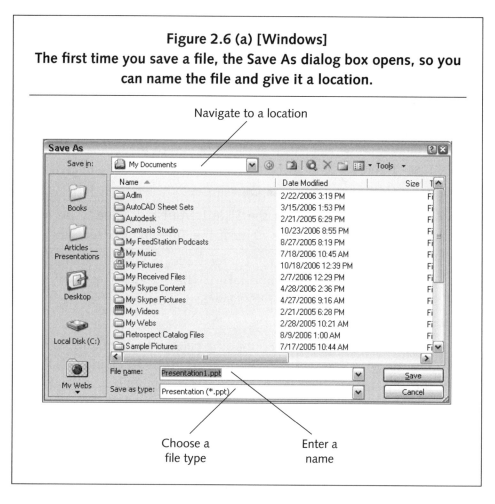

Navigate to a location

Choose a
file type

Enter a
name

took this from the title slide. Leave the Save As Type box at its default setting and click Save. This saves the file in the same format as the version of PowerPoint you're using.

 Create a new folder for each presentation. You can then place all the images and other media in the same folder. All the related files will be easy to find and you'll have fewer problems later on if you need to move the presentation.

From now on, you should click the same Save button every five to ten minutes to ensure that you don't lose your work in case of a computer crash. After all, a teacher's time is precious!

Figure 2.6 (b) [Mac]
**The first time you save a file, the Save As dialog box opens, so you
can name the file and give it a location.**

Enter a name

Navigate to a location

Choose a file type

If you want to make a copy of your PowerPoint file, you can do so within
PowerPoint. In fact, you can save it under a different name. Choose File ➤ Save
As and use the same procedure you used when saving the file for the first time.
(In PowerPoint 2007, click the Office button and choose Save As.) However, you
must either change the location or the file name to create a copy.

Now that you know how to save a presentation, you can break from your session whenever you want and go back to it when you have time. In Mac versions, choose PowerPoint ➤ Quit. In Windows versions, click the Close button at the upper-right corner of the PowerPoint window. You open a PowerPoint file in the same way you open any other file that you create on your computer.

ADDING TEXT

You've added a little bit of title text, but now it's time to add some text on the main part of the slide. Although pictures are ideal, sometimes you need words! A simple way to add text is to use a layout that contains bulleted text. Because this layout is the default layout, it's easy to add.

Slide 3 should be displayed. Follow these steps to add the next slide:

HOW TO DO IT

- *Windows 2000:* Click Common Tasks ➤ New Slide.

- *Windows 2002/2003:* Click the New Slide button on the Formatting toolbar.

- *Windows 2007:* On the Home tab, in the Slides group, click New Slide. Note that in PowerPoint 2007, the Title and Content layout lets you add either images or text.

- *Mac 2001/X/2004:* Choose Insert ➤ New Slide and choose the Bulleted List Slide. Or, in the Formatting palette, click the Bulleted List Slide in the Add Objects section. (You may have to scroll down to find it.)

 For *Windows 2002/2003:* If the Slide Layout task pane is visible, you may want to close it (click the X at its top) so you can see the slide better.

In all versions, click in the slide title area and type **How does water travel?** Then follow these steps for all versions:

Click in the slide body area and type the following lines. Don't add a period after each line. Press Enter to move to the next line. Don't press Enter after the last line or you'll create a fifth bullet.

- **Precipitation: from the clouds to the ground or bodies of water**
- **Evaporation: from bodies of water to the air**
- **Transpiration: evaporation from the leaves of plants**
- **Runoff: through soil and porous rock and in rivers and streams**

We show all the words in bold here (our convention for words you need to type), but when you do it, make only the terms bold. That's because you want the students to make note of them—for a future test! Follow the steps:

HOW TO DO IT

- *Windows 2000/2002/2003:* Select Precipitation: and click the Bold button on the Formatting toolbar.
- *Windows 2007:* Select Precipitation: and click the Bold button on the Home page, in the Font group.
- *Mac 2001/X/2004:* Select Precipitation: and click the Bold button in the Text section of the Formatting palette. Do the same for the other terms. Your slide should look like Figure 2.7.

 You can select the text and press Ctrl+B (Windows)/ ⌘+B (Mac) to make the text bold.

ENTERING AN OUTLINE IN POWERPOINT

We want one more text slide. You could enter the text using the same technique you used for the previous slide, but this time you'll use a different technique, entering text on the Outline tab. If the left pane shows thumbnails

Figure 2.7

**The completed text slide includes important terms that you want
your students to know.**

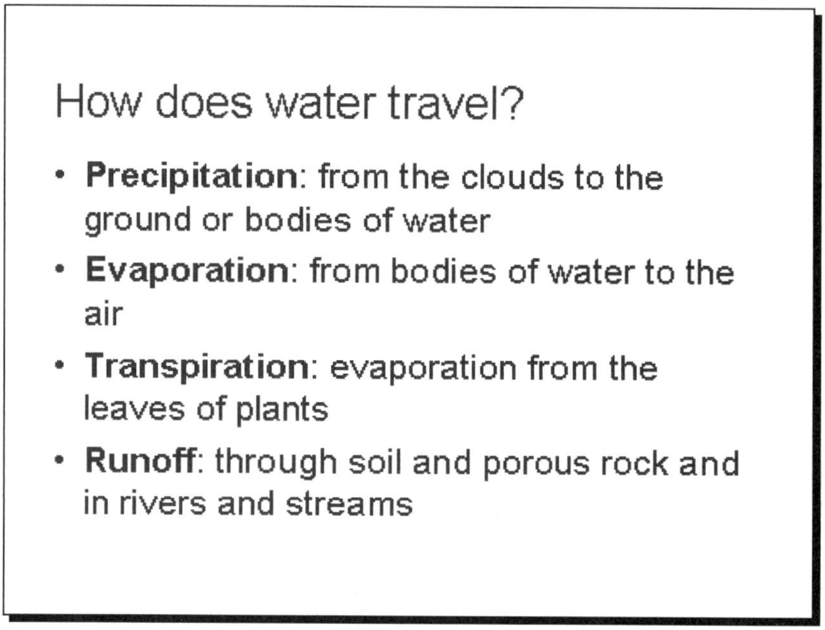

How does water travel?

- **Precipitation**: from the clouds to the ground or bodies of water
- **Evaporation**: from bodies of water to the air
- **Transpiration**: evaporation from the leaves of plants
- **Runoff**: through soil and porous rock and in rivers and streams

of your slides, click the Outline tab (Windows only). The Outline tab is shown in Figure 2.8.

Using the same method you used for the previous slide, insert a new slide using the default layout. In the Outline tab, you'll see the number 5 (because this will be the fifth slide) and a small slide icon.

Click next to the slide icon and type **Why does water travel?** Press Enter. This creates a new slide, which is not what you want. We'll fix it in a minute.

Next to the icon for slide 6, type **The sun heats the earth, which evaporates water.**

Don't press Enter. Instead, you want to turn the title of slide 6 into body text for slide 5. This is called *demoting* text, because body text is considered to be on a lower level than title text. First, select the text (in the Outline pane) that you just typed and then follow the steps:

Figure 2.8
You can enter text in the Outline tab.

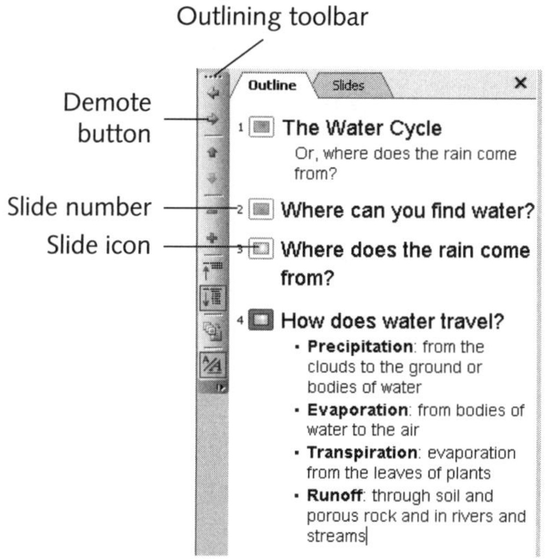

Outlining toolbar

Demote button

Slide number

Slide icon

Outline / Slides

1 ☐ **The Water Cycle**
  Or, where does the rain come from?

2 ☐ **Where can you find water?**

3 ☐ **Where does the rain come from?**

4 ☐ **How does water travel?**
  • **Precipitation**: from the clouds to the ground or bodies of water
  • **Evaporation**: from bodies of water to the air
  • **Transpiration**: evaporation from the leaves of plants
  • **Runoff**: through soil and porous rock and in rivers and streams

HOW TO DO IT

- *Windows 2000/Windows 2002/2003:* Click the Demote button on the Outlining toolbar (shown in Figure 2.8).

- *Windows 2007:* Right-click the text and choose Demote from the shortcut menu.

- *Mac 2001/X/2004:* Choose Increase Indent from the Outlining toolbar.

The text now becomes bulleted text for slide 5. Now click at the end of the text, press Enter, and type the following lines of text, pressing Enter after the first two lines shown here:

- **Evaporation causes water to rise and cool.**

- **Cooling condenses water into rain or snow.**

- **The weight of the water in the clouds causes it to fall again to the surface.**

Figure 2.9
Slide 5 was created in the Outline tab.

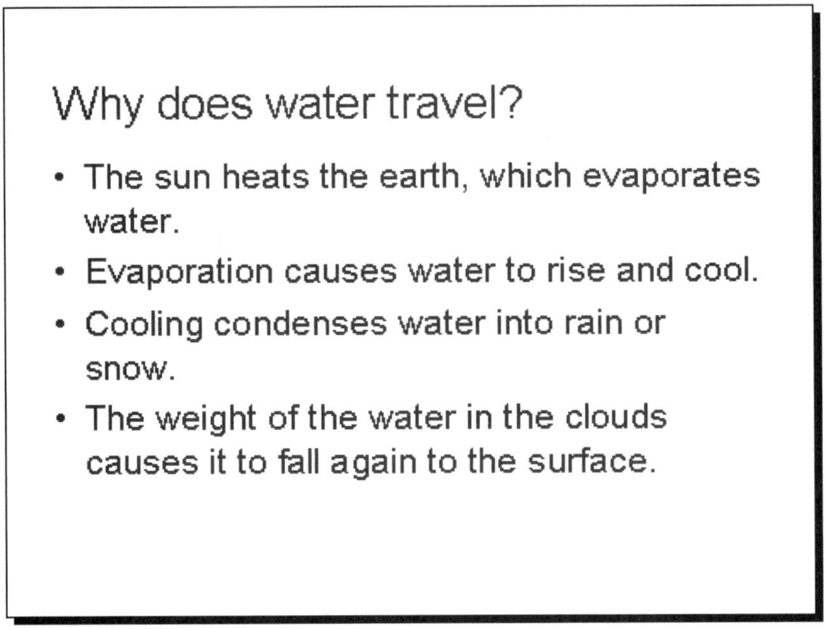

Why does water travel?

- The sun heats the earth, which evaporates water.
- Evaporation causes water to rise and cool.
- Cooling condenses water into rain or snow.
- The weight of the water in the clouds causes it to fall again to the surface.

Don't press Enter after the last line. Your slide should look like Figure 2.9. Now is a good time to save your presentation again!

SPOTLIGHT: IMPORTING AN OUTLINE

You can create an entire presentation by typing an outline in Microsoft Word or even in a simple text editor. This makes the most sense when you have a lot of text. It's great when you already have the text saved in a file. Here are the rules:

- *Text at the margin becomes a slide title.*
- *Press Tab once to indent text; this text becomes bulleted text.*
- *Don't use any blank lines; they come into PowerPoint as empty slides.*

Figure 2.10 shows a sample outline for slides 4 and 5 of our water cycle presentation.

To import the outline, follow these steps:

- *Windows 2000/2002/2003: Choose File ➤ Open. In the Open dialog box, choose All Outlines from the Files of Type drop-down list. Navigate to your outline and double-click it.*

- *Windows 2007: Click the Office button and choose Open. In the Open dialog box, choose All Outlines from the Files of Type drop-down list. Navigate to your outline and double-click it.*

- *Mac 2001/X/2004: Choose File ➤ Open. In the Open dialog box, choose All Outlines from the Files of Type drop-down list. Navigate to your outline and double-click it.*

MOVING AROUND A PRESENTATION

It's time to go back to the second and third slides and add the images. Since you're on slide 5, you need to get back to slide 2. There are many ways to move around a presentation. Follow these steps to go to slide 2.

Figure 2.10

If you want, you can prepare the text in a word processor or text editor and import it into PowerPoint to create your slides.

How does water travel?
    Precipitation: from the clouds to the ground or bodies of water
    Evaporation: from bodies of water to the air
    Transpiration: evaporation from the leaves of plants
    Runoff: through soil and porous rock and in rivers and streams
Why does water travel?
    The sun heats the earth, which evaporates water.
    Evaporation causes water to rise and cool.
    Cooling condenses water into rain or snow.
    The weight of the water in the clouds causes it to fall again to the surface.

As you've probably figured out, you could use these same techniques to move in the opposite direction through your presentation. For example, at the very bottom of the Slide pane's scrollbar is the Next Slide button.

ADDING IMAGES

With slide 2 on your screen, you're ready to insert an image. This slide asks, **Where can you find water?** The image is just to get the students thinking, so let's find a photograph of a body of water. Almost any beautiful photo will do. Of course, you might have a photo that you took, but we went to stock.xchng at www.sxc.hu and searched for *underwater fish.* We found an image we liked and noted that the image license says that it can be used in printed books, so we decided to use it in this book.

 An interesting source for images is students' artwork. With their permission, you can scan their work, save it as a picture file, and insert it in a PowerPoint project.

To download an image from a Web site, right-click (Win)/Ctrl-click (Mac) the image and choose Save Image As, or something similar (the exact words vary with the browser you're using).

You'll then be able to save the file onto your computer. At this point, you may have an opportunity to change the file's name. If so, use a name that will help you remember what's in the image.

Note that you can set the location of downloaded files in your browser; otherwise, the file is saved in a default location. If the location of the file isn't the same folder as your presentation, move it now. It's always wise to keep associated files in the same folder as your presentation. In Windows, you can use Windows Explorer. On the Mac, open the HD (hard drive) icon. Drag the file from its current location to the folder containing your presentation.

Inserting Image Files

With slide 2 displayed and your chosen image file safely saved in the same folder as your presentation, follow these instructions to insert the photo:

HOW TO DO IT

- *Windows 2000:* Choose Insert ➤ Picture ➤ From File. Navigate to the file and click Insert. You'll then need to move it to the desired location. You may need to resize it as well.

- *Windows 2002/2003:* In the content placeholder on the slide, click the Insert Picture icon. Find and select your image file and click Insert.

- *Windows 2007:* In the content placeholder on the slide, click the Insert Picture from File icon. Find and select your image file and click Insert.

- *Mac 2001/X/2004:* In the content placeholder on the slide, click the Insert Picture from File icon. Find and select your image file and click Insert, or double-click the image file.

PowerPoint sizes the image to the placeholder. Your slide should look like Figure 2.11.

You don't need to use the content placeholder to insert pictures; you can insert a picture anywhere on a slide. To do so, Choose Insert ➤ Picture ➤ From File. Navigate to the file and click Insert. (In PowerPoint 2007, click the Insert tab and then click the Picture button.) You'll then need to move the image to the desired location. You may need to resize it as well.

Figure 2.11
Our slide now has a title and a beautiful photo of fish in the ocean.

Where can you find water?

Inserting Clip Art

For slide 3, we could use another photograph, but for a change of pace, we'll use some clip art. The slide asks where the rain comes from, so obviously we need an image of rain. Click slide 3 in the Outline tab, or use one of the other methods previously described to move from slide to slide. As you can see, slide 3 has a content placeholder (except in PowerPoint 2000).

Follow the instructions to insert some clip art.

HOW TO DO IT

 • *Windows 2000:* Choose Insert ➢ Picture ➢ Clip Art. In the Microsoft Clip gallery, type **rain** in the Search for Clips text box and press Enter. Choose one of the images and click OK.

- *Windows 2002/2003:* Click the Clip Art icon in the place-holder. The Select Picture dialog box opens. Type **rain** in the Search Text box and press Enter or click Go. Choose one of the images and click OK.

 - *Windows 2007:* Click the Clip Art icon in the placeholder. The Clip Art task pane opens. In the Search In drop-down list, make sure Everywhere is checked so that you look in all possible locations (including on Microsoft's Web site). In the Results Should Be drop-down list, check Clip Art but uncheck all the other options (photographs, movies, and sounds). In the Search For text box, enter **rain** and press Enter or click Go. Click one of the images to insert it.

 - *Mac 2001/X/2004:* Click the icon in the placeholder. The Clip Art dialog box appears. Choose All Pictures in the Show option. Type **rain** in the Search box and click the Search button. Choose one of the images and click Insert.

We chose an image of people with umbrellas. Note that we avoided clip art with clouds, because that would give away the obvious answer!

The image you chose may be too small. You'll get a chance to fix that in the next section.

You don't need a content placeholder to insert clip art. You can choose Insert ➤ Picture ➤ Clip Art to open the Clip Art Gallery dialog box or task pane where you can search for clip art. (In PowerPoint 2007, display the Insert tab and click the Clip Art button.)

Editing Images

The clip art image we chose is too small; it looks like a postage stamp! Click it to select it and drag one of the corners outward.

 Dragging by any side (rather than a corner) will distort the image.

Then click and drag the clip art to center it, as shown in Figure 2.12.

Figure 2.12

Figure 2.12
Slide 3 now has some clip art to represent the topic of rain.

Where does the rain come from?

You have many other options for editing images. The next sections explain how you can modify an image in PowerPoint.

Changing coloring, contrast, and brightness

We chose a very bright picture. Perhaps you think that a rainy day shouldn't be so bright. You can change the coloring, contrast, and brightness. You don't need to use these tools for this image, but you should know how to use them for other projects.

For all these procedures, you need to select the image first.

HOW TO DO IT

- *Windows 2000/2002/2003:* The Picture toolbar appears, shown in Figure 2.13 (the Windows version is the image on the top). If the toolbar doesn't appear, choose View ➤ Toolbars ➤ Picture. To display shades of gray (called *grayscale*), click the Image Control button and choose Grayscale. Choose Watermark to make the image very light and faint. You might do this for an image that you want to place behind text. To increase or decrease the contrast, click the More Contrast or Less Contrast button until you get the result you want. To increase or decrease the brightness (lightness), click the More Brightness or Less Brightness button until you get the result you want.

- *Windows 2007:* Click the Format tab of the ribbon. To display grayscale, in the Adjust group, click Recolor and choose one of the gray options. You also have other coloring options that you can choose. To change contrast, click Contrast and choose one of the options. To change brightness, use the Brightness button.

- *Mac 2001/X/2004:* The Picture toolbar appears. (The Mac version is the Figure 2.13 image on the bottom.) If the toolbar doesn't appear, choose View ➢ Toolbars ➢ Picture. To display shades of gray (called *grayscale*), click the Image Control button and choose Grayscale. Choose Watermark to make the image very light and faint. You might do this for an image that you want to place behind text. To increase or decrease the contrast, click the More Contrast or Less Contrast button until you get the results you want. To increase or decrease the brightness (lightness), click the More Brightness or Less Brightness button until you get the results you want.

 On the Mac only, if you choose Effects, you can add some genuinely artistic effects to your picture, such as embossing it, or making it look like a charcoal, dry brush, and many more.

Cropping an image

You may not want to use all of an image. You can crop away the edges of any image. For example, in the picture we used, you may not like the black border.

To crop an image, select the image and follow the instructions here.

Figure 2.13
Use the Picture toolbar to edit images. [Windows; top; Mac; bottom]

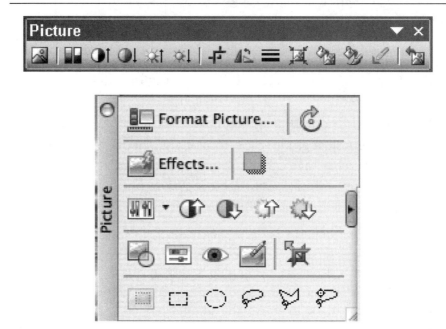

HOW TO DO IT

- *Windows 2000/2002/2003:* Click the Crop button on the Picture toolbar. You see bars on each side and on the corners of the image. Drag a bar inward on any side or corner until you get the results you want.

- *Windows 2007:* Click the Crop button in the Size group of the Format tab. You see bars on each side and on the corners of the image. Drag a bar inward on any side or corner until you get the results you want.

- *Mac 2001/X/2004:* Click the Crop button on the Picture toolbar. You see bars on each side and on the corners of the image. Drag a bar inward on any side or corner until you get the result you want.

Compressing pictures

Images, especially photographs, can be very large. You don't need high-resolution images in a presentation because the screen can't display all the detail. Large images result in large files, which load slowly and can sometimes crash a computer. Therefore, you should compress pictures if you can.

Unfortunately, PowerPoint 2000 and earlier Mac versions don't offer this feature. You may be able to find some outside software to accomplish this for you. For example, the software that comes with digital cameras may be able to compress images. In fact, you should be especially certain to compress photos that you take with a digital camera, because they are very large.

For the versions that can compress pictures, select an image and follow these instructions:

HOW TO DO IT

- *Windows 2002/2003:* Click Compress Pictures on the Picture toolbar. Choose the Screen or Web/Screen setting. Click OK.

- *Windows 2007:* On the Format tab, in the Adjust group, click Compress Pictures. Click Options for more settings. Choose the Screen or Web/Screen setting. Click OK.

- *Mac 2004:* Choose File ➢ Save As. Click the Options button in the dialog box. The Preferences dialog box opens. Check the Compress Graphic Files check box. From the Image Quality pop-up list, choose one of the options, such as Medium. Click OK. Give the file a new name (you can add "compressed" after the current name) and click Save.

 PowerPoint 2007 offers a special feature, called Picture Styles, which quickly applies formatting to pictures. First, select an image. On the Format tab, in the Picture Styles group, place the mouse cursor over an option to see how it looks. You can click the More (down) arrow for more styles. Continue to move the mouse over styles until you find one that you like.

For more formatting options, select a picture, right-click (Win)/Ctrl-click (Mac) it, and choose Format Picture. The Format Picture dialog box opens where you can try out other settings.

ADDING SHAPES

PowerPoint has its own drawing tools that you can use to create your own graphics. You can fill them with a solid color, a gradient, or a picture—or no fill at all. You can choose an outline color or use no outline.

For our water cycle presentation, we wanted to add some arrows to depict the concept of a cycle.

Inserting Shapes

In order to add the water cycle diagram, first add a new slide after the second image (the clip art), using the Title Only layout. See the earlier section of the chapter on how to add a slide with a layout. See the "Adding a Slide" and "Choosing a Layout" sections, earlier in this chapter, for instructions on adding a slide and specifying a layout.

Click in the title area and type **The Water Cycle**.

Follow the instructions to add the two arrows. At this point, don't worry about their size, placement, or formatting.

HOW TO DO IT

- *Windows 2000/2002/2003:* On the Drawing toolbar, choose AutoShapes ➤ Block Arrows ➤ Curved Right Arrow. Click in the middle of the slide to insert the arrow. On the same toolbar, choose Draw ➤ Rotate or Flip ➤ Flip Vertical. Choose AutoShapes ➤ Block Arrows ➤ Curved Left Arrow and click somewhere to the right of the first arrow.

- *Windows 2007:* From the Insert tab, click the Shapes button. In the Block Arrows section, click Curved Right Arrow. Click in the middle of the slide to insert the arrow. Click the Format tab that appears. In

---

the Arrange group, Click Rotate ➤ Flip Vertical. Again from the Insert tab, insert the Curved Left Arrow and click somewhere to the right of the first arrow.

- *Mac 2001/X/2004:* On the Drawing toolbar, choose AutoShapes ➤ Block Arrows ➤ Curved Right Arrow. Click in the middle of the slide to insert the arrow. On the same toolbar, choose Draw ➤ Rotate or Flip ➤ Flip Vertical. Choose AutoShapes ➤ Block Arrows ➤ Curved Left Arrow and click somewhere to the right of the first arrow.

Your slide should look something like Figure 2.14.

As you can see, the arrows should be larger and they need to be lined up. We'll take care of those tasks a little later on in this chapter.

Figure 2.14
These two arrows are the basis for a diagram on the water cycle.

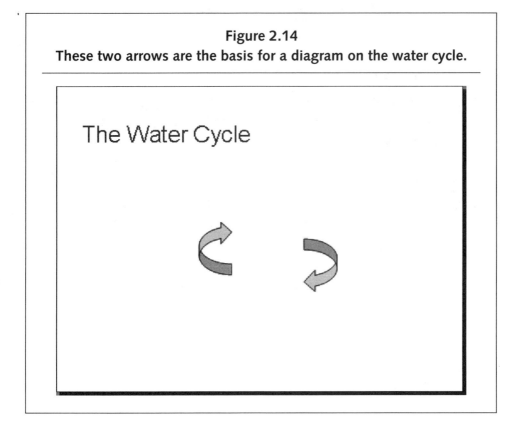

Using the Slide Master

Now, because the slides are so plain, we'd like to add a little decoration on them. This will be a simple bar under the title of each slide. The slide master lets you format the entire presentation. For example, you can set the font, font size, and font color for the presentation here. Also, any image that you place on the slide master appears on every slide. We'll place the bar on the slide master so that it automatically appears on each slide.

 Except for PowerPoint 2000, all versions let you have more than one slide master for a presentation.

To add an object—or a background—to the slide master, you need to display the slide master. Use these instructions to access the slide master.

HOW TO DO IT

- *Windows 2000/2002/2003:* Choose View ➤ Master ➤ Slide Master. You can also press Shift and click the Normal view button at the lower-left corner of your screen. (To return to Normal view, choose View ➤ Normal or click the Normal view button at the lower-left corner of your screen.)

- *Windows 2007:* Click the View tab and click the Slide Master button in the Presentation Views group. To make changes to all layouts, click the Master, which is the first (largest) thumbnail in the left pane. You can also press Shift and click the Normal view button at the lower-right corner of your screen. (To return to Normal view, click Normal on the View tab or click the Normal view button at the lower-right corner of your screen.)

- *Mac 2001/X/2004:* Choose View ➤ Master ➤ Slide Master. (To return to Normal view, choose View ➤ Normal or click the Normal view button at the lower-left corner of your screen.)

Figure 2.15
The slide master provides formatting for the entire presentation or for each slide that uses that slide master.

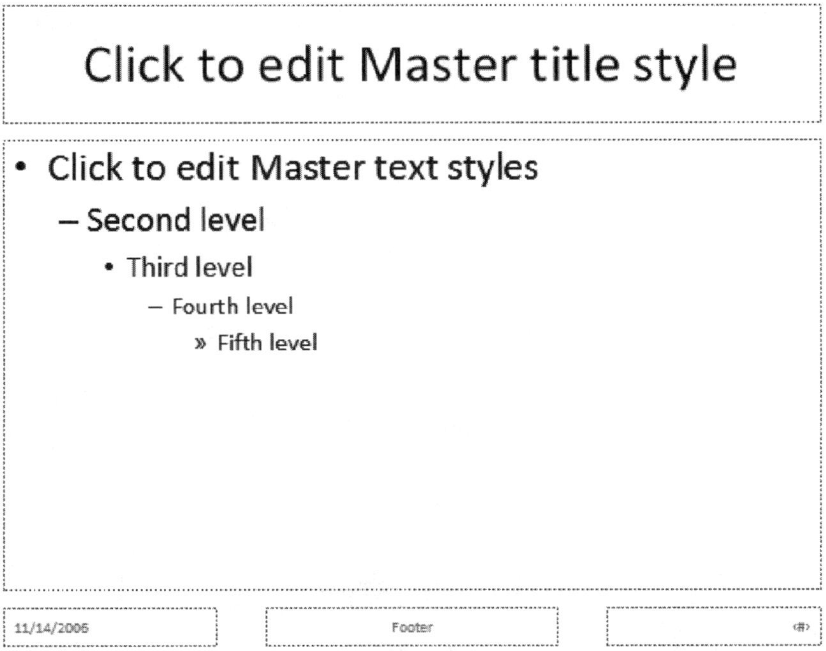

Click to edit Master title style

- Click to edit Master text styles
  - Second level
    - Third level
      - Fourth level
        » Fifth level

11/14/2005   Footer   ‹#›

You should now see the slide master, as shown in Figure 2.15.

To insert the bar, we'll add a rounded rectangle shape to the slide master. If the Drawing bar is not displayed, choose View ➢ Toolbars ➢ Drawing. (You don't need to display the toolbar in PowerPoint 2007.) Follow these instructions:

HOW TO DO IT

- *Windows 2000/2002/2003:* On the Drawing toolbar, choose AutoShapes ➢ Basic Shapes ➢ Rounded Rectangle. Click and drag from the lower-left corner of the title's placeholder and to the upper-left corner of the *Object Area*, where the body slide text goes.

- *Windows 2007:* From the Insert tab, click the Shapes button. In the Rectangles section, choose Rounded Rectangle. Click at the lower-left corner of the title's placeholder and again at the upper-left corner of the *Object Area*, where the body slide text goes.

- *Mac 2001/X/2004:* On the Drawing toolbar, choose AutoShapes ➤ Basic Shapes ➤ Rounded Rectangle. Click at the lower-left corner of the title's placeholder and again at the upper-left corner of the *Object Area*, where the body slide text goes. Your slide should look like Figure 2.16.

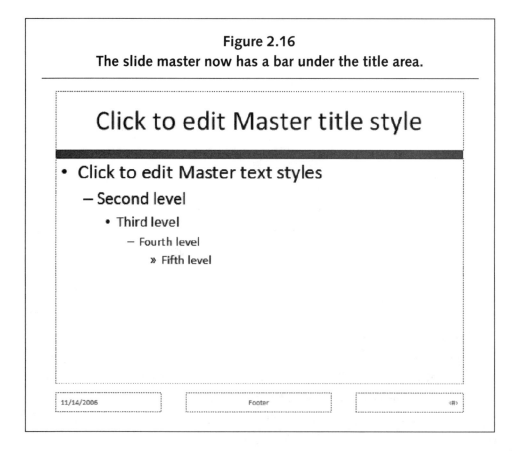

Figure 2.16
The slide master now has a bar under the title area.

Click to edit Master title style

- Click to edit Master text styles
  - Second level
    - Third level
      - Fourth level
        » Fifth level

11/14/2006   Footer   〈#〉

Editing and Formatting Shapes

You have lots of control over how your AutoShapes (or Shapes in PowerPoint 2007) look. In this section, we'll format some shapes.

Formatting fills and outlines

Given the topic of the presentation, perhaps a little water-related decoration is in order. To add it, let's format the fill of the rounded rectangle you just inserted.

Follow these instructions to change the fill and outline of the bar:

HOW TO DO IT

- *Windows 2000/2002/2003:* Double-click the shape to open the Format AutoShape dialog box. In the Fill section, click the Color drop-down list. Choose Fill Effects and click the Texture tab. Scroll down, choose the Water Droplets swatch, and click OK. In the Line section, click the Color drop-down list and choose Aqua. Click OK.

- *Windows 2007:* Double-click the shape to display the Format tab. Click the Shape Fill button and choose Texture. Choose Water Droplets. Click the Shape Outline button and choose one of the Aqua tints.

- *Mac 2001/X/2004:* Double-click the shape to open the Format AutoShape dialog box. In the Fill section, click the Color drop-down list. Choose Fill Effects and click the Textures tab. Scroll down, choose the Water Droplets swatch, and click OK. In the Line section, click the Color drop-down list and choose Aqua. Click OK.

You can see the Format AutoShape dialog box in Figure 2.17.

Note that you have many more options for formatting objects. You can adjust their transparency, change the width of outlines, and so on. For example, to adjust transparency, drag the Transparency slider in the Fill section of the Format AutoShape dialog box. Also, if objects overlap, you can change which object appears on top or below. Right-click the selected object and choose one of the suboptions of the Order menu item. (In PowerPoint 2007, look for the Bring to Front and Send to Back items.)

Figure 2.17

The Format AutoShape dialog box lets you specify fills, outlines, and more.

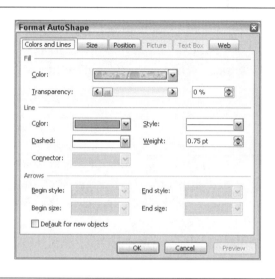

In PowerPoint 2007, you have other special effects available, such as reflections, glows, and soft edges. From the Format tab, click the Shape Effects button. You can also choose from preset Shape Styles to format shapes.

Exit the slide master by clicking the Normal view button or follow the instructions in the previous "Using the Slide Master" section of this chapter. Figure 2.18 shows one of the text slides with the bar.

Removing background graphics from a slide

There's only one problem. The title slide also has a bar in the same location, but it doesn't look very good on that slide. Because title slides are often laid out differently, PowerPoint has a special tool for this situation. First, return to the slide master, following the instructions in the "Using the Slide Master" section earlier in this chapter.

Figure 2.18
The slides all have a bar under the title area, filled with water droplets.

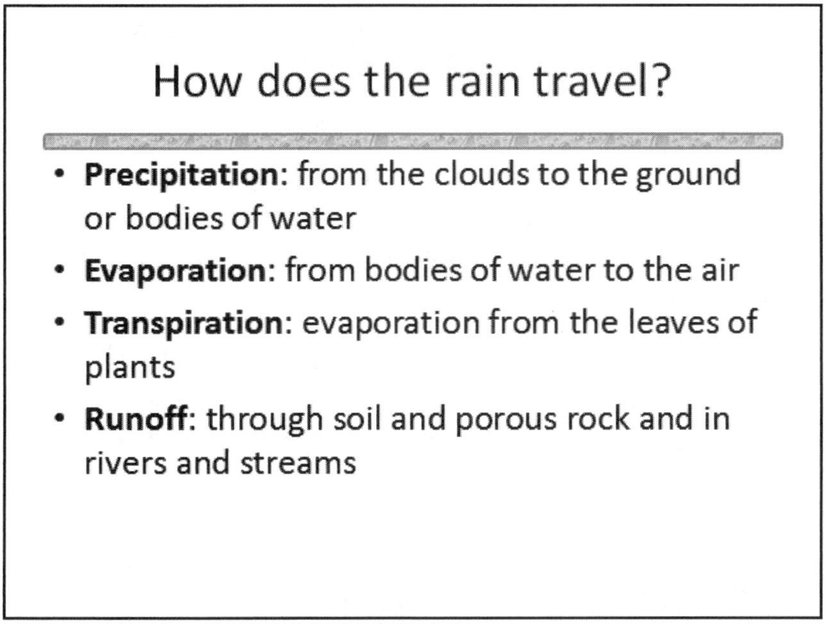

How does the rain travel?

- **Precipitation**: from the clouds to the ground or bodies of water
- **Evaporation**: from bodies of water to the air
- **Transpiration**: evaporation from the leaves of plants
- **Runoff**: through soil and porous rock and in rivers and streams

---

HOW TO DO IT

- *Windows 2000/2002/2003:* From the slide master, choose Insert ➤ New Title Master. The title master appears in the slide pane. Click the bar you just created and press the Delete key.

- *Windows 2007:* From the slide master, click the Slide Master at the top to display it in the slide pane. Click the bar and press Ctrl+X to cut it to the Clipboard. Click the Title and Content layout (which should be the third box from the top) to display it. Press Ctrl+V. This moves the bar to the Title and Content layout; it will now only appear on slides using that layout and won't appear on the title slide.

- *Mac 2001/X/2004:* From the slide master, choose Insert ➤ New Title Master. The title master appears in the slide pane. Click the bar and press the Delete key.

Exit the slide master by clicking the Normal view button.

What would you do if you wanted to remove the background image from a slide that wasn't a title slide? You can do that too, although we don't need to for this presentation. These are the steps you would take if you wanted to remove a background image (that you placed on the slide master) from another slide.

HOW TO DO IT

- *Windows 2000/2002/2003:* Display the slide. Choose Format ➤ Background. In the Background dialog box, check the Omit Background Graphics from Master check box and click Apply.

- *Windows 2007:* Display the slide. On the Design tab, in the Background group, check the Hide Background Graphics check box.

- *Mac 2001/X/2004:* Display the slide. Choose Format ➤ Background. In the Background dialog box, check the Omit Background Graphics from Master check box and click Apply.

Resizing and aligning shapes

We want to make the arrows for our water cycle diagram larger and we need to align them. It's easy to resize selected objects by dragging on their handles. But in this case, we want to make sure that they're exactly the same size, so we'll use a different method.

To resize objects precisely, follow these instructions from Normal view:

HOW TO DO IT

- *Windows 2000/2002/2003:* Display the slide with the two arrows. Double-click the left arrow to open the Format AutoShape dialog box and click the Size tab. In the Scale section, change the height to 200% and the width to 150%. Click OK. Do the same for the right arrow.

- *Windows 2007:* Display the slide with the two arrows. Double-click the left arrow to display the Format tab. In the Size group, click the dialog box launcher arrow on the right to open the Size and Position dialog box. In the Scale section, change the height to 200% and the width to 150%. Click OK. Do the same for the right arrow.

- *Mac 2001/X/2004:* Display the slide with the two arrows. Double-click the left arrow to open the Format AutoShape dialog box and click the Size tab. In the Scale section, change the height to 200% and the width to 150%. Click OK. Do the same for the right arrow.

The arrows are now big enough, but we now need to align the arrows so they're at the same level on the slide. We also want to center the arrows to leave room for some text on either side. Follow the instructions:

HOW TO DO IT

- *Windows 2000/2002/2003:* Click the left arrow, then press Shift and click the right arrow to select them both. On the Drawing toolbar, choose Draw ➢ Align or Distribute ➢ Align Top. Pass the cursor over one of the arrows until you see a four-headed arrow and drag to center the arrows on the slide.

- *Windows 2007:* Click the left arrow, then press Shift and click the right arrow to select them both. On the Format tab, in the Arrange group, choose Align ➢ Align Top to align the tops of the arrows. Pass the cursor over one of the arrows until you see a four-headed arrow and drag to center the arrows on the slide.

- *Mac 2001/X/2004:* Click the left arrow, then press Shift and click the right arrow to select them both. On the Drawing toolbar, choose Draw ➢ Align or Distribute ➢ Align Top. Pass the cursor over one of the arrows and drag to center the arrows on the slide.

Inserting and editing text boxes

We're almost done with this slide, except for some animation that we'll add later on. We need to add two text boxes describing the basics of the water cycle. Follow these instructions.

HOW TO DO IT

- *Windows 2000/2002/2003:* Choose Insert ➤ Text Box (or click the Text Box button on the Drawing toolbar). In the upper-left section of the slide's body area, drag from the left margin to the left arrow, leaving some room on each side. Type **Water moves up through evaporation and transpiration**. Add another text box on the lower-right section of the slide and type **Water moves down through precipitation and runoff**.

- *Windows 2007:* Click the Insert tab. In the Text group, click the Text Box button. In the upper-left section of the slide's body area, drag from the left margin to the left arrow, leaving some room on each side. Type **Water moves up through evaporation and transpiration**. Add another text box on the lower-right section of the slide and type **Water moves down through precipitation and runoff**.

- *Mac 2001/X/2004:* Choose Insert ➤ Text Box (or click the Text Box button on the Drawing toolbar). In the upper-left section of the slide's body area, drag from the left margin to the left arrow, leaving some room on each side. Type **Water moves up through evaporation and transpiration**. Add another text box on the lower-right section of the slide and type **Water moves down through precipitation and runoff**.

Your slide should look like Figure 2.19. If you want to change the size or placement, select a text box and drag on a handle to resize it, or drag it to a different location.

You may want to change the size, color, or font of the text in the text box. You can choose a size, color, or font that appeals to you. To do so, follow the instructions:

HOW TO DO IT

- *Windows 2000/2002/2003:* Select the text. On the Formatting toolbar, click the Font drop-down list to change the font, click the Font Size drop-down list to change the font size, and click the Font Color drop-down list (which is also on the Drawing toolbar) to change the color.

- *Windows 2007:* Select the text. The mini toolbar appears (it's translucent; if it doesn't appear, right-click the text). Click the Font drop-down list to change the font, click the Font Size drop-down list to change the font size, and click the Font Color drop-down list to change the color.

- *Mac 2001/X/2004:* Select the text. In the Font section of the Formatting palette, click the Font drop-down list to change the font, click the Font Size drop-down list to change the font size, and click the Font Color drop-down list (which is also on the Drawing toolbar) to change the color.

When was the last time you saved your presentation?

Figure 2.19
The completed water cycle diagram.

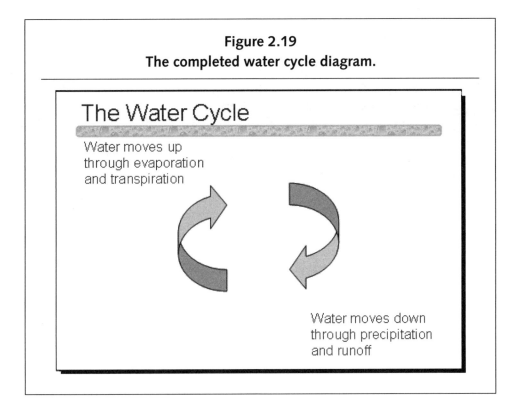

Using Charts and Diagrams

PowerPoint can create excellent graphs (often called charts) based on spreadsheet data. We won't create a graph in this presentation, but we discuss them in Chapter 3. They are especially important in science and math lessons for older students.

 Diagrams provide a way to present content in a visual way. You may feel that a diagram will make a point more visually. Although we won't cover this feature, you can try it out yourself. To insert a diagram, click the Insert Diagram or Organization Chart button on the Drawing toolbar or choose Insert ➤ Diagram from the menu. (In PowerPoint 2007, click SmartArt on the Insert tab.)

> PowerPoint 2007 has improved charting capabilities with a closer connection with Excel. Also, SmartArt diagrams offer more options than in previous versions, including the ability to automatically convert bulleted text to a diagram.

ADDING A BACKGROUND

If you've seen other PowerPoint presentations, you may have noticed that many of them have a background design on each slide. You don't need to add a background design (or color), but you can if you want to.

When you add a background, watch out for two potential problems:

- *Distracting graphics or color.* Research shows (see Appendix A) that distracting graphics hinder learning. This is not surprising. So don't add a pretty background or unnecessary images just because you can. The role of a background is to enhance, not to distract. You can use a background to give a hint of the topic.

- *Lack of legibility.* Whenever you add a lot of color to a background, you run the risk of making text hard to read. The contrast between the background color and the text should be very high.

See Chapter 4, "Understanding Best Practices," for more information on this topic.

Except for the small droplet-filled bar, we didn't add a background to our final presentation on the water cycle, but you may still want to do so. In any event, this is a skill you should know for other projects. You can make your own decision.

Follow along and practice adding backgrounds. If you like the result, keep it. Otherwise, you can choose Edit ➤ Undo (Undo on the Quick Access toolbar in PowerPoint 2007) and undo your changes.

There are three ways to add a background:

- Choose a template (or a theme, in PowerPoint 2007).

- Add a background to the slide master.

- Add a background to one or more individual slides.

For instructions to display the slide master, see "Using the Slide Master" earlier in this chapter. The next few sections explain how to add backgrounds.

Choosing a Template

PowerPoint provides backgrounds for you and the simplest way to add a background to a presentation is to use one of them. Follow these steps:

HOW TO DO IT

- *Windows 2000:* When you first start PowerPoint, choose Design Template from the PowerPoint dialog box. The New Presentation dialog box opens with the Design Templates tab on top. Choose a design and click OK. If you're already in a presentation, click the Common Tasks button and choose Apply Design Template. In the Apply Design Template dialog box, choose a template and Apply.

- *Windows 2002/2003:* Click the Design button to display the Slide Design task pane. Click one of the design templates.

- *Windows 2007:* Click the Design tab. In the Themes group, click the More (down) button to display all the themes. (Themes are similar to templates.) Hover the cursor over any theme to see what it looks like on the slide. When you find one you like, click it.

- *Mac 2001/X/2004:* From the Formatting palette, click the Slide Design button in the Change Slides panel and choose a slide design. Or choose Format ➤ Slide Design, choose a design, and click Apply.

Except in PowerPoint 2000, you can add more than one template (or theme). Select the slides that you want to use from the Slides tab and choose Apply to Selected Slides. (If you don't see this option, try right-clicking and using the shortcut menu.)

Creating a Background for an Individual Slide

You can create a background for a slide. In this case, you're not using the slide master or a template (or theme); you're just creating a unique background and applying it to one or more slides.

Solid Backgrounds

The simplest type of background is a solid color. It's not distracting, but it's not very interesting either. Remember that you can just leave the default white background if you want. Add some black text and you can be sure that your text will be legible!

 A dark solid background (dark blue or black) looks very elegant with light font colors (yellow, white). Such backgrounds are great for projects about outer space!

If you want to add a solid background to one or more slides, follow these instructions:

HOW TO DO IT

- *Windows 2000/2002/2003:* Select the slide(s) in the Slides tab (or in Slide Sorter view). Choose Format ➤ Background. In the Background dialog box, shown in Figure 2.20, click the drop-down list and choose one of the colors or choose More Colors to specify any color you want in the Colors dialog box. Click Apply.

- *Windows 2007:* Select the slide(s) in the Slides tab (or in Slide Sorter view). On the Design tab, in the Background group, click the dialog box launcher arrow on the right to open the Format Background dialog box. Choose the Fill category and choose the Solid Fill option. From the Colors drop-down list choose a color or choose More Colors to specify any color you want in the Colors dialog box. Click Close.

- *Mac 2001/X/2004:* Select the slide(s) in the Outline pane (or in Slide Sorter view). Choose Format ➤ Slide Background. In the Background dialog box, shown in Figure 2.20, click the drop-down list and choose one of the colors or choose More Colors to specify any color you want in the Colors dialog box. Click Apply.

Figure 2.20
You can give slides any background you want from the Background dialog box.

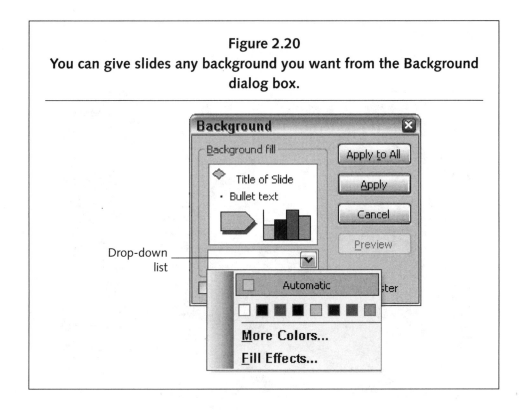

Drop-down list

To format the background in the slide master, open the slide master first, using the instructions in the "Using the Slide Master" section. Clicking Apply applies the background to the entire presentation.

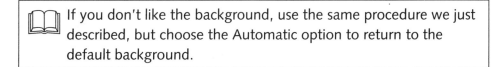 If you don't like the background, use the same procedure we just described, but choose the Automatic option to return to the default background.

Gradient Backgrounds

A gradient background changes the color gradually along the slide. You can create several types of gradients, but make sure that your text is very clear everywhere on the slide. In this case, we made the text white so it would show up clearly. Figure 2.21 shows a slide with a gradient background.

Figure 2.21
A slide with a gradient background.

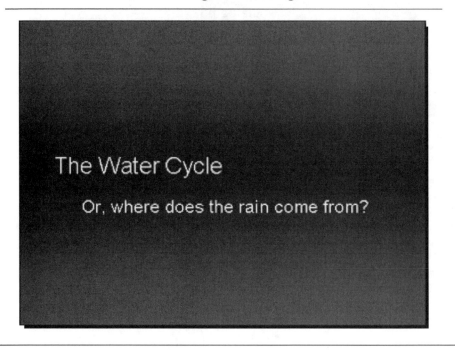

To add a gradient background, follow these directions:

HOW TO DO IT

- *Windows 2000/2002/2003:* Select the slide(s) in the Slides tab. Choose Format ≻ Background. In the Background dialog box, click the drop-down list and choose Fill Effects. On the Gradient tab, choose one of the Colors options and select the color or colors that you want. Try out the various shading styles and variants. Click OK. Click Apply. To format the background in the slide master, open the slide master first, as explained earlier, and follow the same procedure. Clicking Apply applies the background to the entire presentation.

- *Windows 2007:* Select the slide(s) in the Slides tab. On the Design tab, in the Background group, click the dialog box launcher button on the right to open the Format ➤ Background dialog box. Choose the Fill category and choose the Gradient Fill option. Choose a type, direction, and angle. Choose the number of colors (*stops*) by clicking Add. For each stop, specify the position and color. Click Close. To format the background in the slide master, open the slide master first, as explained earlier, and follow the same procedure (but the Background group is on the Slide Master tab).

- *Mac 2001/X/2004:* Select the slide(s) in the Slides tab. Choose Format Background. In the Background dialog box, click the drop-down list and choose Fill Effects. On the Gradient tab, choose one of the Colors options and select the color or colors that you want. Try out the various shading styles and variants. Click OK. Click Apply (or Apply to All to format the entire presentation). To format the background in the slide master, open the slide master first, as explained earlier, and follow the same procedure. Clicking Apply applies the background to the entire presentation.

Picture Backgrounds

The most beautiful backgrounds are pictures, but pictures are most likely to interfere with your text. They also increase the size of your PowerPoint file (especially if you don't compress them). Figure 2.22 shows a slide with a picture background. To make sure that the text would still be clear, we darkened the photo and reduced the contrast in addition to changing the text color to white.

 Fill a text placeholder or text box with an opaque or partially transparent fill. This hides the background enough so that the text is clear. See "Editing and Formatting Shapes" earlier in this chapter for instructions.

Figure 2.22
A picture background can make a lovely slide.

The Water Cycle

Or, where does the rain come from?

To add a picture background, follow these instructions:

HOW TO DO IT

- *Windows 2000/2002/2003:* Select the slide(s) in the Slides tab. Choose Format ➤ Background. In the Background dialog box, click the drop-down list and choose Fill Effects. On the Picture tab, click the Select Picture button. Select a picture and click Insert. Click OK. Click Apply (or Apply to All to format the entire presentation). To format the background in the slide master, open the slide master first, as explained earlier, and follow the same procedure. Clicking Apply applies the background to the entire presentation. You can also have this background on any number of slides if you copy and paste the slide.

- *Windows 2007:* Select the slide(s) in the Slides tab. On the Design tab, in the Background group, click the dialog box launcher button on the right to open the Format Background dialog box. Choose the Fill category and choose the Picture or Texture Fill option. Click the File button, select a picture, and click Insert. Click Close. To format the background in the slide master, open the slide master first, as explained earlier, and follow the same procedure (but the Background group is on the Slide Master tab).

- *Mac 2001/X/2004:* Select the slide(s) in the Slides tab. Choose Format ➤ Background. In the Background dialog box, click the drop-down list and choose Fill Effects. On the Picture tab, click the Select Picture button. Select a picture and click Insert. Click OK. Click Apply (or Apply to All to format the entire presentation). To format the background in the slide master, open the slide master first, as explained earlier, and follow the same procedure. Clicking Apply applies the background to the entire presentation.

 Don't forget that if you make a change that you don't like, you can choose Edit ➤ Undo to undo the change. In PowerPoint 2007, click the Undo button on the Quick Access toolbar.

MOVING A SLIDE

You now have six slides in your presentation. Of course, you could add many more, depending on how detailed you want your lesson plan to be.

Sometimes you decide that you want to change the order of the slides, or delete a slide. In this section, we explain how to accomplish these tasks.

Using Slide Sorter View

Slide Sorter view provides you with thumbnails of all of your slides in one place. Slide Sorter view is a good place to move and delete slides. To enter Slide Sorter view, follow these instructions:

HOW TO DO IT

 • *Windows 2000/2002/2003:* Click the Slide Sorter button at the lower-left corner of your screen, or choose View ➤ Slide Sorter.

 • *Windows 2007:* Click the Slide Sorter button at the lower-right corner of your screen, or display the View tab and click the Slide Sorter button.

 • *Mac 2001/X/2004:* Click the Slide Sorter button at the lower-left corner of your screen, or choose View ➤ Slide Sorter.

Figure 2.23 shows the water cycle presentation in Slide Sorter view. You can see that each slide displays a number beneath it.

Dragging a Slide to a New Position

The first text slide defines some terms relating to the water cycle but it comes after the diagram, which uses those terms. Let's move the text slide with the definitions before the water cycle diagram. Follow these instructions.

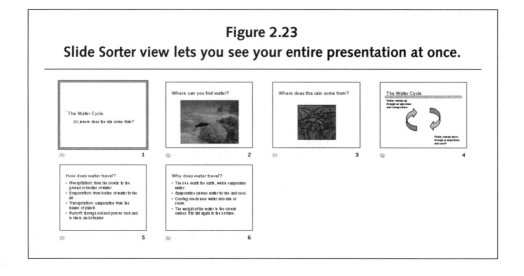

Figure 2.23
Slide Sorter view lets you see your entire presentation at once.

HOW TO DO IT

- *All versions:* In Slide Sorter view, click slide 5 ("How does water travel?"). Drag it between slides 3 and 4.

Copying and Pasting a Slide

Sometimes you want to create a new slide that is similar to an existing slide. An easy way to do this is to copy the slide and then paste it. This makes a duplicate of the slide. We won't do this for this presentation, but here are the steps for future reference:

HOW TO DO IT

- *Windows 2000/2002/2003/2007:* Select the slide that you want to copy. Press Ctrl+C or choose Edit ➤ Copy. Click where you want the new slide to appear. Press Ctrl+V or choose Edit ➤ Paste.
- *Mac 2001/X/2004:* Select the slide that you want to copy. Press ⌘+C or choose Edit ➤ Copy. Click where you want the new slide to appear. Press ⌘+C or choose Edit ➤ Paste.

Deleting a Slide

To delete a slide, select it and press the Delete key.

We're done with Slide Sorter view. To return to Normal view, double-click any slide or click the Normal view icon.

ADDING ANIMATION

The presentation is almost done! In fact, it could stand the way it is, but we would be remiss if we didn't explain how to add some animation. Children love animation, and PowerPoint has lots of animation options. Anything that moves commands attention. In addition, animation can make a point clearer by demonstrating a process.

For our presentation, we'll add three types of animation:

- *Text animation.* Each line of text appears after the previous line, in order.

- *Object animation.* PowerPoint offers lots of options for displaying, moving, and hiding objects.

- *Slide transitions.* You can choose an effect for displaying how slides appear.

 Avoid too much animation. Words or letters flying in and out may be a lot of fun, but after some time, they become annoying. Use your taste and common sense! Think about the age of your students: younger students may be fascinated, but those in high school may not.

Adding Text Animation

You can build up text, line by line, on a slide. You might do this to focus the students' attention on each line as you discuss it. This type of animation is easy to do.

We'll add animation to the two text slides. First, display the new slide 4 ("How does water travel?") so we can animate it. You should be in Normal view. Follow these instructions:

HOW TO DO IT

- *Windows 2000:* Select the body text placeholder by clicking its border and choose Slide Show ➢ Custom Animation. In the Custom Animation dialog box, use the Animation Effect drop-down list to choose Appear.

- *Windows 2002/2003:* Select the body text placeholder by clicking its border and choose Slide Show ➢ Custom Animation. In the Custom Animation task pane, click the Add Effect button and choose Entrance ➢ Appear. (If you don't see the Appear effect, click More Effects.)

- *Windows 2007:* Select the body text placeholder by clicking its border and click the Animations tab. Click the Custom Animation button. In the Custom Animation task pane, click the Add Effect button and choose Entrance ➢ Appear. (If you don't see the Appear effect, click More Effects.)

- *Mac 2001/X/2004:* Select the body text and choose Slide Show Custom Animation. In the Custom Animation task pane, click the Add Effect button and choose Entrance ➢ Appear. (If you don't see the Appear effect, click More Effects.)

You have now created a simple animation that causes each line of text to appear one after the other when you click the mouse. Because the default is to animate text bullet by bullet, you don't have to do anything else. You can preview the result in the Custom Animation task pane/dialog box. We'll also look at it later in Slide Show view.

Display slide 6 and add the same animation to that slide.

Adding Object Animation

You can animate objects on your slides. Object animation offers lots of options that can be both fun and useful. We'll only touch on the subject here, but feel free to try out the different types of animation to see how they look.

We'd like the arrows in the water cycle diagram to *wipe* up or down so that the animation emphasizes the direction of the arrow. First, display your new slide 5, which contains the diagram. Follow these instructions:

HOW TO DO IT

- *Windows 2000:* Select the left arrow and choose Slide Show ➢ Custom Animation. In the Custom Animation dialog box, choose Wipe for the animation effect. Make sure that the direction is From Bottom. Change the speed to Fast. Select the right arrow and add the same animation, but change the direction to From Top.

- *Windows 2002/2003:* Select the left arrow and choose Slide Show ➢ Custom Animation. Click the Add Effect button and choose Entrance ➢ Wipe. (If you don't see the Wipe effect, click More Effects.) In the task pane, make sure that the direction is From

Bottom. Change the speed to Fast. Select the right arrow and add the same animation, but change the direction to From Top.

- *Windows 2007:* Select the left arrow and choose Slide Show ➢ Custom Animation. In the Custom Animation task pane, click the Add Effect button and choose Entrance ➢ Wipe. (If you don't see the Wipe effect, click More Effects.) In the task pane, make sure that the direction is From Bottom. Change the speed to Fast. Select the right arrow and add the same animation, but change the direction to From Top.

- *Mac 2001/X/2004:* Select the left arrow and choose Slide Show ➢ Custom Animation. In the Custom Animation dialog box, choose Wipe for the entry animation effect. Make sure that the direction is From Bottom. Change the speed to Fast. Select the right arrow and add the same animation, but change the direction to From Top. You can program when the animation starts by selecting On Click, With Previous or After Previous. If you select On Click the arrow will appear right after your click. If you select With Previous, the arrow will appear at exactly the same time with the beginning of the slide. When you select After Previous, the arrow will appear after some other animation (first arrow or after an audio file stops playing). Also, you can make the arrow appear from different angles if you select Property. And the Speed options will offer you different duration of the animation.

In PowerPoint 2002 through 2007 for Windows, you can also animate objects along a path. In the Custom Animation task pane, choose Add Effect ➢ Motion Paths. Unfortunately, PowerPoint for the Mac does not offer this excellent animation option.

In all of the preceding animations, we kept the default that starts the animation when you click the mouse. However, you can start animations automatically when a slide is displayed by changing the Start setting to With Previous. The Start setting of After Previous lets you specify a delay (in seconds) between animations.

For more possibilities, click an animation and use its drop-down list to choose Effect Options or Timing if your version has a task pane. If your version has a dialog box, use the tabs to specify other options.

Adding Slide Transitions

Finally, we want to add a simple transition effect from slide to slide. The only purpose for this is to add a bit of spit and polish to the presentation. You'll find this task easiest in Slide Show view, so first enter that view. If you need instructions, see the section "Entering Slide Show View" later in this chapter.

Then follow these instructions to add the slide transition:

HOW TO DO IT

- *Windows 2000:* Choose Slide Show ➢ Slide Transition. In the Slide Transition dialog box, choose Wipe Right from the drop-down list in the Effect section. Click the Medium option. Click Apply to All.

- *Windows 2002/2003:* Click the Transition button. In the Slide Transition task pane, choose Wipe Right (you'll have to scroll down to see it). From the Speed drop-down list, choose Medium. Then click the Apply to All Slides button.

- *Windows 2007:* Click the Animations tab. In the Transition to This Slide group, click the More button (at the right of the Slide Transition gallery) and choose Wipe Right from the Wipes section. From the Transition Speed drop-down list, choose Medium. Click Apply to All.

- *Mac 2001/X/2004:* Choose Slide Show ➢ Slide Transition. In the Slide Transition dialog box, choose Wipe Right from the drop-down list in the Effect section. Click the Medium option. Click Apply to All.

Your presentation is now complete! You're ready to view it full-screen and see how it will look when you deliver it in class.

Be sure to save your presentation before you go on.

 You can find the completed presentation at www.ellenfinkelstein. com/powerpointforteachers.html.

PRESENTING THE SLIDE SHOW

Before you present the slide show in class, review it at home. To avoid mishaps, always rehearse the process of going through the presentation. This section explains the delivery process.

You'll probably use a projector to display the presentation on a screen or the wall. If your school has a projector, someone may be available to show you how to use it. Projectors also come with a manual that you can read. Here we provide some simple steps.

HOW TO DO IT

1. Ideally, you should start with the computer turned off.

2. Make sure that you have the power cord and a computer cable. The computer cable will have a number of pins at one end. The other end may have pins or a USB connector (or both).

3. Take the lens cap off the projector.

4. Connect the projector to the computer using the computer cable. Just match the connectors; if it fits, you have the right place.

5. Connect the power cord to the projector and plug it into an outlet. (Always make sure that the power cord is situated in such a way that no one will trip over it. If necessary, use an extension cord and tape it to the floor.)

6. Turn on the projector. This may involve two switches, one for the projector and one for the lamp. If the computer is on, you should see the computer display on the screen. If not, you'll see some text displaying the projector's name and logo.

7. To raise the picture, use the projector's foot. Look for a release button that lets the foot drop down. You can then adjust the height.

8. Move the projector away from the screen to get a larger display; move it toward the screen to get a smaller display.

9. Adjust the lens to get the best focus. There are usually other buttons that adjust the display in other ways. Most projectors also have a menu for configuring the display.

---

10. If the computer isn't on, turn it on. Laptops generally have a keyboard combination to display on both the laptop's screen and the projector. Look along the F keys. You may have to press a Fn key to access this function. For example, press Fn+F8. (If necessary, check the laptop's manual.)

 Depending on your operating system, you might see a screen that lets you configure the display. Specifically, you can choose to display the same image on both the computer and through the projector, or in some other configuration.

After a brief wait, you should see your computer's display on the screen. If not, close down the computer and turn it on again. Make sure you press the right keyboard combination if you have a laptop. Then look at the troubleshooting section of the projector's manual.

 If you're on a Mac, you may need an adaptor to connect to the projector. Before you're ready to deliver your presentation, check the projector's manual or ask your Information Technology person/department.

When you're done, turn off the projector. If you hear a fan whirring, wait until it turns off before unplugging the projector. The fan cools down the light gradually, which helps it last longer.

Entering Slide Show View

You deliver a presentation in Slide Show view, which shows the presentation full-screen. Here's where all of your work shines!

To enter Slide Show view, click the first slide of your presentation and follow these instructions.

HOW TO DO IT ·

- *Windows 2000/2002/2003:* Click the Slide Show button at the lower-left corner of your screen.

- *Windows 2007:* Click the Slide Show button at the lower-right corner of your screen.

- *Mac 2001/X/2004:* Click the Slide Show button at the lower-left corner of your screen.

To exit Slide Show view, press the Esc key.

Navigating Through Slides

Once you're in Slide Show view, you can do any of the following to move from slide to slide:

- Click the mouse.
- Press the spacebar.
- Press Enter.
- Press the N key.
- Press the right or down arrow.

  If you want to redisplay the previous slide, do any of the following:

- Press the backspace key.
- Press the P key.
- Press the left or up arrow.

  Here are some other keystrokes that you should know when presenting:

- Go to any slide number: type the slide number and press Enter.
- Black out the screen: press the B key.

 Blacking out the screen is a great idea when you want to elaborate on a topic and don't want the students' attention to wander back to the slide (and away from you).

In addition, you can right-click (Win)/Ctrl-click (Mac) to display a shortcut menu with more options. There's a subtle button area at the lower-left corner of the screen that displays the same shortcut menu.

Remember, press Esc to exit Slide Show view. However, you can turn the projector off so that the students don't see Normal view.

Saving Your Project as a PowerPoint Show

You can save your presentation in a format that will open your slides full-screen immediately. This is the way the presentation will look when you show it to your students. By using this format, you'll avoid showing them Normal view and everything will look more polished and professional. This format is called a PowerPoint show.

Wait until you have fully completed creating your presentation. Then follow these steps:

HOW TO DO IT

1. Choose File ➢ Save As.

2. From the Save as Type drop-down list, choose PowerPoint Show (*.pps/*.ppsx).

3. To leave the location and name the same, click Save.

 In Chapter 4, we explain how to print handouts and notes.

SUMMARY

In this chapter, we explained how to create a complete presentation on the water cycle. We discussed how to begin by creating the lesson plan and gathering images. Then we showed how to start a new presentation and add some slides, specifying the appropriate layout. We also explained how to add notes that you could print later.

We covered how to enter text on a slide and in the Outline tab, and how to move around a presentation. We reviewed the process of adding images, both photos and clip art, and how to edit images in PowerPoint. We also discussed backgrounds.

We showed how to use arrow shapes to create a diagram of the water cycle and format them with a fill. We provided steps for aligning the arrows and moving them on the slide. We also explained how to insert a shape on the slide master so it would appear on every slide. We covered moving a slide and copying and deleting slides.

We discussed three kinds of animation: text animation, object animation, and slide transition. Finally, we explained how to present the slide show and navigate through the slides in Slide Show view.

In the next chapter, we will discuss how PowerPoint can incorporate multimedia in learning.

Multimedia and Learning with PowerPoint

Multimedia adds a great deal to the learning process. By involving different areas of the brain and commanding more attention, multimedia increases both retention and understanding. Much research suggests that the more senses employed in learning, the better the retention. (See Appendix A for a description of some of the research.) Multimedia makes learning more fun too, both for the student and for the teacher—which is probably part of the reason why it's effective. In this chapter, we explain what multimedia is, how to incorporate it into PowerPoint, and where to find resources.

WHAT IS MULTIMEDIA?

For the purpose of using PowerPoint, we can define multimedia as images, sounds, music, movies, and animation. (See Chapter 2 for instructions on animating text, objects, and slide transitions.)

Images may include clip art (drawings), photographs, graphs (charts), and diagrams. Practically anything except written words is multimedia. Interestingly enough, if you narrate the text of a slide and insert the narration into the presentation, the narration is multimedia because you're adding sound to text.

Multimedia is something of a buzzword, but don't let that concern you. It's actually very easy to add multimedia to PowerPoint and you don't have to be a multimedia wizard to do it. Sure, the students may be more familiar than their teachers with the latest file types and technology, but believe us: anyone can include multimedia in PowerPoint.

USING MULTIMEDIA EFFECTIVELY

If you've ever seen a sixth grader's first PowerPoint presentation, you'll notice that it's usually very simple. But watch out for the second one! The student will have learned more of PowerPoint's features and tried to use them all. The presentation will include loads of pictures of every conceivable type, animated images (GIFs) running across the slide, a cacophony of sounds—maybe more than one on a slide, and loads of animation everywhere. Words fly, spiral, and bounce onto the slide. By the end of the presentation, everyone has a headache!

Don't discourage that sixth grader. Children love PowerPoint's multimedia features, and eventually they learn that all that movement and noise distracts from the topic of the presentation. But you don't need to fall into the same trap.

Gratuitous images and movement distract and therefore detract from learning. The simple rule is to use multimedia so that it adds to learning. The presentation that Chapter 2 develops on the water cycle shows some good use of multimedia. For example, the simple diagram of the arrows (look back at Figure 2.19) makes the concept of a cycle more clear. By placing arrows next to the appropriate text, and animating the arrows in the direction they point, you help students to quickly comprehend which processes move water up and which move it down.

Here are some ways that multimedia can add to learning:

- *Show a process.* The water cycle diagram is an example of how you can use images and animation to show a process.

- *Visualize a concept.* The well-known food pyramid is an example of a visualization of a concept—in this case, the concept that we should eat a lot of some types of food and less of other types. The pyramid diagram helps make the concept much more understandable.

- *Visualize data.* When you need to portray data that show a trend, such as population growth, a graph portrays the data much more clearly than a list of numbers.

- *Spark creativity and thinking.* In Chapter 2's water cycle presentation, we used a photograph of fish underwater to encourage students to think about where they can find water. Interesting photos can start the creative juices flowing.

- *Draw attention to words.* You can animate words to help focus attention on the point you are currently discussing. For example, you can display one point, discuss that point, then display the next point, and so on.

- *Create a mood.* Music is especially helpful in creating a mood that is conducive to learning. Just as advertisers use music to encourage purchases, a teacher can use music to excite, uplift, and motivate students.

- *Show an example.* If you're talking about deciduous trees, you can show examples of deciduous trees. You can even show speeded-up movies picturing how they change throughout the seasons. Any concept that you're discussing is made more real through the depiction of examples.

- *Provide a metaphor.* If you're trying to explain to students that they sometimes have to work hard to attain a goal, you can show them a steep path as a metaphor, as shown in Figure 3.1. Are you trying to tell them that they can attain anything? Show them a picture of the sky.

Figure 3.1
This slide presents a metaphor for climbing toward a goal.

Sometimes, you have to climb upwards to get to the goal.

- *Add to the fun.* Music and sounds can simply add to the fun and make children laugh. In an interactive quiz, you can add the sound of applause when they choose the right answer. (Chapter 5 explains how to create this type of quiz.) All teachers have had the experience of children paying more attention and learning more when they're having fun.

Keep your slides simple. As long as your animation adds to the learning process and your slides aren't overly busy, you'll be using multimedia effectively. In Chapter 4, we discuss best practices, including those for multimedia.

USING IMAGES

Except in rare instances, all presentations should include images. In Chapter 2, we explained how to add, edit, compress images, and more. (See the "Adding Images" section in that chapter.) We discussed adding images using a slide layout with a content placeholder and adding images from an image file.

It's useful to understand something about image files. You should certainly be able to know if a file is an image that you can insert into PowerPoint. You can tell the image type from its filename extension (the part after the period, as in rose.jpg). Table 3.1 lists the most common types of image files that you can use in a PowerPoint project.

 In Windows, if you see only file names and not their extensions, right-click the Start button and choose Explore. (In Windows Vista, then press Alt to display the menu.) Choose Tools ➢ Folder Options and click the View tab. In the Folder Options dialog box, uncheck the Hide Extensions for Known File Types check box and click OK.

 To display filename extension in Mac's 10.4 OS, choose Finder, then Preferences. Click the Advanced button, and check the Show All File Extensions check box. For earlier OS's, if the file does not have an extension, you can add any picture extension you want; click on the name of the file, add a period, and type an extension.

Table 3.1
Image File Types.

Image File Type	Description
JPEG (.jpg, .jpeg)	This bitmap (made of dots) format is good for photographs.
GIF (.gif)	This bitmap format is good for simple images and supports transparency.
PNG (.png)	This bitmap format is good for photographs and supports transparency.
BMP (.bmp)	This bitmap format creates large files. It's good for printing.
WMF (.wmf)	This is a vector (made of lines) format in Windows.
TIFF (.tif, .tiff)	This bitmap format is seen in scanned images. It's good for printing.
PICT	This is a bitmap format for the Mac.

Here are some other sources for inserting images into PowerPoint:

- *Copy and paste.* You may have an image in another file, such as a Word document. In this case, you can open the Word document, select the image, copy it to the Clipboard, display a slide in PowerPoint, and paste the image onto the slide.

- *Scan.* If you have an image in a book or article, or want to use students' artwork, you can use a scanner to create an electronic image file that you can insert into PowerPoint. (Be careful about copyright issues when scanning printed materials.)

- *Photograph.* You can take photos with a digital camera, upload them to your computer, and insert them into PowerPoint.

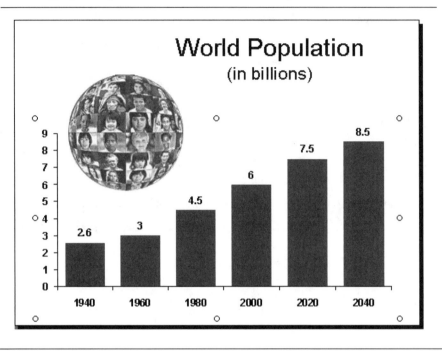

Figure 3.2
A graph helps students visualize the implications of data.

- *Search the Web.* The World Wide Web is full of images. For example, to search Google for images, type images.google.com in your browser's address window. Again, watch out for copyrights.

See the end of this chapter for information on sources of multimedia files.

Creating Graphs

Graphs (called charts in PowerPoint) let you visually display data. You can create bar charts, line charts, pie charts, and more. Figure 3.2 shows a slide with a graph depicting past and projected world population. Trends like these are hard to visualize without a graph. Graphs are especially useful for science and math projects.

Inserting a graph

To create a graph, use a slide with a content placeholder that includes a chart icon. (See the sections "Choosing a Layout" and "Inserting a Slide with a Specified Layout" in Chapter 2 for more information.) Follow these instructions to insert a graph:

HOW TO DO IT

 • *Windows 2000/2002/2003:* Click the Insert Chart icon on the slide. You see a graph and a datasheet, shown in Figure 3.3, filled with dummy (sample) data. Insert your data to replace the dummy data and delete any rows or columns that you don't need. (Click on a row or column head and press Del.) You can also copy and paste data from a spreadsheet, such as Microsoft Office Excel.

 • *Windows 2007:* Click the Insert Chart icon on the slide. In the Insert Chart dialog box, choose the type of chart you want (column, line, pie, and so on). Click OK. If you have Excel, it opens where you can enter your data. (If not, you see a data-sheet like the one shown in Figure 3.3.) When you're done, click the PowerPoint window again to see the result on your slide. You can also copy and paste data from an existing Excel spreadsheet.

 • *Mac 2001/X/2004:* Double-click the chart placeholder on the slide. You see a graph and a datasheet, similar to that shown in Figure 3.3, filled with dummy (sample) data. Insert your data to replace the dummy data and delete any rows or columns that you don't need. (Click on a row or column head and press Del.) You can also copy and paste data from a spreadsheet, such as Microsoft Office Excel. When you're done, choose Graph ➤ Quit & Return to Presentation from the PowerPoint menu.

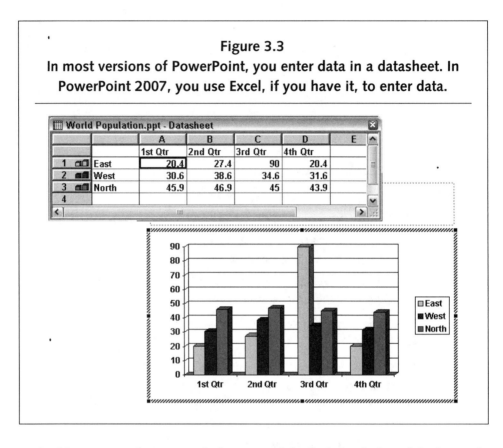

Figure 3.3

In most versions of PowerPoint, you enter data in a datasheet. In PowerPoint 2007, you use Excel, if you have it, to enter data.

At this stage, you have a graph, but you might find that it doesn't look exactly as you would like it to. The next section explains how to edit a graph.

Editing a graph

Graphs are very flexible. Besides changing the chart type (bar, line, pie), you can change the colors, axes, gridlines, and just about everything else in the chart. Follow these instructions to edit a graph:

HOW TO DO IT

- *Windows 2000/2002/2003:* Double-click the graph to enter editing mode. Choose Chart ➤ Chart Type to change the chart to a column,

---

line, pie, or other type of chart. Choose Chart ➤ Chart Options to change options relating to the title, axes, gridlines, the legend, data labels, and the data sheet. Use the Data menu to switch which data appear on the X axis. Finally, double-click any specific element in the chart to open a dialog box where you can format that element. For example, to change the fill of the columns, double-click them to open the Format Data Series dialog box where you can use the Patterns tab to change the fill.

- *Windows 2007:* Select the chart. Use the Design tab of the ribbon to choose a chart style, switch rows and columns, or change the layout. Use the Layout tab to edit individual components of the graph. Finally, use the Format tab to change shape styles, change fills and outlines, and add shape effects.

- *Mac 2001/X/2004:* Double-click the graph to enter editing mode. Choose Chart ➤ Chart Type to change the chart to a column, line, pie, or other type of chart. Choose Chart ➤ Chart Options to change options relating to the title, axes, gridlines, the legend, data labels, and the data sheet. Use the Data menu to switch which data appears on the X axis. Finally, double-click any specific element in the chart to open a dialog box where you can format that element. For example, to change the fill of the columns, double-click them to open the Format Data Series dialog box where you can use the Patterns tab to change the fill.

Creating Diagrams

You can use diagrams to display processes, steps, and relationships. Some versions of PowerPoint include a feature that creates diagrams, but you can also make your own. Figure 3.4 shows a radial-type diagram that portrays the relationship between the three branches of government in the United States.

Here's how to insert a diagram.

Figure 3.4
You can use diagrams to portray relationships.

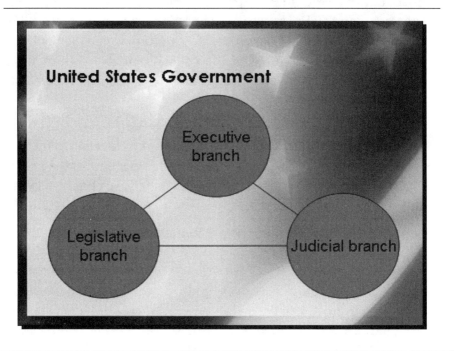

HOW TO DO IT

- *Windows 2000:* This version does not contain diagrams.

- *Windows 2002/2003:* Use a content layout or choose Insert ➢ Diagram. The Diagram Gallery, shown in Figure 3.5, appears. Choose a diagram type and click OK; the diagram appears on your slide and the Diagram toolbar appears. Use the "Click to Add Text" areas to add text labels. Use the Diagram toolbar as follows:

  - To add a shape, click Insert Shape.

  - To delete a shape, select it and press Delete.

- To switch to another type of diagram, use the Change To button on the toolbar.

- To make size adjustments, use the Layout button's drop-down list.

- To turn off AutoLayout, which gives you more flexibility to redesign the diagram, choose Layout ➤ AutoLayout. Do the same to turn AutoLayout back on.

- To change the style (fill and outline) of the shapes, choose Auto-Format to open the Diagram Style Gallery and choose one of the options.

- To reverse the direction of the diagram, click Reverse Diagram.

- *Windows 2007:* Use a content layout or click SmartArt on the Insert tab. (Diagrams are called SmartArt in PowerPoint 2007.) In the Choose a SmartArt Graphic dialog box, choose a diagram type and subtype. Then enter text in the text areas. Use the SmartArt Tools Design and Format tabs as follows:

  - To add a shape, click Add Shape on the Design tab.

  - To delete a shape, select it and press Del.

  - To switch to another type of diagram, click the More button in the Layouts group of the Design tab and then choose More Layouts to reopen the Choose a SmartArt Graphic dialog box.

  - To make size adjustments, use the Shapes group of the Format tab.

  - To change a shape, click Change Shape in the Shapes group of the Format tab.

  - To change the style (fill and outline) of the shapes, use the Smart-Art Styles group of the Design tab, including the Change Colors button.

  - To reverse the diagram, click Right-to-Left in the Create Graphic group of the Design tab.

- *Mac 2001/X/2004:* This version does not contain diagrams.

Figure 3.5
Choose the diagram type that best fits your concept.

In PowerPoint 2007, diagrams (SmartArt Graphics) have been enhanced with many more options. Also, you can convert existing bulleted text to a diagram—select the text, and choose Convert to SmartArt Graphic in the Paragraph group of the Home tab.

ADDING SOUNDS, MUSIC, AND NARRATION

Sounds and music add life to a presentation. With young children who cannot yet read, narration of the instructions is a must. As already noted, applause is a great way to reward a correct answer in a quiz. Music can create a mood that enhances a presentation, as long as it doesn't compete with the content. Of course, sound may not be appropriate if students are going to use the computer in a quiet library.

Adding a Sound or Music File

Sound and music files come in various types and you need to know which types of files you can insert into a presentation. Here are the most common file types that you can use:

- .aif, .aiff

- .mid, .midi

- .mp3

- .wav

- .wma, .asf

First, of course, you need to find a sound or music file. (A music file is just a sound file that contains music.) This is the hard part, because many sounds and most pieces of music are copyrighted. PowerPoint comes with a few sounds (such as applause) and some music in the Microsoft Office Clip Organizer that you can use. (See the end of this chapter for more information about sound resources.) If you have a file that you want to use, make sure you keep it in the same folder as the presentation.

In Chapter 2, we developed a presentation on the water cycle. A great start to that presentation would be a thunderclap—it would certainly get the students' attention! To add the sound, open the presentation that you created in Chapter 2. If you didn't follow through in Chapter 2, you can go to www.ellenfinkelstein. com/powerpointforteachers.html and find the same water cycle presentation. Download it and open it in PowerPoint.

Display the first slide of the presentation. Here is how you can add a thunder sound to that slide.

HOW TO DO IT

- *Windows 2000:* Choose Insert ➤ Movies and Sounds ➤ Sound from Gallery. (If you had a sound file, you would choose Sound from File.) In the Insert Sound window, enter **thunder**. If you find a file, click it and choose Insert Clip. If not (we didn't), click the Clips Online button to go to the Microsoft Office Online Clip Art page. In the Search box, enter **thunder**. Then click the Search button's down arrow and choose Sounds. When you get the results, you can play them to see which one you want. Follow the instructions to download the sound. You can open it directly in the Clip Gallery. There, click the sound and choose Insert Clip from the submenu. When prompted, choose to play the sound automatically.

- *Windows 2002/2003:* Choose Insert ➤ Movies and Sounds ➤ Sound from Clip Organizer. (If you had a sound file, you would choose Sound from File.) The Clip Art task pane opens. Enter **thunder**. If you find a file (we didn't), click it to insert it. If not, click Clip Art on Office Online at the bottom of the task pane to go to the Microsoft Office Online Clip Art page. In the Search box, enter **thunder**. Then click the Search button's down arrow and choose Sounds. When you get the results, you can play them to see which one you want. Follow the instructions to download the sound. You can open it directly in the Clip Organizer from where you drag the sound onto the slide. When prompted, choose to play the sound automatically.

- *Windows 2007:* On the Insert tab, go to the Media group and click the Sound button's down arrow. Choose Sound from Clip Organizer to open the Clip Art task pane. (If you had a sound file, you would choose Sound from File.) Type **thunder** in the Search For box. We found several options. (These were the same that we found online in other versions. If you don't find them, click Clip Art on Office Online and see the instructions for Windows 2002/2003.) Place the cursor over any sound, click its down arrow, and choose Preview/Properties, where you can play the sound. Drag the one you like onto the slide. When prompted, choose to play the sound automatically.

- *Mac 2001/X/2004:* Choose Insert ➤ Movies and Sounds ➤ Sound from Clip Gallery. (If you had a sound file, you would choose Sound from File.) The Clip Gallery task pane opens. Enter **thunder**. If you find a file (we didn't), click it to insert it. If not, click Online at the bottom of the task pane to go to the Microsoft Office Online Clip Art page. In the Search box, enter **thunder**. Then click the Search button's down arrow and choose Sounds. When you get the results, you can play them to see which one you want. Follow the instructions to download the sound. You can open it directly in the Clip Organizer, from where you drag the sound onto the slide. When prompted, choose to play the sound automatically.

Drag the sound icon just off the slide, because you won't need to click it (since it will play automatically).

When you're done, click the Slide Show icon to go into Slide Show view. (See Chapter 2 for instructions.) The thunder should play automatically and create a dramatic start for your presentation!

If you want control over when a sound plays, choose to play it when clicked (rather than automatically), then click the sound icon that PowerPoint places on the slide to play the sound.

Either way, you can play the sound in Normal view by double-clicking the sound icon.

 You can find the completed water cycle presentation, with sound, at www.ellenfinkelstein.com/powerpointforteachers.html.

Adding Background Music

Some PowerPoint projects are meant for the student to run alone, rather than for a teacher to present. In this case, no one is talking during the presentation. You may want to add background music to create a pleasant or invigorating mood.

When you add a music file, as explained in the previous section on adding sounds, as soon as you go to the next slide the music stops. To play music throughout the presentation, first insert it from a file or from the Clip Art pane or dialog box, as also explained in the previous section. Then follow these instructions.

HOW TO DO IT

- *Windows 2000:* Select the sound icon and choose Slide Show ➤ Custom Animation to open the Custom Animation dialog box. On the Multimedia Settings tab, in the Stop Playing section, enter **999** in the After X Slides text box. If the sound is too short to last throughout the presentation, you can *loop* it (play it over and over). Click More Options to open the Sound Options dialog box, where you can see the total play time listed. Check the Loop Until Stopped check box and click OK twice to close both dialog boxes.

- *Windows 2002/2003:* Right-click the sound icon and choose Custom Animation from the shortcut menu to open the Custom Animation task pane. Click the arrow to the right of the sound in the task pane and choose Effect Options to open the Play Sound dialog box with the Effects tab displayed, as shown in Figure 3.6. In the Stop Playing section, enter **999** in the After X Slides text box. Click OK. If the sound is too short to last throughout the presentation, you can *loop* it (play it over and over). Right-click the sound icon and choose Edit Sound Object. In the Sound Options dialog box, you can see the total play time listed. Check the Loop Until Stopped check box and click OK.

- *Windows 2007:* Select the sound icon. On the Animations tab, click Custom Animations to open the Custom Animation task pane. Click the arrow to the right of the sound in the task pane and choose Effect Options to open the Play Sound dialog box with the Effects tab displayed, as shown in Figure 3.6. In the Stop Playing section, enter **999** in the After X Slides text box. Click the Sound Settings tab to see the total playing time. Click OK. If the sound is too short to last throughout the presentation, you can *loop* it (play it over and over). Click the Sound Tools Options tab that appears. Check the Loop Until Stopped check box.

- *Mac 2001/X/2004:* Select the sound icon and choose Slide Show ➤ Custom Animation to open the Custom Animation dialog box. If the audio file is not selected, select it in the Select to Animate dialog box. On the Options tab, in the Stop Playing section, check the Play Using Animation order check box. Then check the After option, and enter **999** in the text box. If the sound is too short to last throughout the presentation, you can *loop* it (play it over and over). Check the Loop Until Stopped check box. Click OK.

Figure 3.6
Use the Play Sound dialog box to continue playing a sound, such as music, during all the slides in your presentation.

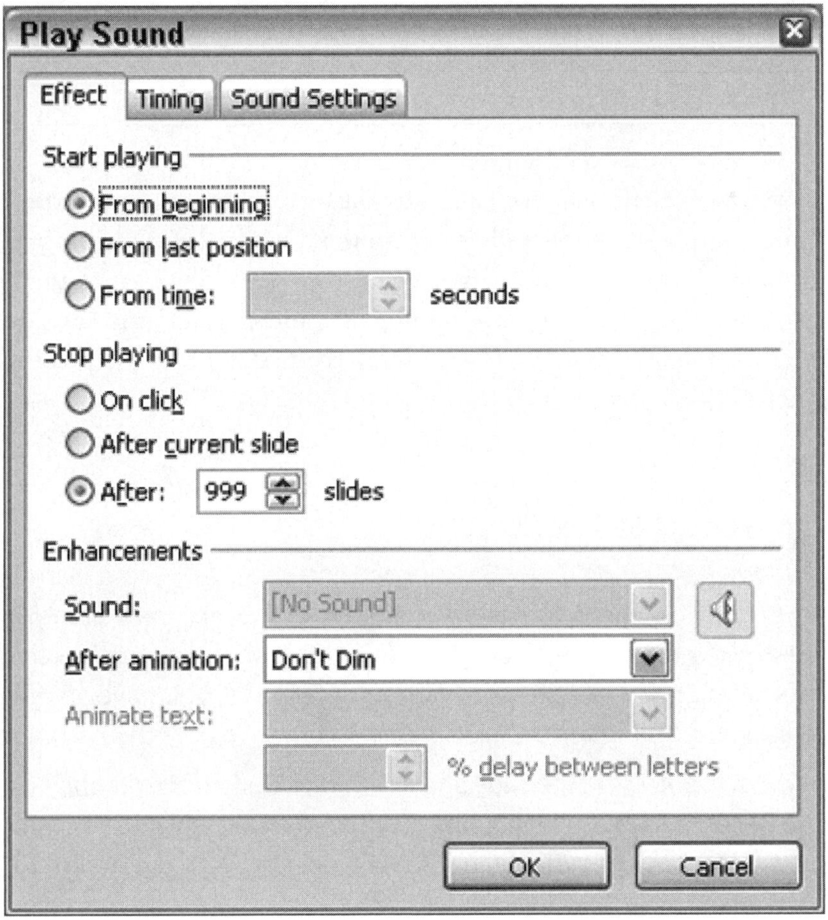

Adding Narration

You can add your own voice to a presentation. To do so, you use the Narration feature of PowerPoint. As we discussed earlier, this is essential for younger children who can't read instructions. The other common use for narration is as a substitute for a live presentation. For example, students who are out sick could view the presentation, with your narration, when they return. You might even e-mail the presentation to them.

 Long periods of narration may lag or function erratically. Also, long narration makes a presentation file very large. An alternative is to place the content of your verbal presentation in the Notes pane, as we explained in Chapter 2.

First, you need a microphone. The better the microphone, the better the sound, but if your computer came with a microphone, try it before buying a more expensive one. Depending on the type of microphone, connect it to the Mic In connector or a USB port on your computer. (You may have to look at your computer's manual to find it.) Then display the first slide of the presentation. Here's how to add narration to a presentation:

HOW TO DO IT

- *Windows 2000/2002/2003:* Choose Slide Show ➢ Record Narration to open the Record Narration dialog box. You go immediately into Slide Show view. Start talking! When you finish a slide, click with the mouse to go to the next slide. When you're done, you have an option to save the timing for the slides. Click No to save only the narration.

- *Windows 2007:* On the Slide Show tab, click Record Narration to open the Record Narration dialog box. You go immediately into Slide Show view. Start talking! When you finish a slide, click with the mouse to go to the next slide. When you're done, you have an option to save the timing for the slides. Click Don't Save to save only the narration.

- *Mac 2001/X/2004:* Choose Slide Show ➢ Record Narration to open the Record Narration dialog box. Click Record. You go immediately into Slide Show view. Start talking! When you finish a slide, click with the mouse to go to the next slide. When you're done, you have an option to save the timing for the slides. Click No to save only the narration.

In the Record Narration dialog box, click Set Microphone Level to test the microphone's volume. Click Change Quality to choose the quality of sound; a higher quality sounds better but creates larger files. Check the Link Narrations In check box to create separate files—this gives you more control if you want to edit the narration. Click the Browse button to specify a location, which should be the same as your presentation file.

USING VIDEO

You can insert a movie, also called *video*, onto a slide. The video may include sound. Video is usually created with a camcorder; these days usually a digital camcorder is used. If you have one available to you (perhaps your school's art department has one), you can go outside on a rainy day and shoot a minute of video of the rain, for example. (Make sure you don't damage the camcorder in the rain!) Many digital cameras can also shoot video. You can find video online but be careful about copyright restrictions.

 You can insert animated GIF files into a presentation. These are very short, line-drawing animations and they play only in Slide Show view. You can find several relating to rain either in the Clip Art task pane or on Microsoft's Clip Art page by searching for **rain** under the Animations category. Follow the instructions for inserting any image, as explained in Chapter 2. Go into Slide Show view to see them move.

To insert video, you need to find or create a video file, because PowerPoint doesn't come with any. The most common types of files are .mpeg, .avi, and .wmv. PowerPoint on the Mac also supports .mov files. Move or copy the file to the same folder as your presentation *before* inserting it, otherwise the video will not play if you move the presentation! (If you need to show the presentation on another computer, be sure to copy both the presentation and the video files.) Then display the slide where you want the video and follow these instructions.

HOW TO DO IT

- *Windows 2000/2002/2003:* Choose Insert ➤ Movies and Sounds ➤ Movie from File. Navigate to the movie file, click it, and click Open. You can choose to play the movie automatically or when clicked.

- *Windows 2007:* On the Insert tab, choose Movie ➤ Movie from File. Navigate to the movie file, click it, and click Open. You can choose to play the movie automatically or when clicked.

- *Mac 2001/X/2004:* Choose Insert ➤ Movies and Sounds ➤ Movie from File. Navigate to the movie file, click it, and click Insert. You can choose to play the movie automatically or when clicked.

Although you seem to be inserting the movie file, you are only linking to it; the file does not become part of your presentation. You can double-click the video in Normal view to play it, or go into Slide Show view.

 You can adjust the size of the movie window by selecting it and dragging on a corner handle. However, if you change the size significantly, the quality may suffer.

MULTIMEDIA RESOURCES

Finding images, sounds, music, and video can be a challenge. The main sources for content are as follows:

- *Microsoft Clip Art gallery.* Although clip art usually means line art, the Clip Art gallery includes photographs as well. Microsoft Office offers a large selection of images that you can use. Choose Insert ➤ Picture ➤ Clip Art to open the Clip Art task pane or dialog box. You can search for images by typing a key-word in the Search text box. If you use the Clip Art gallery, you don't need to save the images as a separate file.

- *Microsoft Clip Art and Media homepage.* You can find thousands more images, sounds, and animated GIFs by going to Microsoft's online clip art center. In the Clip Art task pane/dialog box, click the Clip Art on Office Online link. If you don't have that link, go to http://office.microsoft.com/en-us/clipart/default.aspx. (This is the U.S. site.)

- *The Internet.* The Internet is full of multimedia files. Many are copyrighted and not all are free. However, many sites offer access to their huge collections for a very reasonable fee. Just search for clip art, photos, video, sounds, or music.

- *Your own photos and videos.* If you have a digital camera or camcorder, go out and take pictures or video! You can easily insert them into PowerPoint.

- *Student art or recordings.* If students give you permission, you can use their drawings (scanned), computer art, photos, music, and videos.

We've collected a list of online resources and placed them on the companion Web site at www.ellenfinkelstein.com/powerpointforteachers.html.

SUMMARY

In this chapter, we explained how to insert multimedia content into a PowerPoint presentation. We covered inserting and editing graphs (charts), creating diagrams, inserting sound files, adding background music, adding narration, and inserting video. Multimedia content makes any presentation more lively and interesting.

In the next chapter, we explain best practices when using PowerPoint.

Understanding Best Practices

chapter
FOUR

PowerPoint is so easy and so much fun to use and offers so many features that you can easily get carried away and overdo it—too much design, text, animation, and imagery. Remember, the point of using PowerPoint in the classroom is to enhance the educational process. In this chapter, we explain some best practices that ensure that PowerPoint aids, rather than detracts from, learning.

BACKGROUNDS

Many people start a new PowerPoint presentation by choosing a background or template that provides lots of color and design. Of course, the background you use should depend on the content of the presentation and the age of the students.

However, for most classroom situations, you want the knowledge to come to the forefront. An overly decorative background distracts students; they look at the images, which are often irrelevant, rather than the central concepts, whether text, images, or charts.

 Patrick Douglas Crispen, faculty training and support coordinator for California State University at Long Beach, wrote about the use of PowerPoint in education in his presentation, "Now That I Know PowerPoint, How Can I Use It to TEACH?" He notes, "We

> forget that the primary goal of any classroom PowerPoint presentation isn't to entertain but rather to teach." He also points out that there is a "huge difference between a business PowerPoint presentation and a classroom PowerPoint presentation." (For the full presentation, see this book's companion Web site at www.ellenfinkelstein.com/powerpointforteachers.)

One useful technique is to provide a lively background for the first slide. This entices students to see what's next. Then tone it down for the rest of the slides. You can leave the rest of the slides completely blank, but you can also use a more subtle background. For example, you could create a top bar (or left bar) that contains design elements from the first slide's background.

Unless you're working with PowerPoint 2000, you can have more than one slide master, and therefore more than one background, per presentation. In PowerPoint 2000, you need to use a trick to get the same look. Note, however, that PowerPoint 2000 allows you to create a separate background for title slides, using the Title Master, which we discussed in Chapter 2.

In Chapter 2, in the "Using the Slide Master" section, we explained how to add a background to the slide master of a presentation. We also explained how to add a background to an individual slide in "Adding a Background" in that same chapter. Review those sections if necessary. Here we explain how to add a second slide master, which creates a second background.

HOW TO DO IT

- *Windows 2000:* Display the Slides tab of the left pane. Click the first slide you want to change. Press the Control (Ctrl) key and click any other slides you want to change, so that they're all selected. Right-click in the Outline tab and choose Background from the shortcut menu. Use the Background dialog box, as explained in Chapter 2, to add a background to those slides.

- *Windows 2002/2003:* Choose View ➤ Master ➤ Slide Master to display the slide master. Choose Insert ➤ New Slide Master. Right-click the slide master and choose Background to use the Background dialog box to add a background to the new slide master. You can also choose a template from the Slide Design task pane. (To display the task pane, choose View ➤ Task Pane. Click the down arrow at the right end of the task pane's title and choose Slide Design.) Choose View ➤ Normal View. To add the new background to any slide, display the slide and choose the background from the Slide Design task pane, where it now appears.

- *Windows 2007:* From the View tab, choose Slide Master to display the slide master. On the Slide Master tab, choose Insert Slide Master. Right-click the first layout of the new slide master and choose Format Background to use the Format Background dialog box to add a background to the new slide master. You can also click Themes to add a theme's background to the new slide master. Click Close Master View. To add the new background to any slide, display the slide and click the Design tab. Choose the background from the Themes gallery.

- *Mac 2001/X/2004:* Choose View ➤ Master ➤ Slide Master to display the slide master. Choose Insert ➤ New Slide Master. Right-click (or press the Control key) on the slide master and choose Slide Background to use the Background dialog box to add a background to the new slide master. Or, you can choose a design from the Design folder. From Normal view (View ➤ Normal View), select the slides that you want for which you want the new background. Choose Format ➤ Slide Design and choose a design. Select the Apply to the Current Slide option. Click Apply.

AGE-APPROPRIATENESS

How to best use PowerPoint depends on the age of your students. For young children, lots of color, sounds, and animation keep their interest and make learning fun. By fifth or sixth grade, these techniques are still useful, but should be toned down. That's because the intellectual level of the content is higher and should take greater precedence.

By middle and high school, extraneous "noise" should be at a minimum, so as not to interfere with the content. However, that doesn't mean the presentation should be full of bulleted text and nothing else. Instead, it means the following:

- Use images that add to the knowledge, such as diagrams and charts.
- Use images that encourage creativity and critical thinking.
- Use animation that portrays processes, such as the water cycle we described in Chapter 2.

SPECIAL EFFECTS

As we explained in the previous section, bright colors, sounds, lots of images, and animation need to be used appropriately, based on the age of your students. However, in all situations, you want to keep the special effects simple and coordinated. In this section, we explain some basic principles.

Color Schemes

When designing a presentation for any age, decide on the colors you want to use and then stick to them. For younger children, your colors might be bright, primary colors. For older children, you might use toned-down colors, depending on the topic.

PowerPoint comes with a default *color scheme* (called *theme colors* in Power-Point 2007), but you can change it. Each color scheme (or set of theme colors) has several colors that are applied to different elements on a slide, such as text and AutoShape fills. Changing the color scheme is a good skill to know, because the color schemes that come with PowerPoint were designed for business use, and they may not be ideal for your classroom.

A color scheme creates a unified look for a presentation and helps avoid that chaotic look you've probably seen too often.

HOW TO DO IT
- *Windows 2000:* To choose a new color scheme from a list, choose Format ➢ Slide Color Scheme. In the Color Scheme dialog box, choose one of the color schemes on the Standard tab and click Apply

---

to All. To create your own color scheme, click the Custom tab, shown in Figure 4.1. Click any of the colors from the list and click the Change Color button to open the Color dialog box, where you can choose a new color.

- *Windows 2002/2003:* To choose a new color scheme from a list, choose Format ➤ Slide Design. From the Slide Design task pane, click Color Schemes to open the Color Scheme task pane. Choose one of the options to apply it to the presentation. To create your own color scheme, click Edit Color Schemes at the bottom of the task pane to open the Edit Color Schemes dialog box with the Custom tab on top, shown in Figure 4.1. Click any of the elements from the list and click the Change Color button to open the Color dialog box for that element, where you can choose a new color.

- *Windows 2007:* On the Design tab, click the Colors button in the Themes group and choose one of the sets of theme colors. To create your own theme colors, click Create New Theme Colors at the bottom of the list. Click any of the colors from the list to open a sampling of colors; you can also click More Colors to open the Colors dialog box for a full range of color options.

- *Mac 2001/X/2004:* To choose a new color scheme from a list, choose Format ➤ Slide Color Scheme. In the Color Scheme dialog box, choose one of the color schemes on the Standard tab and click Apply to All. To create your own color scheme, click the Custom tab, shown in Figure 4.1. Click any of the colors from the list and click the Change Color button to open the Colors dialog box, where you can choose a new color.

Animation Effects

Animation can enhance learning in a powerful way, but it can also become a distraction. Little animated figures dancing across the screen at odd moments just don't help the learning process. An entrance animation for every piece of text—such as the text spiraling in—soon grows tiresome.

Figure 4.1
**Use the Custom tab of the Color Scheme (or Edit Color Scheme)
dialog box to create a custom color scheme in all versions
except PowerPoint 2007.**

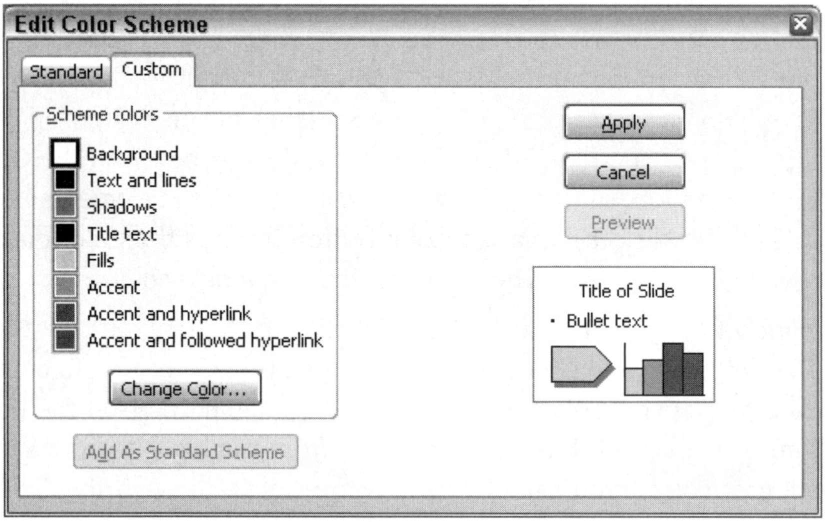

Young children especially love movement, but make it integral to the lesson. You don't want balls gratuitously bouncing all around the slide while you're asking children to decide which shape is the triangle. A better place for the motion is on the positive reinforcement slide. They quickly get the message that they made the right choice and can enjoy some fireworks. As we've mentioned before, using animation to depict a process is totally appropriate. Examples include the water cycle animation presented in Chapter 2 and animation showing the revolution of planets around the sun, the life cycle of a frog, and so on.

See Chapter 2 to learn how to add animation to a presentation.

Sounds

Use sounds and music in the same way that you use animation—with attention to their appropriateness to the lesson. As with animation, sounds are often best for younger children and useful for positive reinforcement. However, adding a sound to every slide soon gets annoying and the students tune out. In fact, sounds can distract from the content and actually hinder learning.

Many students, especially in elementary and middle school, are fascinated with loud special effects like explosions, lasers, ricochets, and so on. Once your children start creating their own presentations, you may need to impose some reasonable restrictions or your classroom will sound like a battlefield.

Background music can introduce a mood that may be appropriate in certain situations, but don't use it just because you can. The students may pay more attention to the music than to the lesson!

A good idea is to use nature sound files as background sounds when the project deals with natural phenomena. Here are some examples:

- The sound of crickets would enhance the effect of a dark forest in the summer.
- The sound of birds, frogs, and insects would be suitable as a background for forests, jungles, and swamps.
- Water sounds would be an excellent accompaniment for your water-related projects.

You can find such sounds on the Internet if you search in your favorite search engine; try typing **nature. wav sound files,** for example. Make sure the sound files are not copyright-protected. Wav files are short, and to create a continuous background effect you would need to loop the sound. (Look for the instructions on looping in Chapter 3.) Of course, you can record your own sounds; a digital tape recorder makes it easiest.

Be sure to consider where the students will access the presentation. Sounds are simply not appropriate if students don't have headphones and will run the presentation in class while other students are involved with different activities.

See Chapter 3 to learn how to add sound to a presentation.

BULLETS ARE BORING

Slide after slide of bulleted text gets boring very quickly. On the one hand, you don't want to overdo the special effects; on the other hand, you don't want to retreat to nothing but text in the same format throughout the presentation. Figure 4.2 presents a tongue-in-cheek illustration of this.

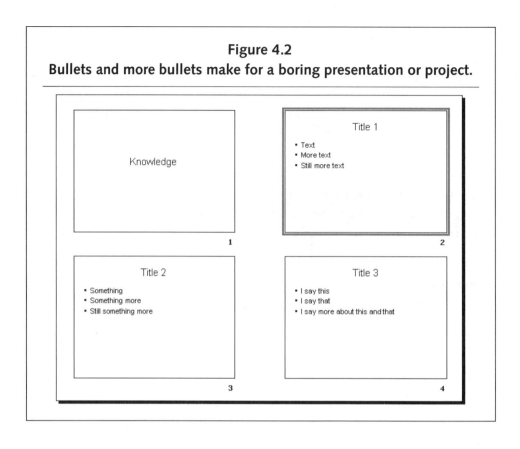

Figure 4.2
Bullets and more bullets make for a boring presentation or project.

Try to think how you can depict concepts visually. Sometimes, you can cover an entire slide with an image and use that to jump-start a discussion. For example, if you're discussing the topic of recycling, show a mountain of garbage and ask the students where it comes from and where it goes.

We've already discussed how you can use an animated diagram to show a process or cycle. Remember, you can use this diagram in place of a slide with text. A graph is often much more effective than text.

Another interesting technique is to place one or two complete sentences on a slide to state a fact or a concept. You can then discuss the topic as long as you want. One way to do this is to use the Title and Content/Picture layout, which provides you with a title placeholder and an image placeholder. In Figure 4.3, we moved the title place-holder to the left side and resized it. We also moved the content/picture placeholder to the right and resized that as well. This gave us more room for text.

Figure 4.3
One way to avoid bullets is to use full sentences matched with images.

In Shakespeare's time, the Elizabethan theatre was a popular form of entertainment

Interior of Swan Theatre in 1596. Found at.
www.fathom.com/course/28701903/session3.html

You can also simply use full sentences in a text placeholder and change the formatting to remove the bullets. For this technique, you would use a Text & Content/Content layout.

HOW TO DO IT

- *Windows 2000/2002/2003:* Select the text placeholder. Choose Format ➤ Bullets and Numbering to open the Bullets and Numbering dialog box with the Bullets tab on top. Click the None option and click OK. If the ruler, shown in Figure 4.4, is not displayed, choose View ➤ Ruler. To remove the first line hanging indent, click anywhere in the text. Drag the hanging indent marker on the ruler all the way to the left, so that it's underneath the first line indent marker. This aligns the text in block format to the left.

- *Windows 2007:* Select all of the text in the placeholder. On the Home tab, click the Bullets button in the Paragraph group to remove the bullets. If the ruler is not displayed, click the View tab and check the Ruler check box. Drag the hanging indent marker on the ruler all the way to the left, so that it's underneath the first-line indent marker. This aligns the text in block format to the left.

- *Mac 2001/X/2004:* Select the text placeholder. Choose Format ➤ Bullets and Numbering to open the Bullets and Numbering dialog box with the Bullets tab on top. Click the None option and click OK. If the ruler, shown in Figure 4.4, is not displayed, choose View ➤ Ruler. To remove the first-line hanging indent, click anywhere in the text. Drag the hanging indent marker on the ruler all the way to the left, so that it's underneath the first line indent marker. This aligns the text in block format to the left.

Remember that bullets set off multiple lines of text; when you get rid of them, make sure that the starting point of each statement is easy to visualize.

USING TEXT WISELY

There's nothing worse than a slide so full of text, especially small text, that no one can read it. Edit, edit, edit! You want the text on a slide to be spare—just enough to express the idea.

Our recommendation is to use only one idea (message, concept) per each slide. The number of slides should not be your concern; it is much better to explain one idea using several slides than to use one slide to explain several ideas or concepts. For example, describing the genres used by Shakespeare, it would be wise to list all the genres on one slide, and then to provide detailed explanations using several slides for each genre.

Text should never be smaller than 18 points, and even that is pretty tiny from the back of the room. We used 18-point text for the references in Figures 4.3 and 4.4.

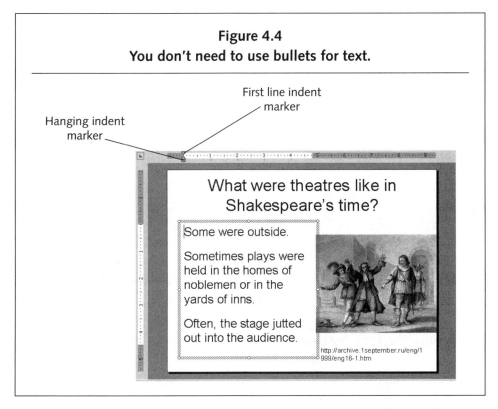

Figure 4.4
You don't need to use bullets for text.

If you simply can't reduce the text any further, split it up onto two or three slides, until each slide has a smaller amount of large, easily readable text.

In addition, always choose font face and color so that the text is legible. Keep the font simple and don't use more than one or two fonts. No fancy fonts! Make sure that the contrast with the background is very high. The best contrast is black text against a white background, but you have lots of other options too, such as dark blue against a pale yellow background. Light backgrounds also feel more like reading a printed text. If you want to use a dark background, use white or yellow text, and use a font that creates thick letter strokes.

THE IMPORTANCE OF CONTEXT

You can use PowerPoint presentations and projects in many different situations and you'll find that, for best results, you'll need to adjust for those situations. Sometimes you're around to expand on the ideas, sometimes you're not. Some projects are for review and others introduce new ideas.

Your Presentation

When you use a PowerPoint presentation to accompany your lesson, you express the concepts yourself and the slides just back you up. This is the type of presentation we created in Chapter 2 on the water cycle. The text indicates important points and terms, and the images, charts, animation, and so on supplement your explanation.

In this situation, the text doesn't need to be complete. If you're using bulleted text, it should be short phrases, just enough so that the students get the idea quickly and then start listening to you. It is appropriate to contract sentences, as long as the message is clear, especially with older students. For example, when you have the title "Macbeth," the text does not have to be "Macbeth was written in 1606"; "Written in 1606" is quite enough. Also, when you have a good picture to support the message, you can use fewer words.

If you're using a chart or diagram, you'll point to the slide as you explain it. A stick or laser pointer is helpful. You can also use the mouse cursor to point. The students should follow along as you identify the various components. You don't need a lot of text to explain, because the chart or diagram should be fairly self-explanatory.

You can even mark the slide temporarily, using the Pointer Options feature. Perhaps you want to circle something that's important. The annotation is not permanent, unless you choose to keep it (available in some versions).

HOW TO DO IT

- *Windows 2000/2002:* In Slide Show view, right-click and choose Pointer Options ➢ Pen. Your cursor turns into a pen, which you can use for underlining, circling, and writing. You can even choose the color of the pen, by choosing Pointer Options ➢ Pen Color and choosing one of the colors.

- *Windows 2003/2007:* In Slide Show view, right-click and choose Pointer ➢ Options ➢ Ballpoint Pen, Felt Tip Pen, or Highlighter (depending on the thickness you want). Your cursor turns into a pen, which you can use for underlining, circling, and writing. You can even choose the color of the pen, by choosing Pointer Options ➢ Ink Color and choosing one of the colors. When you return to Normal view, you see a message asking if you want to keep your markups. Click Yes to do so.

- *Mac 2001/X/2004:* In Slide Show view, Ctrl-click (right-click if you have a two-key mouse) and choose Pointer Options ➢ Pen. Your cursor turns into a pen, which you can use for underlining, circling, and writing. You can even choose the color of the pen, by choosing Pointer Options ➢ Pen Color and choosing one of the colors.

It is a good idea to have an effective navigation method throughout your entire presentation, so that you can easily get to any slide on the project from any other slide. What if a student asks a question about a previously covered slide? It is annoying when the presenter cannot find or get back to some slide; some presenters stop their presentation, return to Normal view, and go to the outline panel to find the needed slide. For tips on how to make your presentation easy to navigate, read Chapter 7.

Viewed as a Class

Some games created in PowerPoint, such as those we introduce in Chapter 8, are viewed by a class as a whole but they're supposed to be self-explanatory. Other presentations run more like a movie; they may have narration and music, but you don't talk during them. They may include automatic timing, so that the slide show runs itself. You show these presentations to the students together as a class.

Although the games work by themselves (once you explain the rules), movie-like presentations need to be clear. If there's narration, that narration does the explaining. If not, the text needs to be more complete than when you are doing the presenting. Instead of sparse text, include fuller explanations. Remember that all the points you want to make need to be stated fully.

Viewed Individually

Many of the projects that we present in this book are viewed individually by students. For example, the review (or quiz) in Chapter 5 is usually used by one student at a time.

These types of projects are interactive in that PowerPoint responds to the students' actions, but the students need to know what actions to take. Therefore, you need to include clear instructions. (If your students ask you what to do, then the instructions aren't clear!)

If you want students to click on a button, add explanatory text to the button. We include these types of instructions when we describe the projects. For example, in Chapter 5, we suggest adding text on or above a button that says, "Click the button to go back to the question." Or you can create an invisible button that covers the entire slide. This technique is appropriate when the only action the students should take is to click to return to another slide.

Students these days are pretty computer-savvy and generally understand the concept of clicking something to choose it, but you may still find that you need to be very explicit. Again, if students need to ask what they should do to use the quiz, then you probably need to add more instructions. For young children, you can narrate the instructions for them to hear.

 See "Adding Narration" in Chapter 3 for detailed instructions.

MAXIMIZING LEARNING

Obviously, the goal of any teaching is learning. Older students like to see a PowerPoint presentation accompany your lecture; whether rightly or wrongly, they think it helps them organize the material better. They also think that you're more organized! Besides, given that many students nowadays are quite experienced with computers, your mastery of PowerPoint should enhance their respect for you.

You can try out various techniques and see which result in higher scores on the unit test. In other words, you can do your own research. Nevertheless, here are some ideas for helping students learn the most.

Helping Students Take Better Notes

According to some research, students do not do a good job of taking notes; they miss most of the important points in their notes. Yet good notes are crucial for learning. How can you use PowerPoint to help students take good notes?

 See Appendix A for more on research related to multimedia and learning.

Students benefit from receiving your notes. Research shows that for fact-based tests (as opposed to tests requiring analysis and synthesis of ideas) students who review the teacher's notes do better on exams than students who use only their own notes. But they also remember more of their own notes (even if they're not very good).

Therefore, the ideal situation is to help students take better notes and also provide them with your notes. These are two separate processes.

Remember, the text in your presentation may be compared to the skeleton of your topic. It shows the main points, expressed briefly. One way to help students take notes is to give them your presentation in a format that provides main points and gives them space to fill in the details. In other words, you add space between the lines of text. Note that the more space you add, the more notes the students will take.

HOW TO DO IT

- *Windows 2000/2002/2003:* Choose File ➤ Send To ➤ Microsoft Office Word. In the Send To Microsoft Office Word dialog box, choose the Outline Only option and click OK. A new Word document opens. Save it. Delete everything except the major topic headings. You can now reformat it and add space between the lines, as appropriate.

- *Windows 2007:* Click the Office button and choose Publish ➤ Create Handouts in Microsoft Office Word. In the Send To Microsoft Office Word dialog box, choose the Outline Only option and click OK. A new Word document opens. Save it. Delete everything except the major topic headings. You can now reformat it and add space between the lines, as appropriate.

- *Mac 2001/X/2004:* Choose File ➤ Send To ➤ Microsoft Word. A new Word document opens. Save it. Delete everything except the major topic headings. You can now reformat it and add space between the lines, as appropriate.

Print copies for each student. Hand out the skeleton outlines to the students before the presentation.

Printing Handouts and Notes

The next step is to give students your complete presentation as a handout after your talk. You don't want to give this to students beforehand; if you do, they'll spend the time reading the notes rather than listening to you. Also, they will assume that the handout includes everything you want them to learn and will take few or no notes at all!

There are several methods for creating handouts. One is the method we described in the previous section, using Microsoft Office Word. This time, however, you don't eliminate any content at all.

Another method is to print the outline of all of your text directly, without going through Word.

HOW TO DO IT

- *Windows 2000/2002/2003:* Choose File ➢ Print. In the Print dialog box, choose Outline View from the Print What drop-down list. Click OK to print.

- *Windows 2007:* Click the Office button and click Print. In the Print dialog box, choose Outline View from the Print What drop-down list. Click OK to print.

- *Mac 2001/X/2004:* Choose File ➢ Print. In the Print dialog box, choose Outline View from the Print What drop-down list. Click Print.

 When you print an outline view, PowerPoint does not include text in AutoShapes (Shapes) or text boxes. Only text in text place-holders is included. You can see what will appear by looking in the Outline tab of the Outline pane.

However, if you have lecture notes, you can give the students much more. As we explained in the "Adding Notes" section in Chapter 2, you can use the Notes pane in PowerPoint to add notes for yourself.

 To print out just the notes, choose Notes Pages from the Print What drop-down list in the Print dialog box.

If you put your lecture notes in the Notes pane, you can provide students with a very complete set of notes that they can use for studying. Use the same procedure we described for creating skeleton outlines in Word, but choose Notes Next to Slides or Notes Below Slides in the Send To Microsoft Office Word dialog box. Figure 4.5 shows a slide using the Notes Below Slides option.

☞ A handout that includes the slides plus your notes is very helpful to students who are out sick on the day of your presentation.

If you have access to software that creates Adobe Acrobat (PDF) files, you can save notes and handouts in PDF format. Then, you can e-mail them to students who missed the presentation.

These techniques can be time-consuming but offer the best combination of encouraging the students to take good notes on their own and giving them your notes.

Providing Electronic Access

Many schools have Web sites on which you can post presentations. Posting student presentations is a great way to make them available to other students and to their parents. If you have an e-mail list of parents, you can e-mail them presentations as an attachment.

Thanks to Patrick Douglas Crispen for many of these ideas.

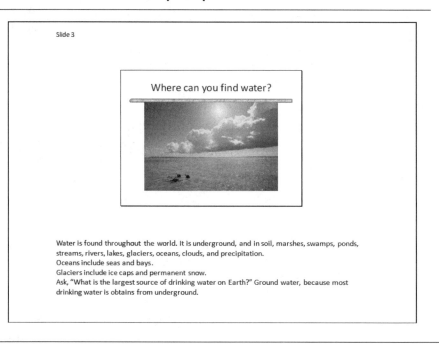

Figure 4.5
Providing students with handouts, including your notes, gives them the most complete packet of information.

Slide 3

Where can you find water?

Water is found throughout the world. It is underground, and in soil, marshes, swamps, ponds, streams, rivers, lakes, glaciers, oceans, clouds, and precipitation.
Oceans include seas and bays.
Glaciers include ice caps and permanent snow.
Ask, "What is the largest source of drinking water on Earth?" Ground water, because most drinking water is obtains from underground.

THE IMPORTANCE OF YOU

Finally, we'll repeat a maxim we've noted before. *You* are the presentation. The PowerPoint file is not the presentation. When you're standing in front of a classroom and using PowerPoint as a visual aid, remember it's just an aid. Don't let it become the master. Games and individually viewed reviews and projects do not, of course, apply.

 If you want to spend some time discussing a topic and the slide has no more to offer, press the letter B key to black out the slide. When you're done, press the letter B again to return to the slide. This focuses the students solidly on you, because the black slide is boring!

SUMMARY

In this chapter, we discussed best practices that will help you use PowerPoint wisely. We explained that you shouldn't use fancy backgrounds and how to use PowerPoint appropriately for the age of your students. We noted that special effects should be simple.

We discussed how to avoid slide after slide of bulleted text and talked about some techniques for using text wisely. We showed how presentations need to vary based on the context in which they'll be used.

We ended the chapter with a discussion about using handouts to help students take better notes and how to create handouts with PowerPoint.

PART TWO

Creating Great Projects Using PowerPoint

Chapter 5: Interactive Reviews

Chapter 6: Interactive Maps

Chapter 7: Menu-Based Projects

Chapter 8: Class Games

Chapter 9: Graded Tests

Now that you know the basics of PowerPoint, you can start creating interactive projects: short reviews (quizzes), clickable maps and pictures, nonlinear presentations, games, and graded tests. Along the way, you'll learn a lot about hyperlinks, buttons, and menus. You'll be able to use these skills to create your own projects.

Interactive Reviews

When the main part of your project is ready, it is time to add an activity that will enhance retention. In this chapter, you will learn how to create interactive PowerPoint projects: short quizzes or reviews. Their format makes these activities look like quizzes, but their role is not so much to test knowledge as to review the material. In our experience, students enjoy such activities immensely. When created with humor and ingenuity, these activities can be extremely effective!

CHOOSING THE IMPORTANT POINTS

A quiz with multiple-choice questions at the end of a project is a great tool for enhancing retention. You offer a number of slides with questions and several choices, from which the students select the right answer. As you saw in Chapter 1, a wrong choice leads to negative feedback ("Try again!" or "Think again!"), and the right choice leads positive feedback ("Great job!" or "You are sharp!" and so on).

First, you need to decide what parts of your projects should be covered in the quiz. Generally, you want to cover the most important points. These points should not be numerical data, but rather significant concepts. For example, it is not so important to know the exact percentage of water in rivers and lakes; it is more important to know that the amount of freshwater on Earth is many times smaller than the amount of saltwater in the ocean. The objective of such a quiz, or review, is to develop higher-order thinking rather than simple recall.

Writing the Questions

When you are ready to create your quiz, start writing your first question. The instructions we give here assume that you have already created the slides that contain the project content. However, you could create a separate presentation just for the review. You might do this if you are presenting the material to the class as a whole, but are offering the review to individual students when they have their own time in front of a computer.

 At this stage, we assume that you know how to insert a slide, choose a layout, resize and move objects, and so on. For instructions, see Chapter 2.

HOW TO DO IT

- *Windows 2000/2002/2003:* Insert a new slide. Select the layout. The most convenient layout is "Title and Text." Click in the text placeholder that says "Click to add title" and type in your question.

- *Windows 2007:* Insert a new slide. Select the layout. The most convenient layout is "Title and Content." Click in the text placeholder that says "Click to add title" and type in your question.

- *Mac 2001/X/2004:* Insert a new slide. Select the layout. The most convenient layout is "Bulleted Text." Click in the text placeholder that says "Click to add title" and type in your question.

You may need to adjust the size of the text placeholder or move it slightly.

Writing Multiple-Choice Answers

After you enter the questions, it is time to type in your multiple-choice answers.

HOW TO DO IT

- *All versions:* In the text placeholder "Click to add text" enter your first answer. By default, there is a bullet in front of each paragraph, which means that every time you press Enter, there will be a bullet. Therefore, use the Enter key to start each new answer.

The multiple-choice answers should reflect the material in the project and offer one correct answer. As you likely know based on other multiple-choice tests you've created, the incorrect answers should also contribute to the retention of the material; they should look correct and require some thinking before the students make their choice.

For example, if your question is "Which of the following contains the largest amount of water on Earth?" the choices may be:

- Groundwater

- Lakes and rivers

- Oceans, seas, and bays

- Ice caps, glaciers, and permanent snow

The obvious choice is "Oceans, seas, and bays." However, if you want to challenge your students, you may want to reformulate your question along these lines: "What is the largest source of drinking water on Earth?"

Although ice caps, glaciers, and permanent snow may seem to be the correct choice (because the largest amount of freshwater is in solid form), the correct answer is groundwater, because most drinking water is obtained from underground.

It is sometimes a good idea to have a most improbable or even absurd choice, just for fun and for stimulating the activity. For example, for the question "What is the largest source of drinking water on Earth?" one of the choices may be "Coca-Cola" or something like that. In such cases, rely on your own taste, creativity, grade level, and the way you offer the project to the students—either as your presentation to the entire class, as part of home assignment, or as a game. The number of choices is also up to you; we used four, as shown in Figure 5.1.

 To improve the look of the slide, you can use AutoShapes (simply called *Shapes* in PowerPoint 2007) instead of plain text for the questions and answers. Use a blank slide layout. Chapter 2 explained how to insert AutoShapes. When you insert an AutoShape, immediately start typing to add text inside the shape.

Figure 5.1
The first question and answer choices.

> # Which of the following contains the largest amount of water on Earth?
>
> - Groundwater
> - Lakes and rivers
> - Oceans, seas, and bays
> - Ice caps, glaciers, & permanent snow

INTERACTIVITY

Once you have the questions and answers, you need to create a method for the review to let students know if they've chosen the right or wrong answer. This is the process that makes the review interactive. The students act (choose an answer), and PowerPoint reacts appropriately.

 Before continuing, now's a good time to save!

Adding the "Try Again!" Response

The next step is to create the feedback for the correct and incorrect choices. Let's start with the incorrect choice. This will tell students who choose an incorrect answer to try again.

Creating a Link to the "Try Again!" Response

Now you need to link the wrong choices to the "Try again!" slide. This way, when a student chooses a wrong answer, PowerPoint will display the "Try again!" slide. You do this using the hyperlink feature.

Hyperlinks in PowerPoint are like hyperlinks on the Web that you click in your browser. When a student clicks on a link, PowerPoint goes to the link's address. In this case, you'll be linking to another slide (the "Try again!" slide) in the same presentation file. However, as you'll see in Chapter 7, you can link to anywhere on the Internet.

First, go back to your question slide and select one of the wrong choices. Then follow these instructions:

toolbar, click Document ➤ Anchor ➤ Locate. The Select Place in Document dialog box appears. Click the small triangle to the left of Slide Titles, select the title that says "Try again!" and click OK, as shown in Figure 5.2b.

The selected words in the question slide become underlined and change color to blue to indicate that your link is active.

 If you use AutoShapes instead of text, you can click the edge of the shape to select the shape, rather than its text, before inserting the hyperlink. Then students can click anywhere in the AutoShape to activate the link. This makes the AutoShape function more like a button that you use in a Web browser.

Repeat this procedure for the remaining two wrong answers. Do not hyperlink all the wrong choices at once; if you do, when students click the link, the text will change

Figure 5.2a
Creating a link to the "Try again!" response in Windows.

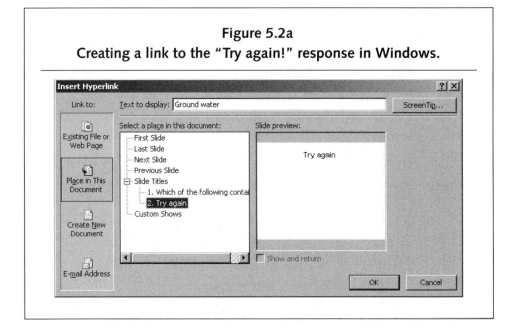

Figure 5.2b
The Select Place in Document dialog box on the Mac.

Select Place in Document

Select an existing place in the document:

First Slide
Last Slide
Next Slide
Previous Slide
▼ Slide Titles
      1. Which of the following contains the largest amount ...
      2. TRY AGAIN!
Custom Shows

Cancel   OK

color for all the linked answers, which will then leave only the one correct answer in the original color—and give away the right answer! (Don't forget to save!)

There is a possibility that a student (or yourself) may miss the linked words and click outside of them. By default, the presentation will advance the show to the next slide, which may not necessarily be the slide linked to the choice. To avoid this, choose Slide Show ➤ Slide Transition, and in the Slide Transition dialog box deselect the On Click check box in the Slide Advance section. In PowerPoint 2007, click the Animations tab, to deselect the On Mouse Click check box.

Creating a Back Link

Each of the wrong choices is now linked to the "Try again!" slide. To check it, click on the Slide Show icon at the bottom of the Outline pane (at the lower-right corner of the window in PowerPoint 2007). Click one of the wrong answers to go to the "Try again!" slide. To get back to the question slide, right-click on the "Try again!" slide and choose Previous.

You can go back to Normal view by pressing the Escape key or right-clicking on the slide and choosing End Show.

However, you don't want to do that in a real-life situation. You want your students to get back to the question slide in one click! There are two ways to accomplish this.

Adding a button

You can add a button to the "Try again!" slide and link the button to the question slide. Students click the button to return to the question.

HOW TO DO IT

 • *Windows 2000/2002/2003:* Choose Slide Show ➢ Action Buttons ➢ Action Button: Back or Previous. Click on the slide to insert the action button. The moment you release the key the Action Settings dialog box appears. In the Hyperlink To drop-down list, choose Slide (you'll need to scroll down) and then choose your question slide in the Hyperlink to Slide dialog box that opens. Click OK. Click OK again.

- *Windows 2007:* On the Insert tab, click the Shapes button. In the Action Buttons section, choose Action Buttons: Back or Previous. Click on the slide to insert the action button. The moment you release the key the Action Settings dialog box appears. In the Hyperlink To drop-down list, choose Slide (you'll need to scroll down) and then choose your question slide in the Hyperlink to Slide dialog box that opens. Click OK.

- *Mac 2001/X/2004:* Slide Show on the main toolbar ➤ Action Buttons ➤ Previous Slide. Click on the slide to insert the action button. The moment you release the key the Action Settings dialog box appears. In the Hyperlink To drop-down list, choose Slide (you'll need to scroll down) and then choose your question slide in the Hyperlink to Slide dialog box that opens (see Figure 5.3). Click OK.

Go back to the "Try again!" slide. You need to tell your students that they have to click the button to go back to the question. You can enter **Click the button to go back to the question** in the text box above the button, or you can type it right on the button (see Figure 5.4). Just click on the button and type. If the text appears too small, select the text and make it larger. Make sure that the button is large enough to hold the text. You can always make it larger—click and drag outward by any corner.

The advantage of creating a back link with an action button is that it offers a nice pictorial of a clickable button, which even produces a visual effect of pressing the button (the left and upper sides of the button change color).

 You can even add a clicking sound effect. In the Action Settings dialog box, check the Play Sound check box and choose Click from the Play Sound drop-down list.

Figure 5.3
The Link to Slide dialog box now links the action button back to the question slide.

Figure 5.3
The Link to Slide dialog box now links the action button back to the question slide.

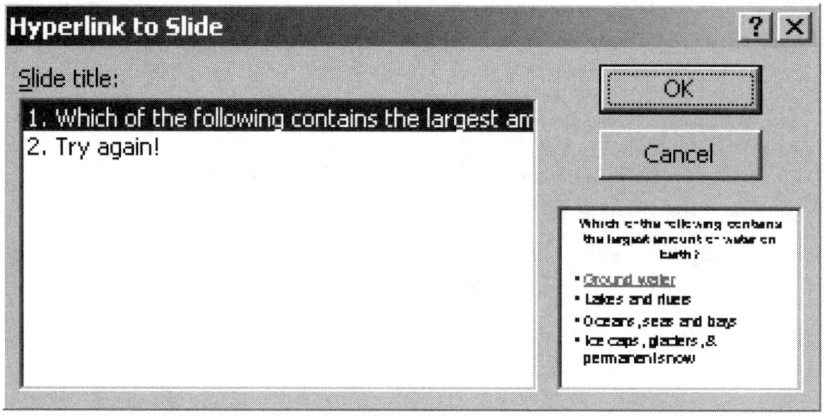

You can change the color of the action button. We described how to change the fill of an AutoShape in Chapter 2.

However, there is a possibility that a student may miss the button and click outside of it. To avoid this, you may either expand the action button so that it occupies most of the slide, or, as we explained earlier in this chapter (in the "Creating a Link to the 'Try Again!' Response" section) you can deselect the On Click check box in the Slide Advance section of the Slide Transition dialog box. (In PowerPoint 2007, click the Animations tab to deselect the On Mouse Click check box.)

Adding an invisible clickable field

Another effective way to create a back link from a feedback slide to the question slide is to insert an invisible clickable button. This button covers the entire slide, so no matter where the student clicks, the presentation returns to the question slide. The first step is to cover the slide with an AutoShape (or shape). Follow these instructions.

Figure 5.4
Typing on the action button.

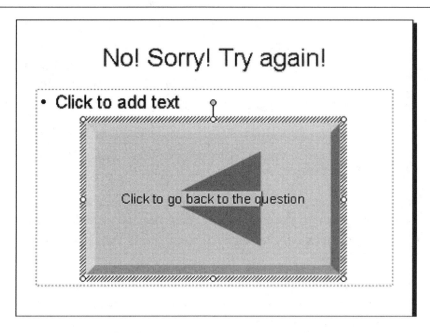

HOW TO DO IT

- *Windows 2000/2002/2003:* In the text placeholder on the "Try again!" slide, type **Click to go back to the question**. On the Drawing toolbar, click on Rectangle (next to AutoShapes). The cursor turns into a small cross. Place the cross at the upper left-hand corner of the slide, then drag diagonally to the opposite corner. When the blue rectangle covers the entire slide, release the mouse button.

- *Window 2007:* In the text box for text on the "Try again!" slide, type **Click to go back to the question**. On the Insert tab, click Shapes and choose the Rectangle. The cursor turns into a small cross. Place the cross at the upper left-hand corner of the slide, then drag diagonally to the opposite corner. When the blue rectangle covers the entire slide, release the mouse button.

- *Mac 2001/X/2004:* In the text box for text on the "Try again!" slide, type **Click to go back to the question**. On the Drawing toolbar click on Rectangle (next to AutoShapes). The cursor turns into a small cross. Place the cross at the upper left-hand corner of the slide, then drag diagonally to the opposite corner. When the blue rectangle covers the entire slide, release the mouse button.

Your slide should look like Figure 5.5.

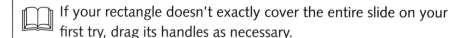 If your rectangle doesn't exactly cover the entire slide on your first try, drag its handles as necessary.

Now that the slide is covered with the rectangle, you need to link the rectangle to the question slide.

HOW TO DO IT

- *Windows 2000/2002/2003:* Select the rectangle and choose Insert ➤ Hyperlink. Click Place in the Document. In the Select a Place in This Document box, choose the question slide from the Slide Titles list.

- *Windows 2007:* Select the rectangle and display the Insert tab. Click the Hyperlink button. Click Place in the Document. In the Select a Place in This Document box, choose the question slide from the Slide Titles list.

- *Mac 2001/X/2004:* Select the rectangle and choose Insert ➤ Hyperlink. On the Web Page/Document/E-mail Address toolbar, click Document ➤ Anchor ➤ Locate. The Select Place in Document dialog box appears. Click the small triangle to the left of Slide Titles, select the title of your question slide, and click OK.

Figure 5.5
The rectangle completely covers the "Try again!" slide.

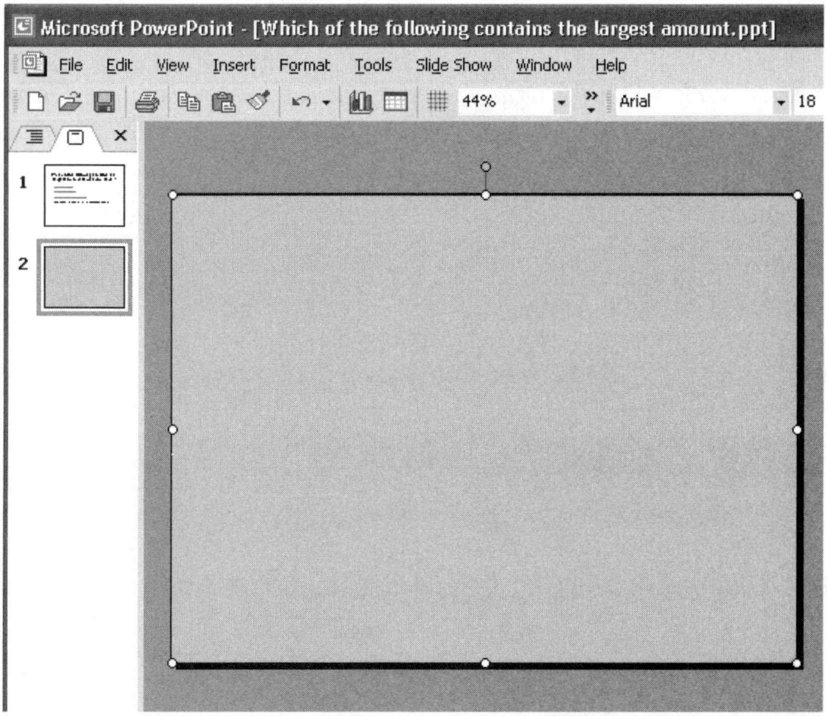

The slide now links back to the question, but the blue rectangle covers the text of the slide. You need to make the rectangle invisible! Follow these instructions:

HOW TO DO IT

- *Windows 2000/2002/2003:* Double-click the rectangle. On the Format AutoShape dialog box Colors and Lines tab, shown in Figure 5.6, choose No Fill from the Color drop-down list in the Fill section. Then choose No Line from the Color drop-down list in the Line section. Click OK.

- *Windows 2007:* Select the rectangle. On the Format tab that appears, click the dialog box launcher arrow at the right side of the Shape

Styles group to open the Format Shape dialog box. With the Fill pane displayed, drag the Transparency slider all the way to the right (100%). Click the Line Color category on the left and again drag the Transparency slider all the way to the right. This makes the rectangle completely transparent and therefore invisible.

- *Mac 2001/X/2004:* Double-click the rectangle. In the Format AutoShape dialog box Colors and Lines tab, choose No Fill from the Color drop-down list. Then choose No Line from the Color drop-down list in the Line section, as shown in Figure 5.6. Click OK.

Figure 5.6
The Format AutoShape dialog box.

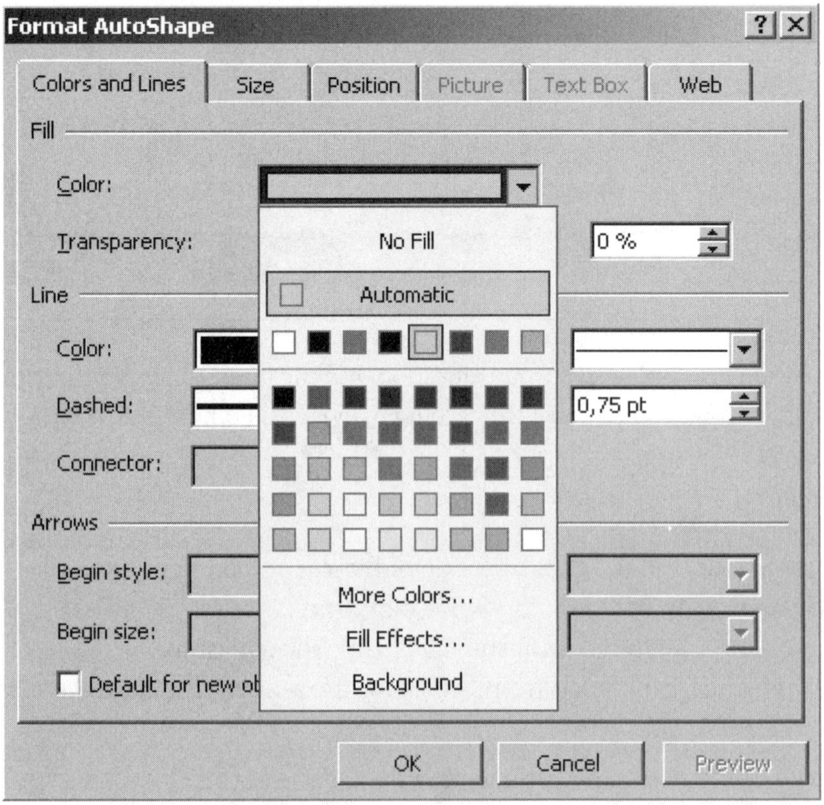

The rectangle becomes transparent, while the whole slide becomes clickable and linked to the desired slide. The advantage of this method is that it guarantees the return to the question slide no matter where you click!

Adding the "Good Job!" Response

One of the choices for the answer is correct. You need to create a "Good job!" slide for positive feedback when the student chooses the right answer. Use the same procedure we explained in the "Creating a Link to the 'Try Again!' Response" section earlier in this chapter, but enter **Good job!** in the title placeholder of the slide.

You then need to link the correct question to this "Good job!" slide. You do this in the same way that you linked the incorrect question to the "Try again!" slide. For instructions, see again "Creating a Link to the 'Try Again!' Response."

Now, when students choose the correct answer, they get positive feedback. Now is a good time to save!

Creating a Forward Link

Logically, after your students select the right choice and receive positive feedback (the "Good job!" slide), the quiz should offer a new question. Let's start with writing a new question. The question we used was, "What is the largest source of drinking water on Earth?"

HOW TO DO IT

- *All versions:* Insert a new slide of the same layout as you used previously. In the title text placeholder, type your new question, as shown in Figure 5.7.

The next step is to create a link from the "Good job!" slide to the next question, the one that you just created. You can do this in the same two ways we explained earlier in the "Creating a Back Link" section. To create an action button, first go back to your "Good job!" slide, and follow these instructions:

HOW TO DO IT

 - *Windows 2000/2002/2003:* Choose Slide Show ➤ Action Buttons ➤ Action Button: Forward or Next. Click on the slide to

---

insert the action button. In the Hyperlink To drop-down list of the Action Settings dialog box, choose Slide (you'll need to scroll down) and then choose your question slide in the Hyperlink to Slide dialog box that opens. Click OK twice to close both dialog boxes.

- *Windows 2007:* On the Insert tab, click the Shapes button. In the Action Buttons section, choose Action Buttons: Forward or Next. Click on the slide to insert the action button. In the Hyperlink To drop-down list of the Action Settings dialog box, choose Slide (you'll need to scroll down) and then choose your question slide in the Hyperlink to Slide dialog box that opens. Click OK twice to close both dialog boxes.

- *Mac 2001/X/2004:* Choose Slide Show ➤ Action Buttons ➤ Next Slide. Click on the slide to insert the action button. In the Hyperlink To drop-down list of the Action Settings dialog box, choose Slide (you'll need to scroll down) and then choose your question slide in the Hyperlink to Slide dialog box that opens. Click OK twice to close both dialog boxes.

Figure 5.7
The next question and answer choices.

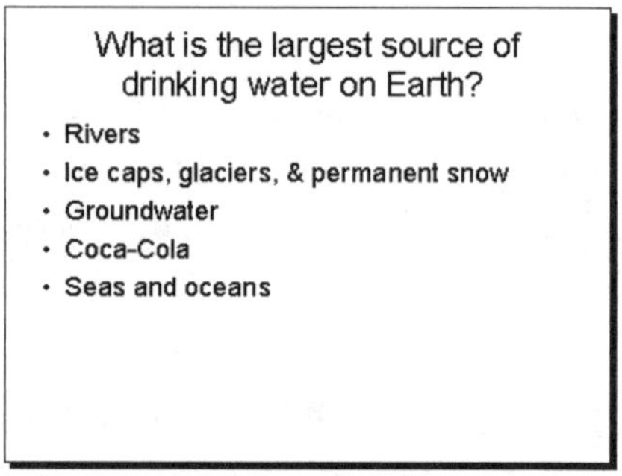

What is the largest source of drinking water on Earth?
- Rivers
- Ice caps, glaciers, & permanent snow
- Groundwater
- Coca-Cola
- Seas and oceans

Don't forget to type **Click on the button to go to the next question** on the action button, as we explained earlier in this chapter.

However, if you prefer the clickable invisible field technique, type **Click to go to the next question** in the text placeholder. Then repeat the procedures, described in the "Adding an Invisible Clickable Field" section for the back link in the "Try again!" slide. You'll need to do the following:

1. Create a rectangle that covers the entire slide.

2. Link the rectangle to the slide with the next question, "What is the largest source of drinking water on Earth?"

3. Make the rectangle invisible.

 A common mistake is creating only one "Try again!" and one "Good job!" slide for all questions. There must be one "Try again!" slide and one "Good job!" slide for each question slide. If you feel that is too much work, copy and paste these slides on the Outline pane or in Slide Sorter view before you create links. In this case, when creating links, you need to rely on the numbers of the feedback slides, because they will all have the same titles.

OPTIONS FOR MORE FUN

It is an excellent idea to add more fun to the feedback slides. You can use pictures or GIF animations—perhaps a picture of a sad face or a crying face for the "Try again!" slide, and a picture of a happy face for the "Good job!" slide. Pictures of fireworks, clapping hands, or the like will also work.

It's also fun to use sounds. You can use the sounds from the Clip Art gallery (Clip Organizer in 2000) or find them on the Internet. Make sure that the sound plays automatically when the slide appears. For more instructions, see Chapter 3.

You can find the completed presentation, Water Cycle Review.ppt, at www. ellenfinkelstein.com/powerpointforteachers.html.

For advanced users: If you use your own sound effect, the sound will play only once—that is, the slide with the negative feedback will only play the sound once, and when the students select another wrong answer, the sound will not play. To avoid that, after you create your "Try again!" slide and insert a back link to the question slide, copy and paste it as many times as the number of wrong choices. Make sure to link each wrong choice to each individual "Try again!" slide. In this case each "Try again!" slide will be activated only once and the sound file will play on each of them. Another option is to add the sound to a slide transition; see Chapter 3 for instructions.

SUMMARY

In this chapter we explained how to create interactive multiple-choice reviews, or quizzes. We showed how to create question slides and link the multiple-choice responses to the feedback slides: either "Good job!" or "Try again!"

We also explained how to create back and forward links using two different techniques: action buttons and an invisible clickable field.

Interactive Maps

I n this chapter, we will explore further the interactive potential of PowerPoint by creating clickable maps and pictures—images on slides that students can click on to get a response. For example, a slide might tell the student to "Click on Africa." When the student clicks, positive or negative feedback appears, depending on whether the answer was right or wrong.

Using this technique, you can create quizzes, reviews, or other learning opportunities that relate to geography or any system that you can visually display on a slide. In this chapter, you will create a geography review project. At the end of the chapter, we offer some other ideas for using this technique. (This chapter is based on techniques that we covered in the previous chapter; if necessary, read Chapter 5 first.)

CREATING A GEOGRAPHY REVIEW

Let's create an interactive map for your students to test their knowledge of the continents. Students will respond to an instruction to click on a continent.

SELECTING AN APPROPRIATE PICTURE

First, you need to find a good picture map. Make sure it contains no names. We used a map from the Clip Art collection.

HOW TO DO IT

- *Windows 2000/2002/2003:* Insert a new slide and choose Title Only layout. (You can choose any layout except Blank.) Choose Insert Picture ➢ Clip Art. In the Insert Clip Art dialog box or task pane, enter **Geography** in the Search For text box. If you find a picture map with all continents, double-click it to insert it on your new slide. If not, see the instructions following this box.

- *Windows 2007:* Insert a new slide and choose the Title and Content layout. On the Insert tab, choose Clip Art. In the Insert Clip Art task pane, enter **Geography** in the Search For text box. If you find a picture map with all continents, double-click it to insert it on your new slide.

- *Mac 2001/X/2004:* Insert a new slide and choose the Title and Text layout. Choose Insert ➢ Picture ➢ Clip Art. In the Insert Clip Art dialog box or task pane, enter **Geography** in the Search For text box. If you find a picture map with all continents, double-click it to insert it on your new slide.

If you don't find a world map in the Clip Art collection, go to this book's companion Web site at www.ellenfinkelstein.com/powerpointforteachers.html and look for the World Map for Chapter 6. Right-click the map and choose Save Image As (or Save Picture As, or something similar, depending on your Web browser) to save the file to your computer. In PowerPoint, choose Insert ➢ Picture ➢ From File (choose Picture on the Insert tab in PowerPoint 2007) to insert the map on your slide.

Make sure that the picture does not cover the Click to Add Title placeholder. Adjust the picture so that it occupies about three-quarters of the main slide area, as shown in Figure 6.1.

Copying and Pasting the Slide

You'll need to make several copies (at least five) of this slide, one for each question. On the Outline pane, click the slide with the map and press Ctrl+C (Windows)/⌘+C (Mac). Then press Ctrl+V (Windows)/⌘+V (Mac) at least four times. You can also right-click on the slide icon in the Outline pane to copy the

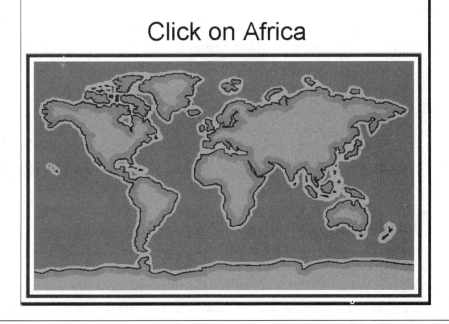

Figure 6.1
Your slide now has a world map on it.

Click on Africa

slide, then click under the icon and right-click again to paste. You can use the Slide Sorter view to do the same. (If you have a two-button mouse for your Mac, you can use the right-clicking instructions.)

Creating Question and Negative Feedback Slides

Now you'll use two of the slides you made to create the first question slide and its negative feedback slide.

HOW TO DO IT

- *All versions:* Return to the first slide and type in the title text placeholder **Click on Africa**. Go to slide 2 and type in the text placeholder **Try again! Click to go back to the question!** This is your negative

---

feedback slide. Then, create a link back to the question slide by adding an invisible clickable field and hyperlinking it to the question slide. This technique is precisely the same as the one we used in Chapter 5. (See "Adding an Invisible Clickable Field" in Chapter 5.)

 Have you saved your presentation file yet?

Now let's create a positive feedback slide, which will also get the user to the next question. Go to slide 3 and type the following in the Click to Add Title text placeholder: **Great job! Now click on Australia.**

Drawing a Hot (Clickable) Spot

Now you need to create a clickable (hot) spot. A clickable spot is an area on a slide that has a hyperlink. This clickable spot will serve as a link to the "Great job!" slide so that when students click on the right location (Africa), they will get positive feedback and can move to the next question. First, go back to the question slide. Then follow these instructions:

HOW TO DO IT

- *Windows 2000/2002/2003:* On the Drawing toolbar, choose AutoShapes ➤ Lines ➤ Freeform. The cursor turns into a cross. Place the cursor anywhere along the contour line of Africa, then click and hold. The cross turns into a pencil. Drag the pencil around the map of Africa, tracing the contour of this continent as accurately as possible. Make sure to connect back to your start point before releasing the mouse button.

- *Windows 2000/2002/2003:* On the Drawing toolbar, choose AutoShapes ➤ Lines ➤ Freeform. The cursor turns into a cross. Place the cursor anywhere along the contour line of Africa, then click and hold. The cross turns into a pencil. Drag the pencil around the map of Africa, tracing the contour of this continent as accurately as possible. Make sure to connect back to your start point before releasing the mouse button.

- *Windows 2007:* On the Insert tab, click the Shapes button and choose Freeform from the Lines section. The cursor turns into a cross. Place the cursor anywhere along the contour line of Africa, then click and hold. Drag the cursor around the map of Africa, tracing the contour of this continent as accurately as possible. Make sure to connect back to your start point before releasing the mouse button.

You have just drawn an AutoShape covering Africa, as shown in Figure 6.2.

Linking the Hot Spot to Positive Feedback

Remember that Africa is the right answer, so its hot spot should link to the positive feedback slide. So the next step is to link the spot to the "Great job!" slide. Follow these instructions:

HOW TO DO IT

- *Windows 2000/2002/2003:* With the AutoShape selected, choose Insert ➤ Hyperlink. The Insert Hyperlink dialog box appears. Click the Place in This Document button and under the Slide Titles group, click on the "Great job! Now click on Australia" slide.

- *Windows 2007:* With the shape selected, display the Insert tab and click Hyperlink. The Insert Hyperlink dialog box appears. Click the

Place in This Document button and under the Slide Titles group, click on the "Great job! Now click on Australia" slide.

- *Mac 2001/X/2004:* With the AutoShape selected, choose Insert ➢ Hyperlink. On the Web Page/Document/E-mail Address toolbar, click Document ➢ Anchor ➢ Locate. The Select Place in Document dialog box appears. Click the small triangle to the left of Slide Titles, select your "Great job! Now click on Australia" slide, and click OK.

The "Great job! Now click on Australia" slide is both positive feedback for the "Click on Africa" question and a new question.

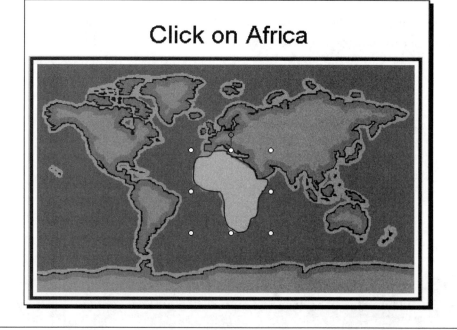

Figure 6.2
The AutoShape covers the continent of Africa.

Click on Africa

The AutoShape may have a blue fill and it has an outline. You need to make the AutoShape invisible. For instructions, see "Adding an Invisible Clickable Field" in Chapter 5.

The next step is to create the hot spot for Australia. On the third slide, use the same technique we explained for Africa to draw a hot (clickable) spot around Australia. Link the hot spot to the next slide, which will be both the positive feedback and the next question. Then make the AutoShape invisible, as you did previously.

Creating a Hot Spot for the Wrong Area

You covered the map of Africa with an AutoShape looking like a contour map of Africa and linked it to the "Great job!" slide. What about the wrong choice? To cover the situation when students click in the wrong location, you need to cover the rest of the map of the world with a clickable spot.

The procedure is exactly the same as the one you used to create the clickable spot for Africa. However, this time, you draw a hot spot on the whole map, leaving out Africa, as shown in Figure 6.3. Never mind that your shape may look like two shapes connected in one or several points; it still is one AutoShape. Make sure you do not release the mouse button until you finish drawing around all the continents, except Africa.

Insert a hyperlink to the "Try again!" slide, so that students see that slide if they click anywhere but Africa.

As we described earlier, you should now make the shape invisible.

Go back to the "Great job!" slide. Now that you know how to create clickable invisible spots, you can make an invisible hot spot to link the wrong choice (everything else but Africa) to a negative feedback slide. You can continue creating questions in this way.

It's now time to save again and go into Slide Show view to see how it all works. You should see that because you created exact copies of the same picture slide, there is no visible transition between slides. As a result, students don't realize that they are looking at different slides. The visual effect is that they see the same slide but with different commands and feedback!

 Make sure that the size and place of the map on the slides remain exactly the same. If there are even slight deviations, the visual effect will be ruined.

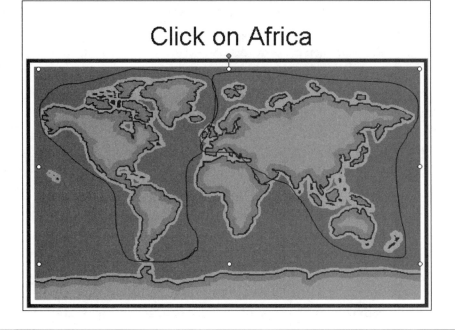

Figure 6.3
Draw a hot spot for the negative feedback.

Click on Africa

ADDING AUDIO OR NARRATION

It is a good idea to add some audio feedback. You can insert a short sound from the Clip Art collection, or perhaps find and save a WAV file from the Web. Insert the sound in the transition to the feedback slides, as described in Chapter 3, in the "Adding Sounds, Music, and Narration" section. You can also use your own narration, as explained in the same section.

TIPS FOR MORE FUN

We don't need to tell you how much children love fun projects. Use your imagination to come up with additional clip art and feedback messages. It is also a great idea to create such projects together with your students—harness their imagination!

Here are some tips:

- Instead of writing in the Click to Add Title placeholder, format the map so that it covers the entire slide, and use text boxes. You will find the text box button on the Drawing toolbar (or on the Insert tab in PowerPoint 2007). In the text boxes, write the same instructions and feedback messages as on the slide titles.

- In addition to positive or negative feedback, provide some prompts; if a student clicks on Australia instead of Africa, you can offer a feedback saying, "This is not Africa, this is Australia! Click again to try once more!" In this case, you need to create several clickable spots on the map, each hyperlinked to an individual feedback slide. The clickable spot on Australia links to the "This is not Africa, this is Australia!" slide, while the clickable map on South America leads to the "This is not Africa, this is South America! Click again to try once more!" slide. Thus, your students not only test their knowledge but also refresh it.

- Use the technique in this chapter for many other subjects. For example, you can make an interactive picture of a cell with clickable components, or a diagram of the water cycle. You can also make interactive graphs (see Chapter 3 to review how to create graphs), pie charts, and much more.

For a completed geography review, see Map of Europe.ppt, on the book's companion Web site at www.ellenfinkelstein.com/powerpointforteachers.html.

SUMMARY

In this chapter we explained how to create interactive maps in PowerPoint.

We showed how to create hot (clickable) spots on an image by drawing Freeform AutoShapes around objects. We explained how to make these AutoShapes invisible and hyperlink them to the feedback slides. Finally, we discussed how to create the visual impression of a static slide with messages appearing on it.

Menu-Based Projects

You can encourage students to explore their own interests if you create a presentation that functions like a Web site, with buttons and links to further content and resources. This is sometimes called a *nonlinear* project because students don't go from slide to slide in order in the presentation. Instead, they click links that can go anywhere— inside the presentation or anywhere on the Internet. In this chapter you will learn how to create such projects.

WHY NONLINEAR?

Many topics have a complex structure. Sometimes it is hard, or even impossible, to cover the topic without having to go back to the beginning. This is especially the case when you're dealing with classifications: you start with a major category, then cover one of the subcategories, then have to get back to the major category to be able to go on to another subcategory.

In Chapter 1, in the "Linear versus Nonlinear" section, we discussed a project on the classification of animals (see Figure 1.7). In this lesson, the major category was animals, and the first slide showed categories of mammals, reptiles and amphibians, fish, and so on. A teacher would cover each of these subcategories as a separate branch. For example, when discussing mammals, you would talk about different types of mammals, specific features, habitats, reproduction, and so on. Then you would go back to the first slide to introduce another subcategory.

This same idea is used in Web sites: a homepage links to the other pages. The menus on the homepage help users choose where they want to go. Then all the subsequent pages have a link back to the homepage.

Just as on a Web site, you can create a "home slide" with a menu. Each choice on the menu will send the students off on a different route. Then you place links on the other slides so students can go back to the menu slide.

 When you offer a nonlinear PowerPoint project as a home assignment, students can use a similar structure to create their own nonlinear projects. This process develops systematic thinking, helping them organize concepts into logical structures, which also enhances comprehension.

In this chapter, we'll create a sample nonlinear project. The topic will be classes of animals, which we have already discussed.

As we explained in Chapter 2, you should start by creating your lesson plan and gathering the information you want to cover. Create an outline of what you want to say and think about how you can depict the concepts visually. Collect images, sounds, animations, and so on, and place them in the same folder where you'll save the PowerPoint presentation.

CREATING SECTIONS

Because PowerPoint requires slides to be in linear order, the first step is to think of the sections of your nonlinear project. In our example, we'll start with mammals as a subcategory so we'll create a section on mammals. Each section will be a few slides long.

 Because a nonlinear project can get quite long, in this chapter, we leave a lot of the content here up to you. You can find a completed project on animals—Animal Categories.ppt—on this book's companion Web site at www.ellenfinkelstein.com/powerpointforteachers.html.

Start by creating a new presentation. Now you're ready to create the first slide of the mammal section.

HOW TO DO IT

- *Windows 2000/2002/2003:* Right-click a blank area of the slide and choose Slide Layout. Choose the Title and Text layout. In the title Text placeholder, enter **Mammals**. In the slide text placeholder, enter **Unlike other animals, mammals have body hair, have three middle ear bones, and nourish their young with milk that females produce in modified sweat glands called mammary glands.**

- *Windows 2007:* Right-click a blank area of the slide and choose Layout. Choose the Title and Content layout. In the title text placeholder, enter **Mammals**. In the slide text placeholder, enter **Unlike other animals, mammals have body hair, have three middle ear bones, and nourish their young with milk that females produce in modified sweat glands called mammary glands.**

- *Mac 2001/X/2004:* Right-click (Windows)/Ctrl-click (Mac without a two-button mouse) a blank area of the slide and choose Slide Layout. Choose the Title and Text layout. In the title text placeholder, enter **Mammals**. In the slide text placeholder, enter **Unlike other animals, mammals have body hair, have three middle ear bones, and nourish their young with milk that females produce in modified sweat glands called mammary glands.**

Insert a new slide with the same layout. In the title text placeholder, enter **Classes of Mammals**, and in the slide text placeholder, enter three lines of text: **Marsupials**, **Monotremes**, and **Placentals**. Now is a good time to save!

Of course, it's entirely up to you how you organize your section on mammals, how many slides you use, and in what order you show these slides. Continue to add slides until you feel you have a good section on mammals.

 It is important that you place some text in the title text placeholder for each slide, so that you can easily hyperlink to the slides using the titles. This is especially important for Mac users because of the way you select slides when you create hyperlinks.

Using the instructions we provided in Chapters 2 and 3, add images, sound, animation, and maybe a video. (If you want, you can add the text and navigation first, and then the images and other elements later.)

Now create a section on insects, using the same technique as for mammals. Continue on to complete the other sections on fish, reptiles and amphibians, and birds.

Save your presentation. You should now have quite a number of slides.

ADDING A MENU SLIDE

Now you need to create a menu slide that will connect all the sections together.

Add a new slide. If you want the menu to be text-based, use the Title and Text (or Title and Content) layout. If you want to add images (remember: a picture is worth a thousand words!), use the Title Only layout. We'll create a menu with pictures and captions.

In all versions, insert the images that you want to use. (See Chapter 2 for instructions.) They should be approximately the same size and very clear. Space them out nicely, leaving room beneath them (or next to them) for the captions.

HOW TO DO IT

- *Windows 2000/2002/2003:* Choose Insert ➢ Text Box or click the Text Box button on the Drawing toolbar. Drag the desired width on the slide under a picture and type the text, such as **Mammals**. If necessary, adjust the placement of the text box relative to the picture. Repeat for all the images.

- *Windows 2007:* On the Insert tab, click the Text Box button. Drag the desired width on the slide under a picture and type the text, such as **Mammals**. If necessary, adjust the placement of the text box relative to the picture. Repeat for all the images.

- *Mac 2001/X/2004:* Choose Insert ➢ Text Box or click the Text Box button on the Drawing toolbar. Drag the desired width on the slide under a picture and type the text, such as **Mammals**. If necessary, adjust the placement of the text box relative to the picture. Repeat for all the images.

Figure 7.1
This is one way to lay out a menu slide. It will function as a menu for the entire project.

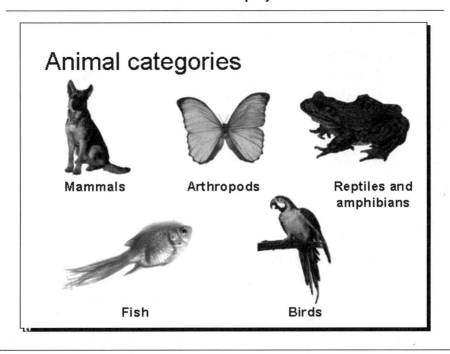

Animal categories

Mammals   Arthropods   Reptiles and amphibians

Fish   Birds

 Once you create your first text box, you can copy it to the Clipboard and paste it as many times as you need and then edit the text as necessary.

You can see our home slide in Figure 7.1.

When you create a menu, you need to line up the text or objects and distribute them evenly. If you don't, the menu can look very messy! PowerPoint offers excellent tools to align and distribute objects.

HOW TO DO IT

- *Windows 2000/2002/2003:* Drag diagonally across two or more objects that you want to line up so that they are selected. From the Drawing toolbar, choose Draw ➤ Align or Distribute and choose the appropriate align option. For example, in Figure 7.1 you would want to top-align each row of images. For a column, you would left-align the objects. To distribute objects evenly, select three or more objects. From the Drawing toolbar, choose Draw ➤ Align or Distribute and choose Distribute Horizontally (for a row) or Distribute Vertically (for a column).

- *Windows 2007:* Drag diagonally across two or more objects that you want to line up so that they are selected. From the Format tab in the Arrange group, choose Align and choose the appropriate aligning option. For example, in Figure 7.1, you would want to top-align each row of images. For a column, you would left-align the objects. To distribute objects evenly, select three or more objects. From the Format tab, choose Align and then choose Distribute Horizontally (for a row) or Distribute Vertically (for a column).

- *Mac 2001/X/2004:* Drag diagonally across two or more objects that you want to line up so that they are selected. From the Drawing toolbar, choose Draw ➤ Align or Distribute and choose the appropriate align option. For example, in Figure 7.1, you would want to top-align each row of images. For a column, you would left-align the objects. To distribute objects evenly, select three or more objects. From the Drawing toolbar, choose Draw ➤ Align or Distribute, and choose Distribute Horizontally (for a row) or Distribute Vertically (for a column).

You can *group* the text box with its image. When you do this, they act as one object. Grouping makes it easier to adjust the placement of the images together with their captions.

If you want to edit the font color or size of the text, select and edit it as explained in Chapter 2. If you have a quiz, enter the words **Take a quiz** somewhere on the menu slide.

Now that the menu slide is ready, you need to move it to the beginning of the presentation, so it will be the starting slide of your project.

 You can also use Slide Sorter view to select, copy, and paste the slide to make it first.

ADDING HYPERLINKS

Now you have the entire project, but it is not organized. You need to sew it—or stitch it—by hyperlinking the slides so that you can easily navigate through the entire project in any direction. This involves three processes:

- Link from each section back to the main menu.

- Create navigation links from slide to slide within each section.

- Link from the main menu to each section.

Note that you could create these hyperlinks in any order you want.

Linking from the Sections to the Menu

Our first step is to link from the last slide of the mammals section back to the menu slide. The idea is that after completing the mammals section, the student would return to the main menu to choose another section. We explained hyperlinking in detail in Chapter 5; look there if you need a review. Here are some brief instructions. Start by displaying the last slide of the mammals section.

HOW TO DO IT

- *Windows 2000/2002/2003:* Choose Slide Show ➤ Action Buttons Home. Click in a suitable place on the slide to place the action button. Accept the default setting of First Slide. Click OK.

- *Windows 2007:* On the Insert tab, click the Shapes button and choose the Home button from the Action Buttons section of the Shapes gallery. Click in a suitable place on the slide to place the action button. Accept the default setting of First Slide. Click OK.

- *Mac 2001/X/2004:* Choose Slide Show ➤ Action Buttons ➤ Home. Click in a suitable place on the slide to place the action button. Accept the default setting of First Slide. Click OK.

 If you think that the main menu might not remain as the first slide (you might want a title slide in front of it), choose Slide from the drop-down list (instead of First Slide) and then choose the main menu slide by its title. This ensures that the hyperlink goes to the main menu, even if you move it so that it is not the first slide.

 Instead of using an action button, you can use any object or picture on the slide, or, for example, a text box containing the words **Return to main menu.** Select the object or words, and hyperlink them to the menu slide.

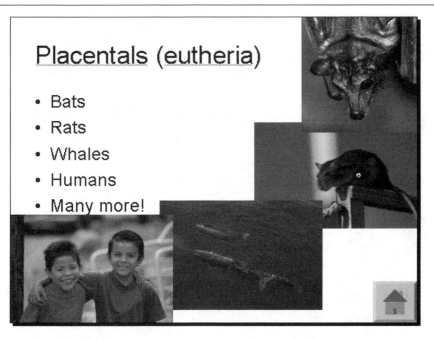

Figure 7.2
The last slide of the mammals section now links back to the menu slide.

Placentals (eutheria)

- Bats
- Rats
- Whales
- Humans
- Many more!

Figure 7.2 shows the last slide of the mammals section with a Home action button.

Add the same back link on the last slide of all of the sections. In fact, it is a good idea to have this link on every slide (except your quiz slides).

 You do not have to create this back link from scratch; just copy and paste the Home button to every slide.

Creating Navigation from Slide to Slide

Once you, or your students, navigate from the menu slide to a section, movement in each section should occur by clicking a Next button. In addition, you can add

Figure 7.3
Each sectional slide has buttons to facilitate navigation
through a section.

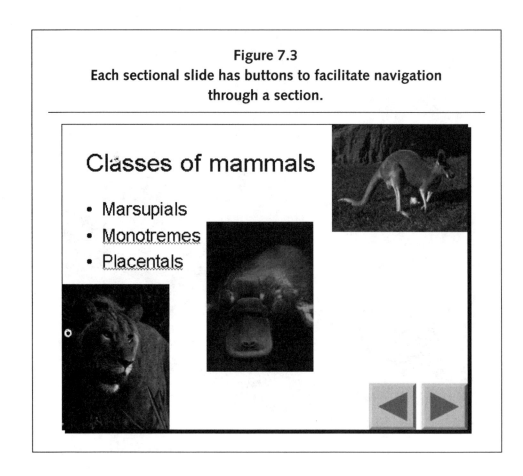

the ability to move backward in a section by creating a Previous button on each slide. Therefore, every slide of your sections should be linked to the previous slide and the next slide, with two exceptions: the first slide of each section should have *only* a Next button and the last slide of each section should have *only* a Previous button. Figure 7.3 shows a slide in the mammals section, on marsupials, with Next and Previous buttons.

Use the same procedure you used to create links to the menu slide, but choose the Forward or Next action button and the Back or Previous action button. Another option is to insert block arrows facing left and right as Next and Previous buttons. Hyperlink these arrows to the appropriate slides, using the Next Slide and the Previous Slide hyperlink options.

Linking from the Menu Slide to the Sections

The final step is to link the menu slide to each of the sections. These links are what make the slide function as a menu. First, display the menu slide. If you need a refresher, see the instructions for hyperlinking in Chapter 5. Here are basic instructions:

HOW TO DO IT

- *Windows 2000/2002/2003:* Select each picture and caption of the menu slide. Choose Insert ➤ Hyperlink and hyperlink the object to the first slide of its corresponding section.

- *Windows 2007:* Select each picture and caption of the menu slide. On the Insert tab, click Hyperlink and hyperlink the object to the first slide of its corresponding section.

- *Mac 2001/X/2004:* Select each picture and caption of the menu slide. Choose Insert ➤ Hyperlink and hyperlink the object to the first slide of its corresponding section.

 You can't hyperlink a grouped object. In PowerPoint 2002 and later, you can click a subobject within a group to select it; then you can hyperlink that object without ungrouping all of the objects.

 When you hyperlink a text box, if you select just the text, the text is underlined and you need to click the text itself to activate the link. If you select the text box itself, by clicking its border, the text isn't underlined and you can click anywhere inside the text box to activate the link.

Navigation can be corrupted or confused if you miss the hyperlinked arrows or buttons and instead click elsewhere on the slide. You want the user to navigate through the entire project using only the hyperlinks. To avoid navigational problems, turn off mouse-clicking for advancing slides.

- *Windows 2000:* Choose Slide Show ➤ Slide Transition. In the Slide Transition dialog box, deselect the On Mouse Click check box in the Advance section. Click Apply to All.

- *Windows 2002/2003:* Choose Slide Show ➤ Slide Transition. In the Advance Slide section of the Slide Transition task pane, deselect the On Mouse Click check box. Click Apply to all Slides.

- *Windows 2007:* On the Animations tab, in the Transitions to This Slide group, deselect the On Mouse Click check box and click Apply To All.

- *Mac 2001/X/2004:* Choose Slide Show ➤ Slide Transition. In the Slide Transition dialog box, deselect the On Mouse Click check box in the Advance section. Click Apply to All.

CREATING HYPERLINKS TO THE WEB

You can provide your students with a lot of information in each section of your non-linear project, but no one can include everything. If students want more information, refer them to Web sites specializing in this particular subject. As you surely know, you'll have to visit each site first to make sure that it is grade- and age-appropriate and educationally valuable. Only then should you provide a link to this site.

- *Windows 2000/2002/2003:* Create a text box or AutoShape and type **Learn more about marsupials!** Go to the Web site, then select and copy the URL address of the site from the address bar. Choose Insert ➤ Hyperlink. In the Insert Hyperlink dialog box, choose Existing File or Web Page and paste the URL in the Address text box (by pressing Ctrl+V). Click OK.

- *Windows 2007:* Create a text box or a shape and type **Learn more about marsupials!** Go to the Web site, then select and copy the URL address of the site from the address bar. On the Insert tab, click Hyperlink. In the Insert Hyperlink dialog box, choose Existing File or Web Page and paste the URL in the Address text box (by pressing Ctrl+V). Click OK.

- *Mac 2001/X/2004:* Create a text box or AutoShape and type **Learn more about marsupials!** Go to the Web site, then select and copy the URL address of the site from the address bar. Choose Insert ➤ Hyperlink. In the Insert Hyperlink dialog box, choose Existing File or Web Page and paste the URL in the Address text box (by pressing ⌘ +V). Click OK.

Figure 7.4 shows a slide with a link to a resource on the Internet.

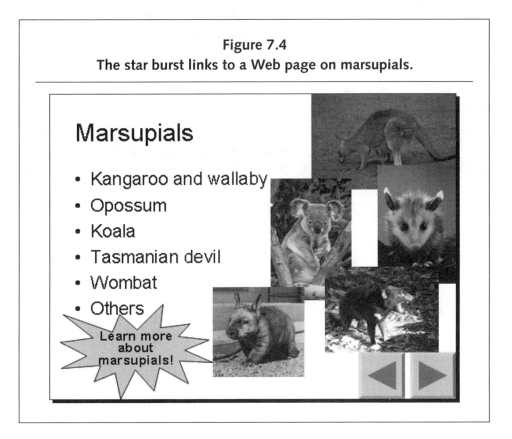

Figure 7.4
The star burst links to a Web page on marsupials.

In most versions of PowerPoint, when you add text to an Auto-Shape, the text doesn't automatically wrap inside the shape. To fit the text nicely in the shape, right-click (Windows)/Ctrl-click(Mac) and choose Format AutoShape. On the Text Box tab, check the Word Wrap Text in AutoShape check box. Another option for fitting text is to reduce the line spacing; choose Format ➢ Line Spacing.

TESTING ALL THE LINKS

You're not done until you test all the links in Slide Show view. Be sure to test both the images and text that you've hyperlinked. Test all outside links to the Web.

When you click a link to the Web, the default browser opens. You may need to show students how to return to the presentation. In Windows, they can use the Windows taskbar. On the Mac, they can close the browser and then click on the PowerPoint window to return to the View Show mode.

SUMMARY

In this chapter we explained how to create nonlinear PowerPoint projects. We showed how to create a menu slide and sections and how to hyperlink them together. We also explained how to set up your project so that a user can only navigate it using hyperlink buttons or objects. Finally, we discussed how to hyperlink to resources on the Web.

chapter EIGHT

Class Games

We do not have to tell you about the importance and effectiveness of games in teaching and learning. All teachers know from their own experience that an interesting and exciting game can enhance memorization and retention of material as well as create an atmosphere of competitive fun in the classroom. Teaching with games is effective in all grades, if you are creative and understand child psychology. PowerPoint is a great tool to help you. This chapter describes several types of class games that you can create with PowerPoint.

MEMORIZATION GAMES

This kind of game uses a very simple but powerful technique of learning by rote based on visual support. Traditionally, it works as follows.

1. Start by writing several sentences (a poem, limerick, piece of news, and so on) on the chalkboard (or whiteboard).

2. Have one of the students read the passage. Spend some time working on grammar, semantics, and so on.

3. Explain that you will remove some words, but the students will read pretending that the erased words are there.

4. After the first reading, erase more words and ask someone else to read.

5. Continue until the students read from the clean chalkboard.

In this way, students learn a passage in a short period of time, contrary to their own expectations and much to their excitement.

This technique is used in teaching foreign languages and English as a second or first language. By learning passages in a short period of time, students learn new words in their natural context and in natural grammatical structures. Although some teachers do not consider learning by rote to be effective in teaching languages, this particular technique, if employed correctly, is regarded by students as a fun game rather than rote memorization.

Using PowerPoint enhances the technique significantly, because you can reuse it as many times as needed without having to rewrite it on the chalkboard, and you can always get back to the original or to the previous slide with the words that have not yet been erased.

Creating a Slide with Complete Text

The first step is to create a slide with the entire text that you plan for students to learn by rote. Our example is "No Enemies," by Charles Mackay, shown in Figure 8.1.

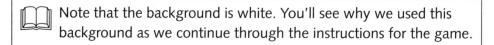 Note that the background is white. You'll see why we used this background as we continue through the instructions for the game.

Next, make a copy of the slide by clicking on the slide's icon on the Outline pane, copying to the Clipboard, and pasting. (See the "Copying and Pasting the Slide" section of Chapter 6 for details.) You can also select the entire slide in the Slides pane (in Normal view). Or in the Slide Sorter view, right-click and choose Copy and then again right-click in an empty area and click Paste.

Creating a Slide with Less Text

Now, you want to start erasing. However, if you delete a word, the text will shrink to remove the space where the word was, and you will lose the visual impression of chalkboard erasing. You want the spaces where the words were erased to remain the same size as the erased words. So, instead of deleting the words, you need to hide them.

Figure 8.1
Some original text to be memorized.

No enemies

You have no enemies, you say?
Alas! my friend, the boast is poor;
He who has mingled in the fray
Of duty, that the brave endure,
Must have made foes! If you have none,
Small is the work that you have done.
You've hit no traitor on the hip,
You've dashed no cup from perjured lip,
You've never turned the wrong to right,
You've been a coward in the fight.

HOW TO DO IT

- *Windows 2000/2002/2003:* Select the word you want to erase. Right-click the word and choose Font to open the Font dialog box, as shown in Figure 8.2. From the Color drop-down list, choose the white color swatch and click OK.

- *Windows 2007:* Select the word you want to erase. Right-click and choose Font to open the Font dialog box. From the Font Color drop-down list, choose the white color swatch and click OK.

- *Mac 2001/X/2004:* Select the word you want to erase. Right-click the word and choose Font to open the Font dialog box, as shown in Figure 8.2. From the Font Color drop-down list, choose the white color swatch and click OK.

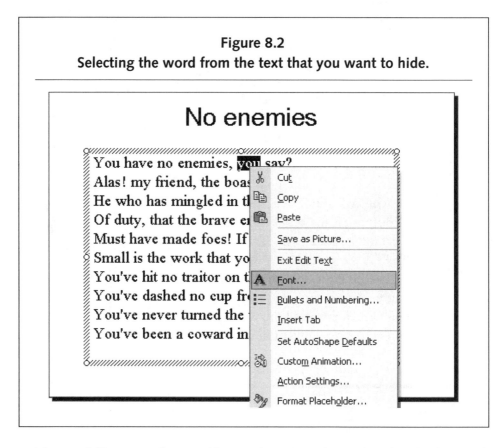

Figure 8.2
Selecting the word from the text that you want to hide.

The word disappears because it's now the same color as the white background, but the space where the word was remains.

Using the same technique, hide several other words that are the easiest to reproduce from the context, for example, the word "you," as shown in Figure 8.3.

Make a copy of the slide with the hidden words. Use the same technique we just described and go on to hide more words. Continue to make copies of each slide and continue hiding more words.

 We suggest you first hide those words that are easiest to ascertain from the context, such as the words "have" and "has." The last words you hide should be the last words in lines. Also, keep the more difficult words like "perjured" and "foe" until the last slide. This will help students memorize them.

Figure 8.3
Hiding more words.

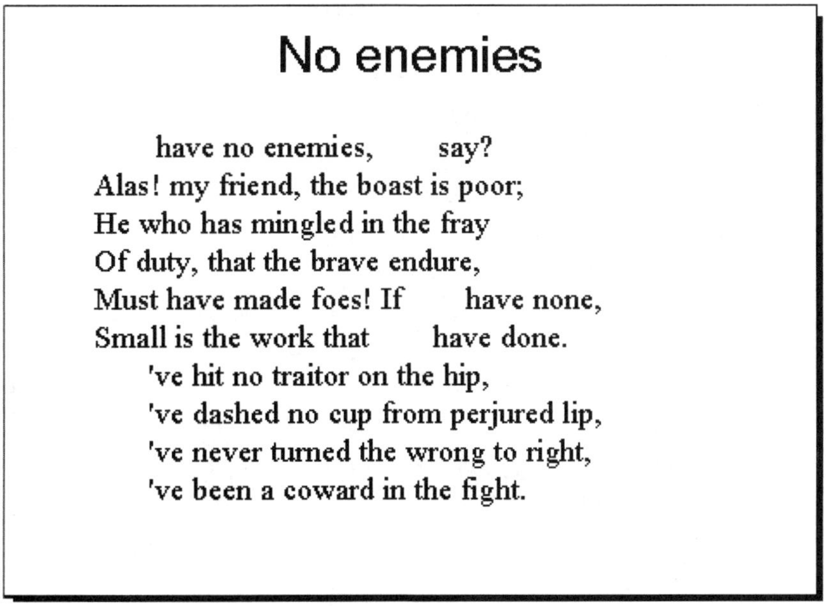

No enemies

have no enemies,   say?
Alas! my friend, the boast is poor;
He who has mingled in the fray
Of duty, that the brave endure,
Must have made foes! If   have none,
Small is the work that   have done.
        've hit no traitor on the hip,
        've dashed no cup from perjured lip,
        've never turned the wrong to right,
        've been a coward in the fight.

When you are done creating slides with the hidden words to the point of almost no words or no words at all, hyperlink the slides with action buttons. (To review how to use action buttons, see Chapter 5.)

Use the Back or Previous action button to hyperlink a slide to the previous one, and the Forward or Next action button to hyperlink it to the next slide. This will help you if the students can't recall a word; you can always go back to the previous slide.

It is also a good idea to insert a hyperlink to the first slide using the Home action button beginning from the third slide. Once you have done one Home button, just copy and paste it on all slides except for the first and second. Your slides will look something like the one in Figure 8.4.

You can play this game as a whole-class contest or use it as a competition between two class groups; you can assign points or not. Of course, the winner or winners will be those who can reproduce the entire piece from the clean screen.

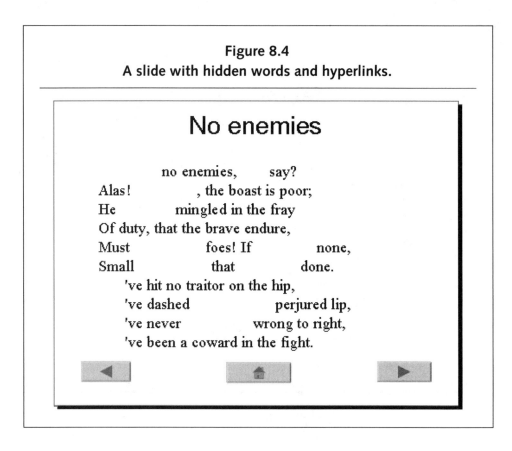

Figure 8.4
A slide with hidden words and hyperlinks.

No enemies

> no enemies,   say?
> Alas!   , the boast is poor;
> He   mingled in the fray
> Of duty, that the brave endure,
> Must   foes! If   none,
> Small   that   done.
>   've hit no traitor on the hip,
>   've dashed   perjured lip,
>   've never   wrong to right,
>   've been a coward in the fight.

Your experience will tell you how many slides to use, how many words to erase per slide, how much time to spend on discussion, which text to choose, and so on. However, we can offer several tips:

- If you do not play a game, but instead call on your students to read the text aloud, start with the weakest and end with the strongest. Allow prompts from classmates. Avoid situations where a student can be put on the spot as a lone contestant, unless you are confident that this particular student can handle that.

- A few days after you've used this technique, have the students recall the piece. It will help them memorize it.

- Do not use this technique with the same class too often; once or twice a semester is best.

This same hiding technique can be used with letters to help spelling. For example, ask your students this question: *What English word consists of nine letters, and if you remove one letter at a time, it will form yet another English word all the way to the last single letter?* Then display a slide with the word "startling." Ask your students which letter they will remove to form a shorter word. Remove "l" (show the slide with the hidden "l"). Ask which letter they will remove next (the second "t"), and show the slide with the hidden "t." Continue the activity (staring-string-sting-sing-sin-in-I). Of course, you can do this with chalk and chalkboard, but PowerPoint is so much more fun!

 You can download Memorization Game.ppt from this book's companion Web site at www.ellenfinkelstein.com/powerpointforteachers.html.

SPELLING GAMES

You can use PowerPoint as a game to help students learn spelling with assigned points. This technique is a simple variant of a multiple-choice review (a quiz) where, say, three words are misspelled, and one is spelled correctly—for example: necesarry, nececery, necessary, nescessary. (Multiple-choice reviews are discussed in Chapter 5.)

To make a multiple-choice review look like a game, you need to assign points to every correct answer, and maybe, negative points for every incorrect answer. Here we offer a more complex variant of a spelling game, in which students have to identify the spelling error in context.

Start by creating a slide with a wrongly spelled word to have the students identify which letter is wrong. To place a word in the context, for example, we entered **Austin is the capitol of Texas**. We deliberately misspelled "capital," because this is one of the most common spelling mistakes.

Here are the steps to create this game:

1. First, create the question slide. Insert a slide with the Title and Text layout. In the title text placeholder, enter **Which letter is incorrect?** In the text placeholder, enter **Austin is the capitol of Texas**. Below the sentence enter several letters with two spaces between them from which the students can choose the incorrect letter, as shown in Figure 8.5.

2. Now create the negative feedback slide. Make a copy of the slide by clicking on the slide icon in the Outline pane, and then copying and pasting (see Chapter 6 for details). Enter in the title text placeholder **Incorrect! Minus 5 points!**

Figure 8.5
This slide shows a misspelled word and letters that include the incorrect letter.

Which letter is incorrect?

Austin is the capitol of Texas

A S I E U O

---

3. The last slide is the positive feedback slide. Copy and paste the slide as before and enter **Correct: CapitAl! Plus 10 points!** in the title text placeholder and enter **I eccept your apology** in the text placeholder for another spelling test, as shown in Figure 8.6.

4. Return to the first slide with the text **Austin is the capitol of Texas**. Hyperlink the **O** to the positive feedback slide (Correct …). Then select each of the other letters separately and hyperlink them to the negative feedback slide (Incorrect! …).

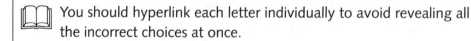 You should hyperlink each letter individually to avoid revealing all the incorrect choices at once.

Figure 8.6
This positive feedback slide contains a new spelling test.

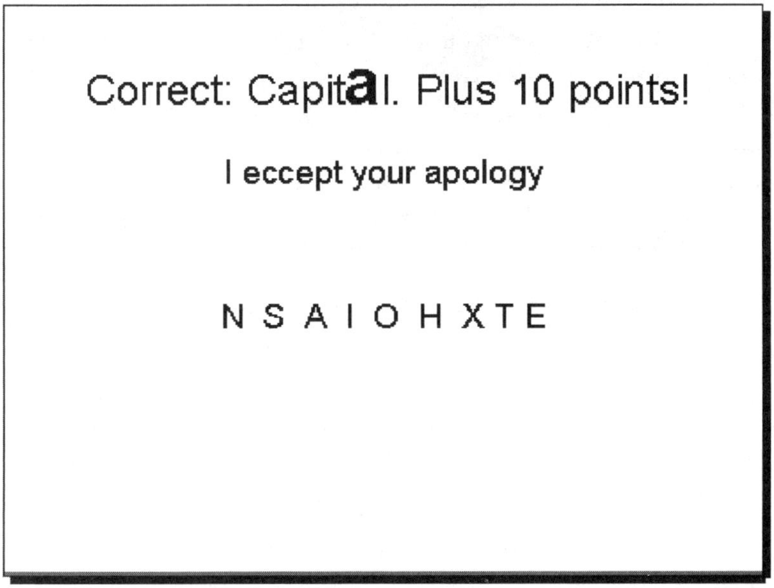

Correct: Capital. Plus 10 points!

I eccept your apology

N S A I O H X T E

5. After you have hyperlinked all the letters, select them. Copy and paste them to the negative feedback slide. Don't forget to save!

6. Create the negative and positive feedback slides for the second question and hyperlink the letter choices on the Correct slide, and so on, until you're done.

Try the game. When you are on the question slide, a wrong choice will bring you to the Incorrect! slide. Because the wrong choices are all linked to this slide, clicking on the wrong choices on this slide does not change anything, they are linked to themselves. Only the right choice will lead to the Correct slide.

When you are done, choose Slide Show ➢ Slide Transition and uncheck the On (Mouse) Click in the Advance Slide section to make sure that the user can navigate only using the hyperlinks. (In PowerPoint 2007, display the Animations tab and you'll find the same check box in the Transition to This Slide group.)

You can play this game with two competing teams, or between individual students. Of course, you should keep the score, or assign a student to do so.

You can use difficult words rather than sentences. The preceding examples are for words whose correct spelling can be identified from the context ("there" and "their," "threw" and "through," "its" and "it's," and so on). For more difficult words visit the Common Errors in English page at www.wsu.edu:8080/~brians/errors/errors.html.

 You can download Spelling Game.ppt from this book's companion Web site at www.ellenfinkelstein.com/powerpointforteachers.html.

WHO WANTS TO BE A MILLIONAIRE? POWERPOINT VERSION

If you want to further develop a PowerPoint multiple-choice quiz or review into a more complex form, you can call it "Who Wants to Be a Millionaire?" for the popular television game that was also based on the idea of multiple choice. Start your first multiple-choice question with 100 points and then go to the next question for 250 points. Every correct choice will be hyperlinked to a next question with the number of points to win. This game can be played with individuals or with two teams. The team or individual who scores the highest wins.

 This is a long game. It's best used at the end of a large topic or a semester to review a considerable amount of material.

The procedure is similar to the one described in Chapter 5 on creating quizzes. There are a few small differences, though. To make things easy, you should create a slide that will function as a template for all the questions. Follow these steps:

1. Start a new presentation, and select the layout with a title and two columns. In the right column enter the number of points, from 100 at the bottom to a million at the top, and in the left column enter **Choice 1**, **Choice 2**, **Choice 3**, and **Choice 4**, as shown in Figure 8.7.

2. Copy and paste the slide thirteen times, using the Outline pane.

3. Create a negative feedback slide that says, **Sorry, wrong choice!**

4. On the first question slide (worth 100 points) enter your first question in the title text placeholder: **What is the world's largest ocean?** In place of the

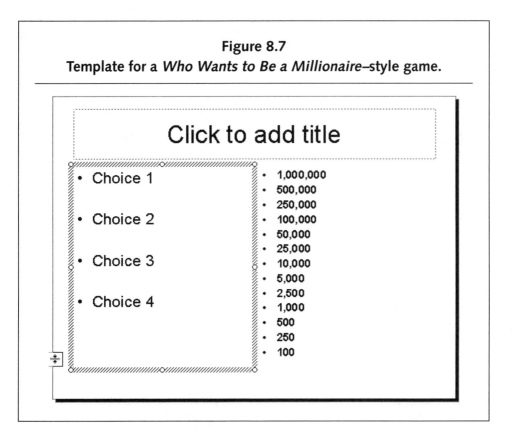

Figure 8.7
Template for a *Who Wants to Be a Millionaire*–style game.

words Choice 1, Choice 2, and so on, enter the names of the oceans: **Atlantic**, **Pacific**, **Indian**, **Arctic**, as shown in Figure 8.8.

5. Select the number 100 and change its color to red. Use the same method we described earlier in this chapter, in the "Creating a Slide with Less Text" section. There you chose the white color swatch. This time, if necessary, choose the More Colors link and click the red color swatch on the Standard tab of the Colors dialog box.

6. Hyperlink individually the wrong choices to the Sorry, wrong choice! slide. Because the game does not allow second attempts, don't hyperlink the negative feedback slide to any other slide. Once a wrong choice has been made, that's the end of the game for that contestant.

7. Create the 250-point question slide by going to a next slide and entering a new (slightly harder) question in the title text placeholder.

Figure 8.8
Creating the first question.

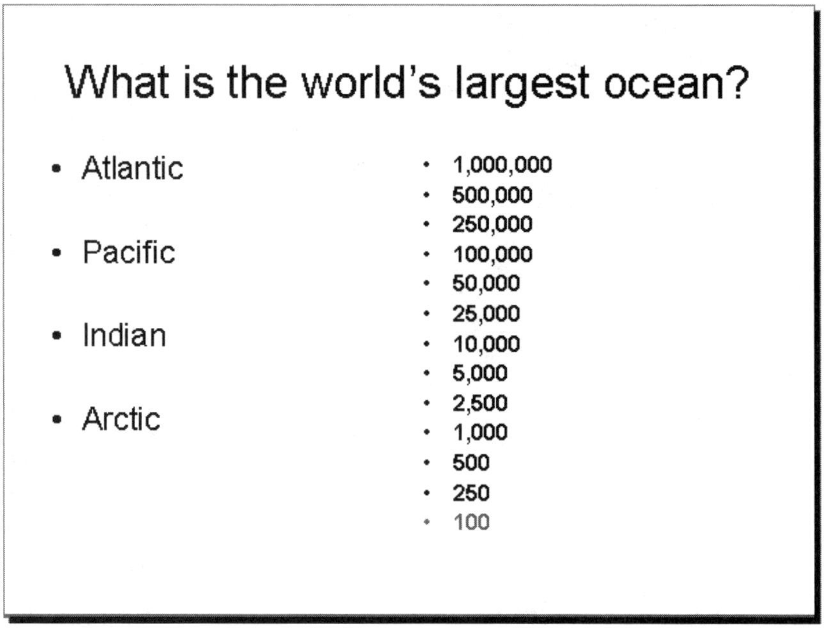

What is the world's largest ocean?

- Atlantic

- Pacific

- Indian

- Arctic

- 1,000,000
- 500,000
- 250,000
- 100,000
- 50,000
- 25,000
- 10,000
- 5,000
- 2,500
- 1,000
- 500
- 250
- 100

8. Enter the choices for the new question.

9. Change the color of 250 to red.

10. Hyperlink the right choice on the 100-point slide to the 250-point slide.

Continue entering new questions and choices and changing the color of the numbers until you finish with the question that's worth a million points. When you are done, use the same technique we described for the previous game to make sure that the user can navigate only via the hyperlinks.

To make the game more realistic, you can add a fifty-fifty choice for especially difficult questions by hyperlinking your question slide to a question slide with only two choices instead of four. You can also add the music played in the show. Search for a midi file for "Who Wants to Be a Millionaire" on the Web.

You can download the template for this game—whowantstobea-millionaire-like.ppt—from this book's companion Web site.

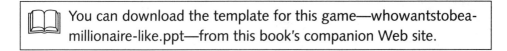 Assign this game as a project to your students and have students play several of these games in your class.

JEOPARDY POWERPOINT VERSION

Jeopardy is a question-and-answer game in which each right answer is connected to a certain amount of money or points. It is clear that the television version of *Jeopardy* is not suitable to play in class, because you don't want your students to compete to be the first to give an answer. Instead, we offer a simplified variant.

1. Insert a new slide with the layout that contains a title and a table.

 You can also use the Title and Content layout. In that case, click the table icon to insert a table.

2. Double-click to add a table. In the Insert Table dialog box, enter four columns and five rows. Click OK.

3. For easier work with the table, click on the border of the title text placeholder and delete it. Stretch the table to the top of the slide.

4. Enter the categories in the cells of the upper row and amounts in the rest of the cells. (See Figure 8.9.)

5. Create slides with questions according to the category and the amount of money.

6. Hyperlink the numbers denoting the amount of money to the question slides. (See Figure 8.10.) To hyperlink a number select it and insert a hyperlink to the desired slide. (See Chapter 5 for details.)

7. Hyperlink the question slide back to the slide with the table and numbers. The best way to do it is to use the Home button from the Action Buttons, in

Figure 8.9
Creating the first slide for a Jeopardy-style game.

Animals	Plants	Minerals	People
$ 100	$ 100	$ 100	$ 100
$ 200	$ 200	$ 200	$ 200
$ 300	$ 300	$ 300	$ 300
$ 400	$ 400	$ 400	$ 400
$ 500	$ 500	$ 500	$ 500

Slide Show. (See Chapter 7 for more details on Action Buttons.) You can also use any AutoShape or any word as a hyperlink back to the table slide. Once you have created such a hyperlink, you can copy and paste it to all the question slides. It is a good idea to disable On Click as the default function of slide advancing from all the slides to prevent "clicking away." Again, see Chapter 7 for more details.

Continue until you have all the questions and hyperlinks ready for all the categories and amounts. When you are done, use the technique we described earlier in this chapter to make sure that the user can navigate only via the hyperlinks.

You can play this game with two or more teams. Each team selects a category. The teacher controls the game. The right answer will lead to a more difficult question; the wrong answer will discontinue the game for that particular team.

Figure 8.10
A slide with the question and hyperlinks.

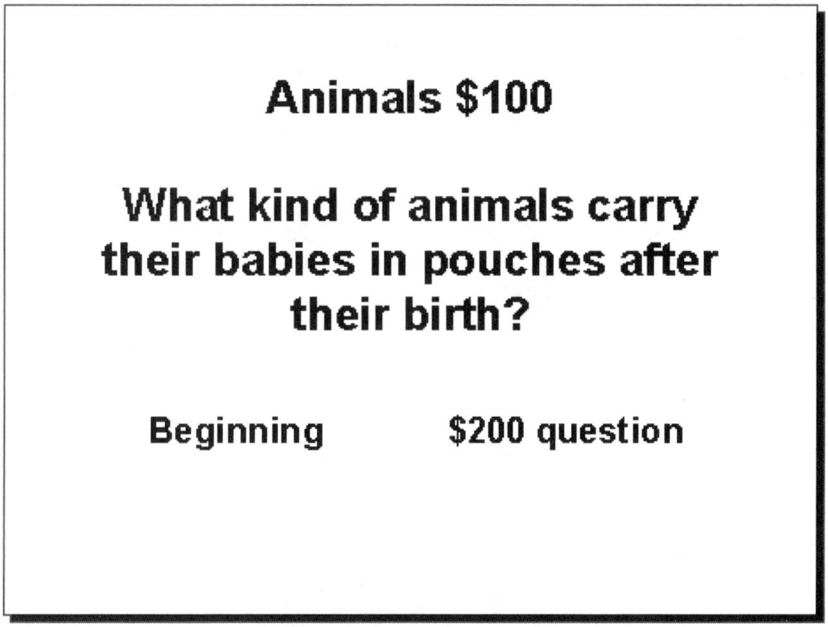

Animals $100

What kind of animals carry their babies in pouches after their birth?

Beginning   **$200 question**

 Download the template for this game—jeopardy-like.ppt—from the book's companion site at www.ellenfinkelstein.com/ powerpointforteachers.html.

MORE GAMES

You can create an infinite number of games using the techniques we describe in this chapter, because the subject matter can be anything you want. As you use the games, you'll probably think of variations that you prefer. Soon you'll have your own repertoire of games.

For more ideas, as well as many games that you can download, see the section on games in Chapter 13.

SUMMARY

In this chapter we explained how to create interactive games using PowerPoint.

We described a memorization game, a spelling game, and two television-style games—one that resembles *Who Wants to Be a Millionaire?* and one based on *Jeopardy*.

Have fun!

Graded Tests

D id you know that you can create a graded test in PowerPoint? In this chapter, we'll show you how. You don't need to be a programmer to complete this chapter, although the technique involves programming. We'll accomplish this by giving you the programming code! If you're ready to delve a little deeper into PowerPoint's capabilities, we encourage you to try this out. However, expect to spend a significant amount of time and focus on this chapter, more than on the others in this book—it's definitely an advanced technique. If you're not interested in creating graded tests, you can skip this chapter.

We want to thank David Marcovitz, who kindly gave us permission to use the code from his book, *Powerful PowerPoint for Educators: Using Visual Basic for Applications to Make PowerPoint Interactive*. You can find out more—and even purchase a copy of the book—by going to www.loyola.edu/edudept/Powerful-PowerPoint. His Web site contains many more examples of code from the book.

POWERPOINT AND PROGRAMMING

Although you don't need to be a programmer to use the information we provide in this chapter, we want to introduce you to the topic of programming Power-Point for several reasons:

- Perhaps you want to try your hand at programming PowerPoint.
- Even if you use someone else's programming code, you need to understand how to use it.

- You should understand what the code actually does.

- You will probably need to modify the code. This won't require programming skills.

The name of the programming language that PowerPoint uses is Visual Basic for Applications, or VBA. In fact, all of Microsoft Office software supports VBA.

Benefits of VBA

Programmers use VBA to automate repetitive tasks, integrate PowerPoint with other applications, and make PowerPoint interactive. It's this last item that is of greatest interest to teachers.

 An easy way to use VBA to automate repetitive tasks without programming is to record a *macro*. A macro is any VBA code that performs a task or responds to a user action. If you need to perform a multistep procedure several times, you can record it the first time, save it as a macro, and use a keyboard shortcut to repeat it whenever you need it. However, Mac versions don't include this ability and neither does PowerPoint 2007, so we don't discuss it in detail here. For more information, search for "Create a Macro" in PowerPoint 2000/2002/2003 Help and look at the "About Macros" and "Create a Macro" topics. In all versions, you can write VBA code to create macros, and this method is the one we discuss in this chapter.

When you use VBA to make PowerPoint interactive, you need a procedure that works in Slide Show view, which viewers use to run through the presentation. Tasks that VBA can accomplish easily for our graded quiz are as follows:

- Request and store the user's name.

- Provide feedback on right or wrong answers in a quiz.

- Track the answers given.

- Add up the number of right answers and the total number of answers.

- Save the results to the presentation.

- Print the results.

Making It Easy

Although VBA is not hard to learn as programming languages go, busy teachers may not have enough time to become proficient at writing the code themselves. Therefore, you can make use of code that others have written. All you need to know is where to store the code and how to run it.

As we already mentioned, in most cases you'll also need to edit the code to customize it for your own questions and answers. Don't worry, we'll provide you with step-by-step instructions.

 You can find the test we use in this chapter on this book's companion Web site at www.ellenfinkelstein.com/powerpoint-forteachers.html. It's called Math Quiz.ppt. When you open this presentation, you'll probably get a warning about enabling macros. The macros in this file are supposed to be there, and without them, the quiz won't work. Therefore, you should choose the option "Enable the macros." You can also download the same presentation without the VBA code, Math Quiz-No VBA.ppt, so that you can work through this chapter and create the VBA without having to create the questions.

Before you start, you should download Math Quiz.ppt from the companion Web site, go into Slide Show view, and take the quiz. This will help you see how it works and make the rest of this chapter easier to understand.

 Whenever you're working with macros, you want to make sure that the only ones in your presentation are the ones you need. It is possible to get a macro that works like a computer virus. To avoid this situation, make sure you have the latest virus-scanning updates for your version of PowerPoint. From the Help menu, choose Check for Updates or something similar (depending on your version). If necessary, speak to the information technology person at your school to arrange this.

CREATING A MULTIPLE-CHOICE TEST

The first step is to create a presentation that contains a multiple-choice test. You do this in the same way that you create an ungraded test. We explained this process in Chapter 5; if you haven't gone through that chapter, you should do so now. The instructions in this chapter assume that you understand the content there.

We suggest that you start by offering only two possible answers for each question, because each answer requires more code. Later, you can add more answers, as we'll explain.

Each question requires separate code, so start with a short test. As you become familiar with this method, you'll feel comfortable adding more questions. The quiz in this chapter has three questions—a very short quiz!

Creating a Cover Slide

Start with a cover slide that introduces the quiz. This slide will also ask for, and store, the student's name. The quiz will then do the following:

- Address the student by name throughout.
- Create a results printout with the student's name on it.
- Create a slide storing the results of the quiz that also contains the student's name.

As you can see, you get a great deal of value from asking the student's name.

HOW TO DO IT

☐ • *Windows 2000/2002/2003:* Start a new presentation. On the first slide, add a title, such as **Welcome to the Linear Algebra Quiz**. From the Drawing toolbar, choose AutoShapes ➤ Action Buttons and choose Action Button: Custom, which is blank. Click on the slide to insert the action button. The Action Settings dialog box opens. For now, click Cancel and immediately enter **What is your name?** Resize the action button to fit the text and move it to a central location, as shown in Figure 9.1.

- *Windows 2007*: Start a new presentation. On the first slide, add a title, such as **Welcome to the Linear Algebra Quiz**. From the Insert tab, choose Shapes ➤ Action Buttons and choose Action Button: Custom, which is blank. Click on the slide to insert the action button. The Action Settings dialog box opens. For now, click Cancel and immediately enter **What is your name?** Resize the action button and move it to a central location, as shown in Figure 9.1.

- *Mac 2001/X/2004*: Start a new presentation. On the first slide, add a title, such as **Welcome to the Linear Algebra Quiz**. From the Drawing toolbar, choose AutoShapes ➤ Action Buttons and choose Action Button: Custom, which is blank. Click on the slide to insert the action button. The Action Settings dialog box opens. For now, click Cancel and immediately enter **What is your name?** Resize the action button to fit the text and move it to a central location, as shown in Figure 9.1.

Figure 9.1
This is a short linear algebra quiz that will be graded.

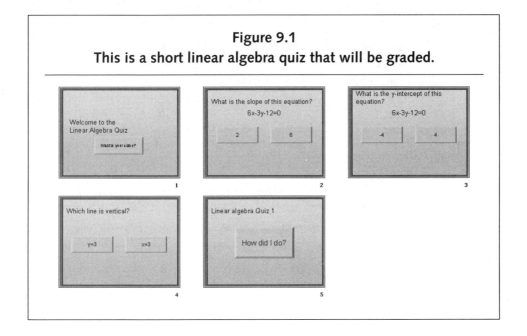

If you want, you can change the size and color of the text, and change the fill and outline of the action button. For instructions, see Chapter 2.

Creating the First Question Slide

The next step is to start creating questions and answers. You can place the question in the title placeholder. The answers reside on action buttons. In our example, we added a text box for an equation, but you may wish to format the slide differently. For example, the equation could be part of the slide's title.

 For your first effort, don't change the answers or their order. The VBA code we use assumes the answers we show here. When you're more comfortable with the process, you can make changes.

HOW TO DO IT

- *Windows 2000/2002/2003:* Create a new slide using the Title Only layout. In the title placeholder, enter the question, **What is the slope of this equation?** To add a text box, click Text Box on the Drawing toolbar and drag from left to right on the slide. Enter the equation, **6x – 3y – 12 = 0**. You may need to resize the text box or the text. Insert a Custom Action Button as you did for the previous slide, click Cancel to dismiss the Action Settings dialog box, and enter the first answer, **2**. (This is the correct answer.) We increased the size of the text in the text box. Select the action button and press Ctrl+D to duplicate it. Drag it to the right of the first one and change the text to **6**.

- *Windows 2007:* Create a new slide using the Title Only layout. In the title placeholder, enter the question, **What is the slope of this equation?** To add a text box, click Text Box on the Insert tab and drag from left to right on the slide. Enter the equation, **6x – 3y – 12 = 0**. You may need to resize the text box or the text. Insert a Custom Action Button as you did for the previous slide, click Cancel to dismiss the Action Settings dialog box, and enter the first answer, **2**. (This is the correct answer.) We increased the size of the text in the text box. Select the action button and press Ctrl+D to duplicate it. Drag it to the right of the first one and change the text to **6**.

- *Mac 2001/X/2004:* Create a new slide using the Title Only layout. In the title placeholder, enter the question, **What is the slope of this equation?** To add a text box, click Text Box on the Drawing toolbar and drag from left to right on the slide. Enter the equation, **6x – 3y – 12 = 0**. You may need to resize the text box or the text. Insert a Custom Action Button as you did for the previous slide, click Cancel to dismiss the Action Settings dialog box, and enter the first answer, **2**. (This is the correct answer.) We increased the size of the text in the text box. Select the action button, and copy and paste it to duplicate it. Drag it to the right of the first one and change the text to **6**.

Adjust the size and placement of the objects on the slide to get a balanced layout.

Finishing the Presentation

Now you need to finish the questions and answers. Add a third and a fourth slide as follows; use Figure 9.1 as a guide:

- *Third slide.* The question should be **What is the y-intercept of this equation?** The text box should say **6x – 3y – 12 = 0** (the same equation as the previous slide). The answer on the left should be **–4** and the one on the right should be **4** (the correct answer).

- *Fourth slide.* The question should be **Which line is vertical?** The answer on the left should be **y = 3** and the one on the right should be **x = 3** (the correct answer).

Finally, add a last slide, using the Title Only layout. In the title placeholder, enter a summary. Ours was **Linear Algebra Quiz 1**. Add a Custom Action Button as you did before and enter the text, **How did I do?** Students will click this button to get their quiz results. This completes the structure of the presentation. Don't forget to save!

 In PowerPoint 2007, you need to save in a special format that allows VBA code, called a *macro-enabled presentation.* When you save, choose PowerPoint Macro-Enabled Presentation (*.pptm) from the Save as Type drop-down list.

ADDING THE CODE

With the questions and answers done, you now need to add the VBA code. The code is what makes the action buttons function so that you have an interactive quiz. If you're not writing the code yourself, you usually copy it from another location and place it in your own presentation.

 VBA code that you add becomes part of the presentation file; it is not a separate file.

Opening the VBA Window

VBA has its own window where you work with VBA code. The first step is to open that window, called the Visual Basic Editor. Here you can write and edit code. In your own presentation, do the following:

HOW TO DO IT

- *Windows 2000/2002/2003:* Choose Tools ➤ Macro ➤ Visual Basic Editor. To add an editing window, choose Insert ➤ Module. You see the Visual Basic Editor in Figure 9.2.

- *Windows 2007:* If you don't see the Developer tab (by default, it's *not* displayed), click the Office button and choose PowerPoint Options. Click the Popular item on the left and check the Show Developer Tab in the Ribbon check box. Click OK. Click the Developer tab and click Visual Basic. To add an editing window, choose Insert ➤ Module. You see the Visual Basic Editor in Figure 9.2.

- *Mac 2001/X/2004:* Choose Tools ➤ Macro ➤ Visual Basic Editor. To add an editing window, choose Insert ➤ Module. You see the Visual Basic Editor in Figure 9.2.

Checking Security Settings

PowerPoint provides a way to control macros, because they can contain harmful code. A setting of High is safest, but it doesn't let the macros run. In most cases, a

Figure 9.2
You work with VBA code in the Visual Basic Editor window.

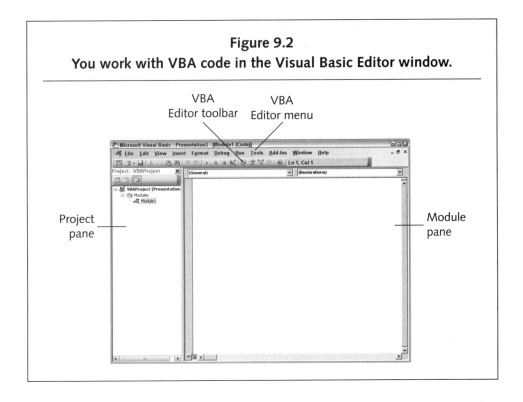

setting of Medium is ideal; at this setting, you need to confirm that you want the macros to run. This provides safety, because macros don't run without your permission. The Mac versions do not have this feature.

HOW TO DO IT

- *Windows 2000/2002/2003:* Choose Tools ➤ Macro ➤ Security. Choose Medium (if not already selected) and click OK.

- *Windows 2007:* Click the Office button and then click the Power-Point Options button. Click the Trust Center category, then click the Trust Center Settings button. Choose the Disable All Macros with Notification option (equivalent to Medium). Click OK twice.

- *Mac 2001/X/2004:* This feature is not available on the Mac.

When you open a presentation that contains VBA code, you'll see a dialog box or a bar at the top, allowing you to enable the macro. However, if you don't want this notification to appear when students use a quiz, you can temporarily set the macro setting to the lowest security level.

Pasting in the Code

Now you need some code! As instructed earlier, download the presentation Math Quiz.ppt for Chapter 9 from the book's companion Web site (www.ellenfinkel-stein.com/powerpointforteachers.html). Save it in a location where you can find it again easily. Then open the presentation.

 You may have to click an Enable Macros button to open the presentation. VBA code doesn't work unless you enable the macros.

Now display the Visual Basic Editor again, as explained in the previous section. You'll see all the code in your window. Notice that you see both presentations listed on the left, in the Project pane. (See again Figure 9.2.) You now need to copy the code into your own presentation.

HOW TO DO IT

- *All versions:* Select all the code and copy it to the Clipboard. In the Project pane, double-click Module1 beneath your own presentation. (If necessary, double-click the VBA Project item for your presentation to expand it.) The code window is now blank. Paste from the Clipboard and the code appears in the blank window, as shown in Figure 9.3. Press Ctrl+S (Windows)/⌘+S (Mac) to save the code in your presentation.

 If you try the quiz now, you'll find that it does not work yet. There are several more steps you will need to complete. Continue through the chapter and we'll explain the entire process.

Figure 9.3
The VBA code is now in your own presentation.

```
(General)                          ▼   (Declarations)                    ▼
'Written by David Marcovitz for his book,
'Powerful PowerPoint for Educators:
'Using Visual Basic for Applications to Make PowerPoint Interactive.
'www.loyola.edu/edudept/PowerfulPowerPoint
'edited for PowerPoint for Teachers by Ellen Finkelstein
'Used with permission

Dim numCorrect As Integer
Dim numIncorrect As Integer
Dim userName As String
Dim q1Answered As Boolean
Dim q2Answered As Boolean
Dim q3Answered As Boolean
Dim answer1 As String
Dim answer2 As String
Dim answer3 As String

Sub GetStarted()
    Initialize
    YourName
    ActivePresentation.SlideShowWindow.View.Next
End Sub

Sub Initialize()
    numCorrect = 0
    numIncorrect = 0
    q1Answered = False
    q2Answered = False
    q3Answered = False
End Sub

Sub YourName()
    userName = InputBox(Prompt:="Type your name")
End Sub
```

To avoid confusion, we suggest that you now close Math Quiz.ppt and work only with your own presentation.

Understanding the Code

Of course, you will need to change the code for your own situation. In order to do that, you have to understand it. We'll explain each section of the code and describe exactly what you need to do to customize it for your own quizzes.

Introductory section

The code starts as follows:

```
'Written by David Marcovitz for his book,
'Powerful PowerPoint for Educators:
'Using Visual Basic for Applications to Make
  PowerPoint Interactive.
'www.loyola.edu/edudept/PowerfulPowerPoint
'edited for PowerPoint for Teachers by Ellen
  Finkelstein
'Used with permission
Dim numCorrect As Integer
Dim numIncorrect As Integer
Dim userName As String
Dim q1Answered As Boolean
Dim q2Answered As Boolean
Dim q3Answered As Boolean
Dim answer1 As String
Dim answer2 As String
Dim answer3 As String
```

Note that the first few lines all have an apostrophe (') in front of them. These are comments, and PowerPoint knows not to process them. You can add any comments you want to help you understand the code or to remind you of changes you made. Just put an apostrophe in front of each line. When you click somewhere else, the code turns green, telling you that it is a comment.

The second section defines *variables* and specifies what type of data they use. A variable is a named container for a value. For example, if you name a variable and give it a value of 6, the VBA code remembers that value and can process it anywhere in the code. The first variable, numCorrect, keeps track of the number of correct answers. Obviously, to grade the quiz, the code needs to keep track of this value, so it creates a variable for it. The data types used are as follows:

- *Integer.* A whole number. For example, the number of correct answers must be a whole number.

- *String.* Text. The code will save the name of the student as text.

- *Boolean.* True or false. The three Boolean variables keep track of whether a question has been answered or not. The value is either true or false.

You need to edit this section if you add more questions. As you can see, the code applies to three questions. If you add more questions, just continue both lists. For example, for five questions, the last six lines would expand to the following:

```
Dim q1Answered As Boolean
Dim q2Answered As Boolean
Dim q3Answered As Boolean
Dim q4Answered As Boolean
Dim q5Answered As Boolean
Dim answer1 As String
Dim answer2 As String
Dim answer3 As String
Dim answer4 As String
Dim answer5 As String
```

GetStarted section

The next section of code reads as follows:

```
Sub GetStarted()
    Initialize
    YourName
    ActivePresentation.SlideShowWindow.View.Next
End Sub
```

This is the first *procedure.* A procedure is code that does something. It always starts with Sub and ends with End Sub.

Procedures must have a name with no spaces or symbols, and in our example, all the procedures have an empty set of parentheses after them. The first procedure is called GetStarted.

The GetStarted procedure runs two other procedures, Initialize and Your-Name. The third line after the procedure's name moves the presentation to the next slide.

You can leave this code as is. You don't need to change it when you change your questions and answers.

Note the indenting. The purpose for indenting is to make the code easier to read. You can easily see where the procedure begins and ends because of it. However, indenting is not necessary and doesn't change how the code runs. So don't worry about it too much.

Initialize section

Remember that the GetStarted procedure runs the Initialize procedure. Here is the Initialize procedure:

```
Sub Initialize()
    numCorrect = 0
    numIncorrect = 0
    q1Answered = False
    q2Answered = False
    q3Answered = False
End Sub
```

The Initialize section makes sure that there are no leftover values from the previous student. For each new student, the number of correct and incorrect answers should be zero. No questions have been answered, so the q1Answered and subsequent variables should be set to False. This section makes sure that each student starts with a clean slate.

If you add questions, you need to edit this section. Just continue the listing. For five questions it would read as follows:

```
Sub Initialize()
  numCorrect = 0
  numIncorrect = 0
  q1Answered = False
  q2Answered = False
  q3Answered = False
  q4Answered = False
  q5Answered = False
End Sub
```

Getting the student's name

One of the nice features about this presentation and its code is that it asks the student's name and uses it throughout. Here's the procedure that accomplishes this:

```
Sub YourName()
    userName = InputBox(Prompt:="Type your name")
End Sub
```

An input box is a text box that users can type in. This box prompts the student to "Type your name" and saves the name in the `userName` variable so it can be used later in other code. You don't need to edit this code, although you can if you want to change the prompt. Just substitute other text inside the quotation marks. For example, you might want to type:

```
userName = InputBox(Prompt:="Type your first and last
    name")
```

Positive feedback

If you read Chapter 5, you'll remember that you created a positive feedback slide. The next procedure has the same objective; it displays a message box that says, "You are doing well." Note that it adds that userName variable. If the student enters the name Evan, the message would read, "You are doing well, Evan".

```
Sub DoingWell()
    MsgBox ("You are doing well, " & userName)
End Sub
```

You can easily edit this procedure to change the message. Remember to keep the space after the comma and before the second quotation mark so that there is a space between the comma and the student's name. For example, you might want to change this to the following:

```
MsgBox ("Yes, you got that right, " & userName)
```

Negative feedback

Just as there is positive feedback, there is negative feedback. Here is the procedure that determines what happens when students choose a wrong answer:

```
Sub DoingPoorly()
    MsgBox ("No, that's not the right answer. Try
        again, " & userName)
End Sub
```

It's just like the positive feedback procedure. In the same way, you can change the message if you want.

First answer to the first question

Now comes some more detailed code, but it still isn't too difficult. Remember that you don't need to know how to write it from scratch; you just need to have a general idea of what's going on.

In our quiz, each question has two answers and each answer has its own procedure. You should name the procedure in a way that clearly identifies the answer because you'll need to assign it later to the answer's action button on the slide. Figure 9.4 shows this slide. We'll focus quite a bit on this slide, because all the question slides work the same way.

Note that the correct answer to the question is 2, and this procedure applies to the correct answer.

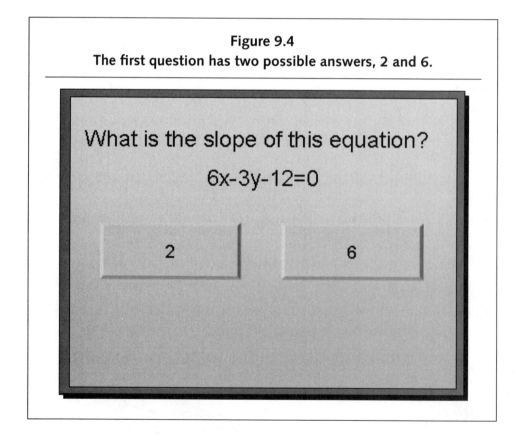

Figure 9.4
The first question has two possible answers, 2 and 6.

What is the slope of this equation?

6x-3y-12=0

2

6

```
Sub Answer1_Two()
   If q1Answered = False Then
      numCorrect = numCorrect + 1
      answer1 = "2"
   End If
   q1Answered = True
   DoingWell
   ActivePresentation.SlideShowWindow.View.Next
End Sub
```

This procedure is named Answer1_Two because it is a possible answer to question 1 and the answer is 2. We could have named it Answer1_2, but that seemed confusing. Here's what the next few lines do:

1. The first few lines say that if the first question has not been answered (and it usually has not been up to this point), then the number of correct answers is now one more than before, because the student just chose the correct answer. This group also specifies that this answer is 2. The code will use this fact later.

2. Then the procedure runs the DoingWell procedure, which we just discussed. That's the positive feedback because the student chose the right answer.

3. Finally, the procedure moves the student to the next slide to tackle the following question.

You need to edit this code for your own question. Remember that this is for the correct answer. Here's how:

• Change the first line, *Sub Answer1_Two()*, so that the last part (Two) reflects the correct answer of your own question. For example, if you're giving a history test and the correct answer is "Civil War," then your first line could read *Sub Answer1_CivilWar()*. This part only names the routine and the name can be anything you want. The main point here is to use a name that you'll recognize easily as the answer. Another point is that the procedure's name cannot contain spaces. We had problems with hyphens, too.

• Change the line that says, *answer1 = "2"* to include the exact correct answer, which is the text on the action button. This is usually the same as the name of the routine, more or less. Your code could read, *answer1* = *"Civil War"*. Note that you can put a space inside the quotation marks.

Second answer to the first question

The first question has a wrong answer, too. What happens if the student clicks the action button with the wrong answer? In this case, the wrong answer is 6. Here's the code:

```
Sub Answer1_Six()
    If q1Answered = False Then
        numIncorrect = numIncorrect + 1
        answer1 = "6"
    End If
    q1Answered = True
    DoingPoorly
End Sub
```

Here's what this code does:

1. The first few lines say that if the first question has not been answered (and it usually has not been up to this point), then the number of incorrect answers is now one more than before, because the student just chose the incorrect answer. (Notice that the code uses the numIncorrect variable instead of the numCorrect variable used in the previous procedure.) This section also specifies that this answer is 6. The code will use this fact later.

2. Then the procedure runs the DoingPoorly procedure, which is the negative feedback procedure we previously discussed, because the student chose the wrong answer.

The code does not move the student to the next question. Instead, the student stays on the same slide. Remember that the DoingPoorly procedure tells the student to try again.

To customize this procedure for your quiz you need to do the following:

- Change the first line, *Sub Answer1_Six()*, so that the last part (Six) reflects the correct answer of your own question. For example, if you're giving a history test and the incorrect answer is "War of 1812," then your first line could read *Sub*

Answer1_War1812(). This part only names the routine and the name can be anything you want. The main point here is to use a name that you'll connect easily to the answer. Remember, no spaces are allowed in the name of the procedure.

- Change the line that says *answer1 = "6"* to include the exact incorrect answer, which is the text on the action button. This is usually the same as the name of the routine, more or less. Your code could read, *answer1 = "War of 1812"*.

More questions

The quiz has two more questions and the procedures for them are very similar to the ones for the first question. Here's the code for the right and wrong answers of the second question:

```
Sub Answer2_minusFour()
   'can't use a hyphen here, so write out "minus"
   If q2Answered = False Then
        numCorrect = numCorrect + 1
        answer2 = "-4"
   End If
   q2Answered = True
   DoingWell
   ActivePresentation.SlideShowWindow.View.Next
End Sub

Sub Answer2_Four()
   If q2Answered = False Then
        numIncorrect = numIncorrect + 1
        answer2 = "4"
   End If
   q2Answered = True
   DoingPoorly
End Sub
```

The only differences are as follows:

- The procedure's name includes *Answer2* instead of *Answer1*.
- The variable on the second line is named *q2Answered* instead of *q1Answered*.

- The variable on the fourth line is named *answer2* instead of *answer1*.

- Line 6 repeats the *q2Answered* variable which was previously the *q1Answered* variable.

The changes you need to make are the same as for the first question—change the name of the procedure on the first line and the answer itself on the fourth line.

Similarly, here's the code for the third question's wrong and right answers. You adjust this in the same way you adjust the first and second questions.

```
Sub Answer3_yequals3()
  'Can't use an equal sign, so write it out
  If q3Answered = False Then
      numIncorrect = numIncorrect + 1
      answer3 = "y=3"
  End If
  q3Answered = True
  DoingPoorly
End Sub

Sub Answer3_xequals3()
  If q3Answered = False Then
      numCorrect = numCorrect + 1
      answer3 = "x=3"
  End If
  q3Answered = True
  DoingWell
  ActivePresentation.SlideShowWindow.View.Next
End Sub
```

Calculating and displaying the results

Now PowerPoint needs to calculate the results and create a slide that displays them. The code to do this is more complicated, because it creates a slide "on the fly," based on the results of the quiz. The process is quite interesting, but you don't need to understand it fully. Figure 9.5 shows an example of the slide that this code creates. As you look through the code, refer to this figure.

Figure 9.5
The PrintablePage procedure creates a slide like this, showing the student the results of the quiz.

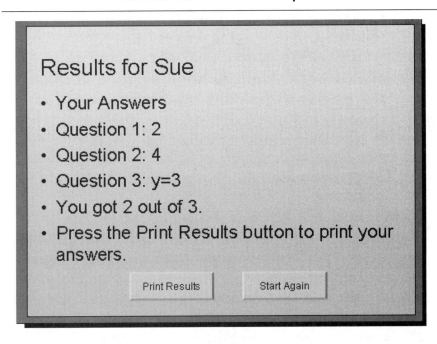

Here's the code:

```
Sub PrintablePage()
  Dim printableSlide As Slide
  Dim homeButton As Shape
  Dim printButton As Shape

  Set printableSlide = ActivePresentation.Slides.
    Add(Index:=6, _
      Layout:=ppLayoutText)
  printableSlide.Shapes(1).TextFrame.TextRange.
    Text = _
      "Results for " & userName
```

```
printableSlide.Shapes(2).TextFrame.TextRange.
    Text = _
        "Your Answers" & Chr$(13) & _
        "Question 1: " & answer1 & Chr$(13) & _
        "Question 2: " & answer2 & Chr$(13) & _
        "Question 3: " & answer3 & Chr$(13) & _
        "You got " & numCorrect & " out of " & _
        numCorrect + numIncorrect & "." & Chr$(13) & _
        "Press the Print Results button to print your
            answers."
Set homeButton = ActivePresentation.Slides(6).
    Shapes.AddShape _
        (msoShapeActionButtonCustom, 400, 450, 150,
            50)
homeButton.TextFrame.TextRange.Text = "Start
    Again"
homeButton.ActionSettings(ppMouseClick).Action =
    ppActionRunMacro
homeButton.ActionSettings(ppMouseClick).Run =
    "StartAgain"
Set printButton = ActivePresentation.Slides(6).
    Shapes.AddShape _
        (msoShapeActionButtonCustom, 200, 450, 150,
            50)
printButton.TextFrame.TextRange.Text = "Print
    Results"
printButton.ActionSettings(ppMouseClick).Action =
    ppActionRunMacro
printButton.ActionSettings(ppMouseClick).Run =
    "PrintResults"
ActivePresentation.SlideShowWindow.View.Next
ActivePresentation.Saved = True
End Sub
```

The first section declares some variables, one as a slide (the slide that the procedure creates) and two as Shapes—the two buttons that you see on the slide in Figure 9.5.

The next statement adds a new slide using the text layout and specifies that it will be slide 6. That's because the presentation has an introductory slide, three questions, and a final slide, or a total of five slides. We'll discuss this statement later, because you need to edit it if you change the number of questions.

The following statement adds text to the title placeholder of the slide. The text says "Results for" and adds the user's name.

Then the code adds the following text in the body of the slide:

- The text "Your answers."

- A list of the student's answers, using the *answer1, answer2,* and *answer3* variables. Now you know why those variables were saved.

- Text that tells the student how many correct answers the student got out of the total. This code uses the numCorrect and numIncorrect variables. Note that although the quiz forces the student to retry until the right answer is chosen, the first answer that the student chooses is the one that counts.

- The text "Press the Print Results button to print your answers."

Now the code adds two action buttons. The first button with the text "Start Again" is placed in a specific location on the slide, and runs the *StartAgain* macro. The second button with the text "Print Results" is placed in another location on the slide, and runs the *PrintResults* macro. We'll discuss those macros next.

The student is on the slide that has a How Did I Do? button. Clicking that button runs the `PrintablePage` procedure that we're discussing. This procedure creates the slide but now needs to move the student to that new slide and that's what the next statement does.

Finally, the procedure saves the presentation because it has added another slide.

That's a lot of code, but luckily you don't have to change much of it to customize it for your own quiz. In fact, if you stick to three questions, you don't have to change anything. If you add questions (which means adding slides), you need to add to the list of questions. The following code lists these questions:

```
"Question 1: " & answer1 & Chr$(13) & _
"Question 2: " & answer2 & Chr$(13) & _
"Question 3: " & answer3 & Chr$(13) & _
```

Copy the last line and paste it following that line, doing so for as many questions as you want. Then change the "3"s to "4"s, and so on, as necessary.

You also need to change the number of the slide in three separate places where the code now uses the number 6:

```
Set printableSlide = ActivePresentation.Slides.
  Add(Index:=6, _Layout:=ppLayoutText)
Set homeButton = ActivePresentation.Slides(6).
  Shapes.AddShape _ (msoShapeActionButtonCustom,
  400, 450, 150, 50)
Set printButton = ActivePresentation.Slides(6).
  Shapes.AddShape _ (msoShapeActionButtonCustom,
  200, 450, 150, 50)
```

As we discussed, the quiz has an opening slide, a slide for each question, and a How Did I Do? slide. Therefore, there are two more slides than questions; in this example, the three-question quiz has five slides. The new slide needs to come next, so it is slide 6. Therefore, if you have five questions, change the index (slide) number to 8. If you have ten questions, change it to 13.

You don't need to change anything else, but if you're inquisitive, here are a couple of other possibilities for changing the code:

- You could change some of the text. For example, instead of "Press the Print Results button to print your answers," you might want to say, "Click the Print Results button to print the answers."

- You could move the buttons by changing the numbers in the "(msoShapeActionButtonCustom, 400, 450, 150, 50)" and "(msoShapeActionButtonCustom, 200, 450, 150, 50)" phrases.

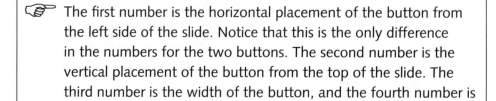 The first number is the horizontal placement of the button from the left side of the slide. Notice that this is the only difference in the numbers for the two buttons. The second number is the vertical placement of the button from the top of the slide. The third number is the width of the button, and the fourth number is its height. All values are measured in pixels.

Printing the results

As we mentioned, the previous procedure creates a button that runs the `PrintResults` procedure and here it is:

```
Sub PrintResults()
  ActivePresentation.PrintOptions.OutputType =
    ppPrintOutputSlides
  ActivePresentation.PrintOut From:=6, To:=6
End Sub
```

Note that the procedure prints out only slide 6, by specifying a range from 6 to 6. Both these numbers need to be changed if you change the number of questions, as we explained in the previous section. So if you change the slide number to 8 in the PrintablePage procedure, you need to change both the From and To numbers to 8 in this procedure.

Starting Over

The final procedure displays the first slide of the presentation. It deletes the slide that calculates the student's score, allowing the student to try again. Then it saves the presentation.

```
Sub StartAgain()
  ActivePresentation.SlideShowWindow.View.
    GotoSlide (1)
  ActivePresentation.Slides(6).Delete
  ActivePresentation.Saved = True
End Sub
```

If you increase the number of questions, you again need to change the slide number in this procedure from 6 to whatever is appropriate, as we've just discussed.

ASSIGNING MACROS TO THE BUTTONS

When the code is customized to your satisfaction, you need a way to run the code. You do this by attaching the procedure (also called a macro) to the action buttons in the presentation. Your quiz won't work until you complete this step. Here's the general procedure:

> **HOW TO DO IT**
> - *All versions:* Select a button. To make sure that you've selected the entire shape and not just text on the shape, click the border of the button. Choose Slide Show ➤ Action Settings. In the Action Settings dialog box, choose the Run Macro option. From the Run Macro drop-down list, choose the appropriate macro. Click OK.

When you follow this procedure, you'll understand why the names of the procedures should be descriptive—they help you choose the right macro in the drop-down list. Table 9.1 shows the buttons and the macros they need to run.

Table 9.1
Macros for Quiz Buttons.

Button	Macro
What is your name?	GetStarted.
2 (the left-most answer button on slide 2)	Answer1_Two
6 (the right-most answer button on slide 2)	Answer1_Six
-4 (the left-most answer button on slide 3)	Answer2_minusFour
4 (the right-most answer button on slide 3)	Answer2_Four
y=3 (the left-most answer button on slide 4)	Answer3_yequalsThree
x=3 (the right-most answer button on slide 4)	Answer3_xequalsThree
How did I do?	PrintablePage

When you've finished assigning macros to buttons, save your presentation and you're ready to test it.

TESTING THE TEST

Yes, you need to test the test. One of the frustrations of working with any programming code is that it has to be perfect; if it isn't, it won't work. Click the first slide, enter Slide Show view and take the quiz, trying out various answers as you go. Be sure to try all the wrong answers as well as the correct ones.

If something doesn't work, write down the problem and go back to the Visual Basic Editor and look at the code. This chapter has given you the information you need to check and edit it. Good luck on your test!

ADDING MORE

As we've discussed throughout this chapter, you can add more questions and answers. Here we summarize the steps you need to take to expand our little quiz.

Creating a Quiz with More Than Two Answer Choices

The quiz we used had only two answer choices for simplicity, but you probably would like to use more, because this makes the test more challenging. It's not hard. Here are the instructions for one slide; repeat them for each slide. This assumes that you already have code for one correct answer and one incorrect answer, according to the example we've been using in this chapter.

HOW TO DO IT

- *All versions:* Create a slide containing four action buttons with one correct answer and three incorrect answers. In the Visual Basic Editor, select the code for the incorrect answer for that question and copy it to the Clipboard. Place the cursor below the next horizontal line and paste the code from the Clipboard. Again place the cursor below the next horizontal line, press Enter and paste again. This

---

adds procedures for two more incorrect answers. Change each procedure's name to reflect the answer and change the fourth line of code to specify the exact answer. For example: `answer1="The Spanish-American War"`.

This procedure creates one correct and three incorrect answers for every question.

Adding More Questions

Three questions are certainly not enough. Here is a summary of the steps you need to take to add more questions.

HOW TO DO IT

- *All versions:* Create more slides with questions and answers. In the Visual Basic Editor, select the code for the last question, including both the right and the wrong answer. Copy it to the Clipboard. Click just below the horizontal line after the last wrong answer and paste from the Clipboard. The editor creates the horizontal lines to separate each procedure.

When you have the additional questions, you need to do the following:

1. Add additional variables in the first section of code, as explained earlier under the "Introductory Section" heading.

2. Add the additional questions in the Initialize section, as explained earlier under the "Initialize Section" heading.

3. For each question, change the number of the question in four locations. Generally, this means changing all the "3"s to "4"s, for all the answers of the fourth question, and so on for each additional question.

4. Change the Sub name and answer for each question. We explain how to do this for correct answers in the "First Answer to the First Question" section. For incorrect answers, look at the "Second Answer to the First Question" section.

5. Add to the list of questions in the PrintablePage section, as we explained under the "Calculating and Displaying the Results" heading.

> If you increase the number of questions, there might be a lot of text on the slide! The text should adjust in size (get smaller) to fit into the text placeholder unless you've formatted the placeholder to resize instead. To check, go into Master Slide view and select the text placeholder. Right-click (Windows)/Ctrl-click (Mac) and choose Format Placeholder or Format (Auto)Shape. On the Text Box tab or category, make sure that the Resize Placeholder/Shape to Fit Text check box is *not* checked. Click OK/Close. If this technique doesn't work, you can eliminate the list of questions in the PrintablePage section to reduce the amount of text on the slide. The statement would then read as follows:
>
> ```
> printableSlide.Shapes(2).TextFrame.TextRange.
>     Text = _"You got " & numCorrect & " out of "
>     & _numCorrect + numIncorrect & "." &
>     Chr$(13) & _"Press the Print Results
>     button to print your answers."
> ```

6. Change the number of the last slide in three places in the PrintablePage section and in two places in the PrintResults section, as we explained under the "Calculating and Displaying the Results" heading.

7. Assign the new macros you've just created to the new buttons, as we explained in the "Assigning Macros to the Buttons" section.

8. Thoroughly test your test!

> You can find a complete quiz with ten questions and four possible answers for each question on the book's companion Web site at www.ellenfinkelstein.com/powerpointforteachers.html. Look for 10-Question Math Quiz.ppt. You can use this presentation as a template for your own quizzes.

SUMMARY

In this chapter, we explained how to create a graded quiz in PowerPoint. Although the presentation requires students to keep trying until they get the right answer, it only stores the first click for each question.

The presentation calculates the number of right answers and the total number of answers. It prints out a results slide and also saves that slide in the presentation for the teacher to refer to later.

We explained how to create the presentation, provided sample code, and described how to customize the code for your own quizzes.

PART THREE

Projects and Resources

Chapter 10: PowerPoint Projects for Pre-Kindergarten to Grade 1

Chapter 11: PowerPoint Projects for Grades 2 to 5

Chapter 12: PowerPoint Projects for Grades 6 to 12

Chapter 13: Online Resources for Teachers Using PowerPoint

Part III offers ideas for specific projects at various age levels, along with some helpful online resources.

PowerPoint Projects for Pre-Kindergarten to Grade 1

I n this chapter we describe projects appropriate for students from pre-kindergarten through first grade. You can use these ideas as a springboard for your own projects. These projects are different from those you would use in later grades, as you'll see in this chapter.

We assume that your students have already learned basic mouse and clicking skills. It takes a little time for them to learn to control the mouse and click a specific button, picture, or word.

FUN IN THE EARLY YEARS

You understand very well that learning for pre-K, kindergarten, and many first-grade students should be fun and not text-based. Children at this age learn by playing; many of them have only rudimentary reading skills.

Because the students are not yet ready to read fast from the screen, all the instructions in your PowerPoint projects should be given orally. You can either tell the students what to do, or record your voice instructions. (See Chapter 3 for details.)

Let's look at the four major areas of learning in these grades: language arts, mathematics, science, and social studies.

LANGUAGE ARTS

Many students in kindergarten and even first grade do not have developed reading skills; some are only beginning to learn letters. We suggest multiple-choice activities that require students to click on the right letter with a negative or positive feedback. (See Chapter 5 for detailed instructions.) For example, you might tell the students to click on the letter A, and then watch the student's response; for independent work (which should be very brief at this age), you may record the commands and feedbacks.

When teaching students the sounds of letters, you can ask them to click the object that starts with a certain letter, such as B. They might choose from a picture of a book, a cat, a duck, and a house.

As soon as children have some reading skills, they can match pictures with words. For example, you can show a picture of a book and ask them to click the word "book." Other choices would typically start with a different letter, such as "cat" or "milk."

PowerPoint projects at this grade level do not necessarily have to be interactive. Simple storytelling can be greatly enhanced by PowerPoint; pictures, short video clips, and musical files can be extremely helpful. You can use clip art, scan your own pictures and pictures of the students, or use pictures from a digital camera in PowerPoint. Describing pictures is always part of teaching at this level; doing this with PowerPoint can be effective and fun.

You can use a PowerPoint presentation in this way to excellent effect to review a class trip during which you've taken pictures. The students can relate parts of the trip, which you can enter (as they speak) in a PowerPoint presentation. Then you can add pictures. When you're done, show them the results of their storytelling and tell the story back to them. Figure 10.1 shows an example of a slide that might result from a trip to the zoo.

Although creating CDs of the presentation for children to take home might be too challenging a project, you may be able to print out the presentation, staple it into a book, and give it to the children.

 You can download a sample story, Our Zoo Trip.ppt, from this book's companion Web site at www.ellenfinkelstein.com/ powerpointforteachers.html.

MATH

Children learn to identify numbers and relate them to the number of objects. PowerPoint projects of this type can be extremely effective. For example, it is easy to

Figure 10.1
Children can tell stories that you can turn into a slide-show "book"
for them with PowerPoint.

We saw some giraffes and zebras.

Ethan Jones

create a PowerPoint project with images (bees, butterflies, beetles, teddy bears, and so on) forming a certain number, and to show the character denoting this number.

Animation here is a good idea too. For example, you show a butterfly on a flower and ask, "How many butterflies can you see?" You click on the slide and the number 1 appears next to the picture. Then you click on the slide again, and another butterfly flies in and lands on the flower. You repeat the question about the number, show the number 2, and so on. Figure 10.2 shows such a project, showing three butterflies and the number 3.

 You can download this project at the book's companion Web site at www.ellenfinkelstein.com/powerpointforteachers.html. The same Web site includes an image of a butterfly (butterfly.wmf) that you can use.

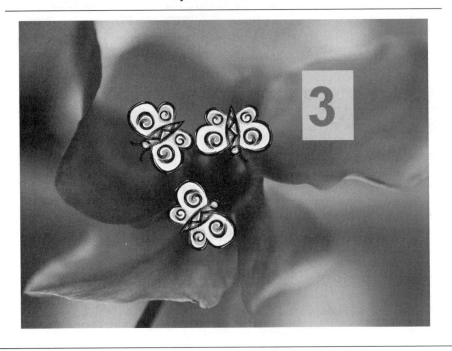

Figure 10.2
Children match numbers with the appropriate number of objects on a slide.

Collecting Images for a Math Project

For such a project, you need the right background and the right images. One option is to leave the background white. If you'll use a colorful background, make sure that the images contrast well; for example, use a darker background and light images.

When you insert multiple images of an object, such as a butterfly, make sure that the image doesn't have a white, square background—it will look ugly and distracting. All images are technically rectangular, but if they have a transparent background, you see only the object itself, such as the butterflies in Figure 10.2.

Start by collecting the images you want to use and saving them in the folder where you will save the PowerPoint presentation.

Only PNG, GIF, and some TIFF image file types can have a transparent background. JPG image files do not support transparency. WMF images are vector images that usually don't have a background, so they also work well in this situation.

Animating the Objects

To create this project, start a new presentation. If desired, insert a flower image as a background. Then insert a picture, such as the butterfly we used, from the Clip Art gallery or from a file. We explain both procedures in Chapter 2. If necessary, move and resize the image; we wanted the butterfly to look as if it were landing on the center of the flower.

You want to create animation, so that one image after another flies onto the slide as the number displayed increases. In our example, we animated a butterfly. The first animation will fly in from the bottom-left corner of the slide, so select the butterfly and use the green rotation handle to face the butterfly so that it's facing the upper-right corner of the slide. (Look at the lower-left butterfly in Figure 10.2.)

HOW TO DO IT

- *Windows 2000:* Select the butterfly and choose Slide Show ➢ Custom Animation. In the middle of the Custom Animation dialog box, click the Effects tab. From the Entry Animation and Sound drop-down list, choose Fly. From the Direction drop-down list just to the right, choose From Bottom-Left. Click the Order and Timing tab. In the Start Animation section, choose the On Mouse Click option. Click OK.

- *Windows 2002/2003:* Select the butterfly and choose Slide Show ➢ Custom Animation. In the Custom Animation task pane, choose Add Effect ➢ Entrance ➢ Fly In. You can adjust the speed of animation in the Speed drop-down list. In the Direction drop-down list, choose From Bottom-Left. In the Start drop-down list, choose On Click.

- *Windows 2007:* On the Animations tab, click Custom Animation. In the Custom Animation task pane, choose Add Effect ➢ Entrance ➢

Fly In. You can adjust the speed of animation in the Speed drop-down list. In the Direction drop-down list, choose From Bottom-Left. In the Start drop-down list, choose On Click.

- *Mac 2001/X/2004:* Select the butterfly. Choose Slide Show ➢ Custom Animation. In the Custom Animation dialog box, click Add Effect. Click the Entrance tab. Choose Fly In. Click OK. From Start drop-down list, choose On Click. From the Property drop-down list, choose From Bottom-Left. From the Speed drop-down list, choose the desired speed. Click OK.

In place of the Fly In effect, you can choose the Crawl In effect, or any other effect that produces the impression of a butterfly flying and landing.

The second step is to animate the number to match the number of butterflies. Insert a text box and type the number **1**. Select this text and choose a very large font so that the kids can easily recognize it. (We used a font size of 96.) If necessary, enlarge the text box and change the text and fill color to get the desired contrast. For instructions, see Chapter 2. Make sure that the text box is located to one side of the slide, so that it isn't on top of the butterflies; look again at Figure 10.2.

Now you're ready to animate the text box.

HOW TO DO IT

- *Windows 2000:* Select the text box. Choose Slide Show ➢ Custom Animation. In the Custom Animation dialog box, on the Effects tab, click the Entry Animation and Sound drop-down list and choose Appear. Click OK.

- *Windows 2002/2003:* Select the text box. Select Slide Show ➢ Custom Animation. In the Custom Animation dialog box, Select Add Effect ➢ Entrance and select Appear or Dissolve In (or any other effect to make the number appear on click). Click OK.

- *Windows 2007:* Select the text box. From the Animation tab, click Custom Animation. In the Custom Animation task pane, choose Add Effect ➢ Entrance ➢ Appear.
- *Mac 2001/X/2004:* Select the butterfly. Choose Slide Show ➢ Custom Animation. In the Custom Animation dialog box, click Add Effect. Click the Entrance tab. Choose Appear. Click OK.

Other animation options are Dissolve In, Checkerboard, or any other effect that makes the number appear when you click it.

 Make sure that the butterfly picture is animated first, and the number 1 is animated second. If not, change the order using the arrows in the Custom Animation dialog box or task pane.

Time to save your presentation! Then go to Slide Show view and test your work. Your show will start with the picture of a flower. When you click, the butterfly flies in. On a second click, the number 1 appears.

The third step is to add more butterflies. You do so as follows:

1. Copy and paste the picture of the butterfly. It pastes almost on top of the original picture.

2. Drag the picture to the desired part of the flower.

3. Rotate it to a different direction. For example, face it toward the upper-left corner of the slide.

4. Animate it as previously described. If it is facing the upper-left corner of the slide, you would choose the From Bottom-Left direction from the Direction drop-down list.

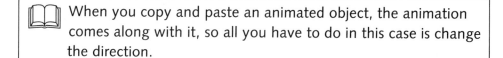 When you copy and paste an animated object, the animation comes along with it, so all you have to do in this case is change the direction.

From the Start drop-down list, choose On Click.

If you want, you can use the Speed drop-down list to make the object move at a desired speed.

Now you need to add the number 2, which you do as follows:

1. Click on the border of the text box to select the text box, making sure that you're not selecting its text.

2. Copy and paste it. A new text box appears almost on top of the old one.

3. Drag it so that it perfectly covers the original text box.

4. Select the number 1 and change it to **2**.

5. Animate it to appear on your click as you did with the previous text box. (The animation should exist already, because you copied and pasted an animated object.)

Don't forget to save. Then test it in Slide Show view.

 If you add an animation that you don't want, click it in the Custom Animation dialog box/task pane and click the Remove or X button.

You can continue until you reach the desired number, such as five or ten.

In case you want to remove one or more butterflies, you can. Then you can count backward, too.

HOW TO DO IT

- *Windows 2000:* The feature is not available.

- *Windows 2002/2003:* Select one of the butterflies. Choose Slide Show ➢ Custom Animation. In the Custom Animation task pane, choose Add Effect ➢ Exit ➢ Fly out. As you did earlier, choose the speed and the direction, and choose On Mouse Click from the Start drop-down list. To change the number, just add another text box with the appropriate number (for example, **3**, if you have four butterflies), as you did earlier.

- *Windows 2007:* Select one of the butterflies. On the Animations tab, click Custom Animation. In the Custom Animation task pane, choose Add Effect ➢ Exit ➢ Fly out. As you did earlier, choose the speed and the direction, and choose On Mouse Click from the Start drop-down list. To change the number, just add another text box with the appropriate number (for example, **3**, if you have four butterflies), as you did earlier.

- *Mac 2001/X/2004:* Select one of the butterflies. Choose Slide Show ➢ Custom Animation. In the Custom Animation dialog box, choose Add Effect ➢ Exit ➢ Fly out. As you did earlier, choose the speed and the direction, and choose On Mouse Click from the Start drop-down list. To change the number, just add another text box with the appropriate number (for example, **3**, if you have four butterflies), as you did earlier.

Notice that the entire animation occurs on one slide.

Using AutoShapes to Teach Math

Kindergarteners and first graders are expected to identify forms, shapes, and colors. Here PowerPoint has a great potential, because of the number of shapes, colors, and drawing features it provides.

The AutoShapes (called just Shapes in PowerPoint 2007) provide ovals, triangles, rectangles, cubes, cans, and many more. To use the AutoShapes, go to the Drawing toolbar and select AutoShapes ➢ Basic Shapes. (In PowerPoint 2007, display the Insert tab and choose Shapes ➢ Basic Shapes.) For more detailed instructions, see "Inserting Shapes" and "Editing and Formatting Shapes" in Chapter 2.

You can change the size and the proportion of the shape by dragging the shape by one of the corners or sides. In this way you can create good material for learning the notions of "large," "larger," "thin," "thinner," and so on.

You can use AutoShapes to contrast, compare, and describe attributes of shapes (corner, side, straight, curved, number of sides) using concrete models (circle, rectangle, square, rhombus, triangle, and so on). Another lesson is to identify congruent shapes (the same size and shape) in a variety of positions and orientations.

Another important expectation for pre-K to grade 1 is to be able to identify patterns. Creating number patterns (2, 4, 6, 8) is easy. A bit more challenging is to create patterns of colors, shapes or sizes. Figure 10.3 is a good example of how you can use PowerPoint to create simple patterns.

The upper pattern is a color pattern; the students are supposed to identify what the next color is. Of course, writing on the slide "What is next?" is optional, and it depends on the level of your students' reading skills. The bottom pattern is a pattern of shapes.

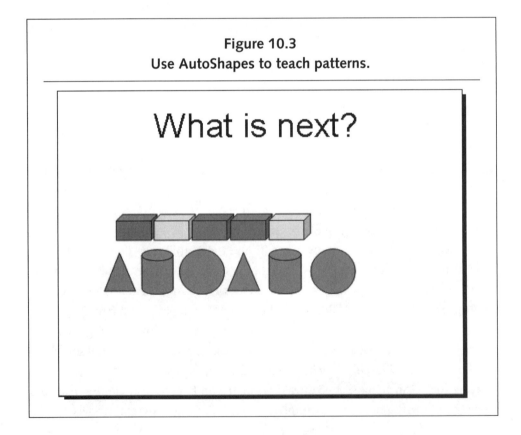

Figure 10.3
Use AutoShapes to teach patterns.

HOW TO DO IT

- *All versions:* Insert a cube from the Basic Shapes section of the AutoShapes (Shapes in PowerPoint 2007). Copy and paste the number of cubes needed for one complete pattern (three, in our case). Arrange them in one line with same distance between them. Change the fill color of the cubes so that they are all different colors. You don't have to repeat this to add another set of cubes (the first two cubes of the second pattern, which are green and blue in Figure 10.3). Click on the green and blue cubes, while pressing the Ctrl (Windows)/ ⌘ (Mac) key. Copy and paste the cubes. Place them right after the red one. Fine-tune the placement.

 To align objects, you can use the arrow keys on your keyboard to finely adjust position and spacing. Also, see Chapter 7 for a discussion of how to use the Align and Distribute features to line up objects.

The procedure for the shapes pattern is similar.

PowerPoint projects with AutoShapes and pictures help develop operational notions and the corresponding vocabulary for pre-K to grade 1 students: *add, subtract, join, remove, take away, put together.*

Another idea for math at the pre-K to grade 1 level is money. These students are expected to be able to count up to a dollar and beyond. Unfortunately, the Clip Art gallery does not contain good pictures of money. You can find such pictures on the Internet or take your own pictures.

SCIENCE

Pre-K to first-grade students need to know parts of the human body, parts of plants, and major domestic and wild animals. We suggest the following projects in PowerPoint:

- *Major parts of plants.* The project can include an interactive map of a plant, showing roots, leaves, and stems. See Chapter 6 for instructions on creating a clickable map.

- *Parts of the human body.* This project can easily be made interactive by including a clickable map of the body. You can also use the technique described earlier for the math project (the butterflies and numbers) to animate the labeling of each part of the body. Instead of using a text box, use one of the Callout AutoShapes. These shapes can point to a part of the body.

- *Differences between living and nonliving objects, between plants and animals.* Ask students to identify the appropriate category as you display pictures, such as a dog, a rock, or a tree.

- *Domestic and wild animals.* Here we suggest a presentation with a short multiple-choice quiz (overview). As a variant of the project, you can talk about animals the kids can pet and those they cannot. To make this interactive, ask students to click on the pictures of animals they can pet with the permission of the owners (dogs, cats, sheep, goats, and so on), and those they must not pet (snakes, possums, raccoons, and so on). See Chapter 5 for instructions on creating a quiz.

> Apart from the scientific value of this project, it can have an important practical value for young children, especially those living in areas where they may encounter snakes, raccoons, rats, scorpions, and other potentially dangerous creatures.

- *Weather patterns.* The seasons of the year can be depicted with great pictures from the Internet; rain, snow, heat, ice, and other natural phenomena are great topics and subjects for your PowerPoint projects.

- *Food.* Show food pyramids, explain what's edible and what is not edible, what's healthy and what is not. The material for the projects is readily available on the Internet. The projects can involve some interactivity, for example, "Click on the type of food that you should eat in moderation."

- *The five senses.* Explain touch, smell, vision, hearing, and taste. This project can easily be made interactive, with clickable pictures.

Of course, the possibilities are limitless.

SOCIAL STUDIES

Some social studies projects for pre-K to grade 1 are as follows:

- *Community workers and their jobs.* This presentation would include pictures of teachers, police officers, firefighters, doctors, construction workers, and so on. You provide explanations of the roles of the community workers and describe their duties. If you take the students on a trip to visit the police or fire station, you can also create a story presentation, as we described earlier for the zoo trip. Be sure to take plenty of pictures while on the trip.

- *Directions and order.* Teach right, left, first, last, and so on. Using arrows is very important! Street signs, such as red and green lights and stop signs, are important for children to recognize. Look for clip art for "traffic" and "stop" and you're sure to find excellent images.

- *Maps of the states and the United States.* Create a presentation showing states or the United States (or another country) on the map and the globe. Create maps of different features of Earth: seas, rivers, islands, and so on. See the instructions on how to create an interactive map in Chapter 6.

- *Transportation.* Create a presentation on cars, trains, planes, boats, and so on.

AN INTERDISCIPLINARY APPROACH

PowerPoint is a great tool for the interdisciplinary approach. This is especially important because you are the only teacher for this grade level. For example, you can include elements of social studies in most PowerPoint projects; the math project on money could include explanations on the ways people use money to purchase food and other goods.

Here are some other examples of interdisciplinary projects:

- Projects on weather patterns can include the ways the weather affects people and their lives.

- Projects on geometry can include the notions of directionality, position, and size.

- Projects on plants and animals can include concepts of preservation of the environment, and the counting of plants and animals.

- Projects on letters can work together with projects on patterns, since reading involves recognizing patterns.

You'll find that a PowerPoint presentation can collect and integrate concepts from many different kinds of lessons.

SUMMARY

In this chapter we suggested some ideas to use in PowerPoint projects in language arts, math, science, and social studies for pre-kindergarten through the first grade. The projects should include as little text as possible, or even no text at all, unless they are specifically designed to teach reading. Most of the projects can be inter-disciplinary, including more than one aspect of learning, such as math, social studies, and so on.

PowerPoint Projects for Grades 2 to 5

I n the previous chapter we discussed some project ideas for pre-kindergarten through the first grade. Sometimes there is no strict distinction between the nature of the projects for grades 1 and 2; some can be used in both grades. However, because children in grades 2 and higher have already acquired some reading skills, PowerPoint projects can involve some text. Following are some ideas for projects, organized by subject. Just as with the projects for the younger students, many projects can and should be interdisciplinary. This is especially important in elementary school, where most classes are taught by one teacher.

Remember that during these grades, you can start teaching students how to use PowerPoint themselves. Most schools start in the fifth grade, but see the "Articles" section of Chapter 13 for a reference to an article about a librarian who taught her second-grade students PowerPoint. Either way, you can start including the students in the process of creating presentations.

LANGUAGE ARTS

You can use PowerPoint with pictures and context clues to confirm meanings of words. On a slide the teacher places two pictures: one of a city and the other of a town, and the words "city" and "town." The students connect the word and the picture (other examples: river-stream, lake-ocean, hill-mountain, and so on). As reading skills and understanding of the written word develops, projects involve phrases and sentences. The students begin to learn how to derive the meaning of a word from a larger context—for example, words that have more than one meaning (ear, table, chest, and so on). A pictorial support is essential here.

As reading skills develop, you can put more text on one slide. Matching words, filling spaces ("Guess the missing word"), comparing right and wrong spellings, completing sentences and more can become the content of your projects. Projects on the parts of speech and sentence, on the use of orthography, synonyms, antonyms, and so on, are included in your teaching. In such "dry" subjects as grammar or spelling, use more pictures and sound effects. Sound effects, especially WAV files, liven up even the driest subject. Use audio files from cartoons and movies that have been popular with students of this age. You can easily find these files on the Web.

PowerPoint is an excellent tool to develop storytelling skills. Students at this age start to write their own stories, which can be entered into a PowerPoint presentation. This is an opportunity to get the students to help you create the presentation; they can come up and type a sentence into the computer. If you're projecting the display on a screen, the entire class can watch the story creation process. This process also is the beginning of teaching them to use PowerPoint.

As we mentioned in the previous chapter, a class trip offers an excellent opportunity to retell the event in the form of a PowerPoint presentation. If you take digital photos during the trip, the students will enjoy seeing them so quickly in the presentation.

PowerPoint language arts projects are especially effective when you use them as a review of the material covered. Here you can use multiple-choice quizzes as games or contests with points or places assigned to the winners or winning teams.

MATH

Math is ideally suited to presentations in PowerPoint because the concepts can be made so visually clear in bright, bold colors. PowerPoint offers you the choice of numerous geometrical shapes to help in this regard.

Teaching Fractions

In grades 2 and 3, students begin to study fractions. PowerPoint is an excellent tool to create projects to explain the concept of fractions, as shown in Figure 11.1.

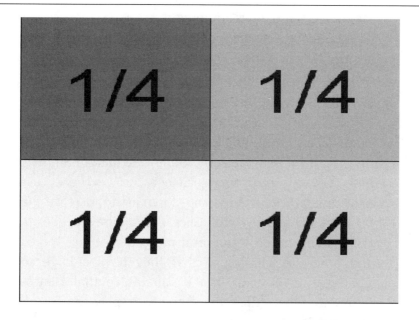

Figure 11.1
A slide representing fractions.

1/4 + 1/4 + 1/4 + 1/4 = 1

Start with a slide using the Title Only layout. Drag the title text placeholder to the bottom of the slide.(You can do this in the slide master to format all slides this way.) Then add the squares (or any other shape you want).

HOW TO DO IT

- *Windows 2000/2002/2003:* On the Drawing toolbar, click the Rectangle button. Press the Shift key (to constrain the shape to a square) and drag a square about one-quarter of the size of the slide, leaving room for a margin. Immediately type

1/4 in the square. Select the text and use the Font Size drop-down list to increase the size; 96 points is about right. Click the square's border to exit text-editing mode. Copy and paste the square three times and drag the squares so that they form a large square. Change the fill color of the squares so that they are all different colors. (Double-click a square to open the Format AutoShape dialog box.)

- *Windows 2007:* On the Insert tab, choose Shapes. Click the Rectangle button. Press the Shift key (to constrain the shape to a square) and drag a square about one-quarter of the size of the slide, leaving room for a margin. Immediately type **1/4** in the square. Select the text and use the mini-toolbar's Font Size drop-down list to increase the size; 96 points is about right. Click the square's border to exit text-editing mode. Copy and paste the square three times and drag the squares so that they form a large square. Change the fill color of the squares so that they are all different colors. (Click the shape to display the Format tab. Click the Shape Fill button.)

- *Mac 2001/X/2004:* On the Drawing toolbar, click the Rectangle button. Press the Shift key (to constrain the shape to a square) and drag a square about one-quarter of the size of the slide, leaving room for a margin. Immediately type **1/4** in the square. Select the text and use the Font Size drop-down list to increase the size; 96 points is about right. Click the square's border to exit text-editing mode. Copy and paste the square three times and drag the squares so that they form a large square. Change the fill color of the squares so that they are all different colors. (Double-click a square to open the Format AutoShape dialog box.)

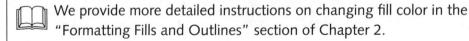 We provide more detailed instructions on changing fill color in the "Formatting Fills and Outlines" section of Chapter 2.

SPOTLIGHT: USING THE PIE SLICE SHAPE

PowerPoint includes an AutoShape (Shape in PowerPoint 2007) called Pie Slice. It's excellent for illustrating fractions, because you can adjust it to any percentage of the whole pie, as shown in Figure 11.2. It starts as three-quarters of a pie. Drag either of the yellow diamonds to change the amount of pie that you see.

Unfortunately, in several versions of PowerPoint, the pie shape is not easy to find. In PowerPoint for Windows 2000/2003/2003, click the AutoShapes button on the Drawing toolbar, and choose More AutoShapes. Either scroll down to find Pie Slice or do a search for it. In PowerPoint for Windows 2007, you can find it in the Basic Shapes section of the Shapes gallery. In PowerPoint 2001/X/2004 (Mac) Basic Shapes are in AutoShapes (on the Drawing Toolbar located normally on the left side).

In the title text placeholder, enter **1/4+1/4+1/4+1/4 = 1.**

Copy and paste the slide. Now you can represent the idea of three-quarters by removing one of the squares, or add another square to represent the idea of five quarters.

 If necessary, press Shift + arrows to fine-tune the alignment of the squares.

You can use the pie slice to create a slide like the one shown in Figure 11.3.

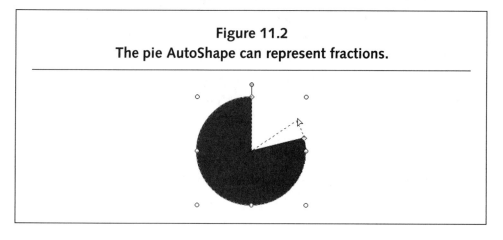

Figure 11.2
The pie AutoShape can represent fractions.

Figure 11.3
Fractions are seen as part of a pie in this slide.

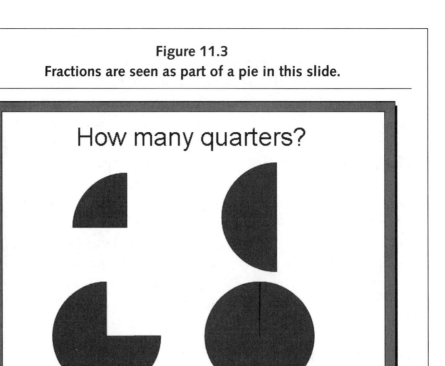

Using similar techniques, you can explain the concepts of subtraction, addition, division, and multiplication. Of course, most teachers introduce these concepts with real objects and let students manipulate them, but PowerPoint lets you introduce new types of objects and show the slides over and over. It provides a good transition from real, three-dimensional objects, to two-dimensional representations of them, to the final level of working with numbers on paper. The bright colors and shapes help students visualize these concepts more clearly.

For example, you can use images of real-world objects, including the stereotypical apples and oranges. You can also use animation to portray the process. In Figure 11.4, we show a series of steps on the concept of division. Unfortunately, all Mac versions and Windows 2000 do not support this type of motion path animation. Yet, because it is so useful, we provide instructions for those of you on more recent Windows computers. For more precise instructions on animating, see "Adding Animation" in Chapter 2.

Figure 11.4
You can animate the division of six apples into two groups.

Share them with a friend

Share them with a friend

Share them with a friend

Share them with a friend

Share them with a friend

Share them with a friend

Share them with a friend

How many do each of you get?

HOW TO DO IT

- *Windows 2000:* This version does not support motion paths.

- *Windows 2002/2003:* Use the Title Only layout. In the title text place-holder, enter **Share them with a friend**. Insert one apple from the clip art collection at the bottom and make it much smaller. Select the apple, copy it to the Clipboard, and paste it six times. Move them to the bottom of the slide. Select the first apple and choose Slide Show ➢ Custom Animation. Click Add Effect ➢ Motion Paths ➢ Draw Custom Path ➢ Line and draw a line from the apple to the upper-right side of the slide. Use the same technique to move the second apple to the upper-left side. Continue until you've moved the apples into two separate groups. Select the title text placeholder, and copy and paste it. Move the copy to the bottom of the slide, where the apples were, and enter **How many do each of you get?** Select the first place-holder and give it an exit animation of Fade. Give the second placeholder an entrance animation of Fade.

- *Windows 2007:* Use the Title Only layout. In the title text place-holder, enter **Share them with a friend**. Insert one apple from the clip art collection at the bottom and make it much smaller. Select the apple, copy it to the Clipboard, and paste it six times. Move them to the bottom of the slide. Select the first apple, click the Animations tab, and click Custom Animation. Click Add Effect ➢ Motion Paths

➢Draw Custom Path ➢ Line and draw a line from the apple to the upper-right side of the slide. Use the same technique to move the second apple to the upper-left side. Continue until you've moved the apples into two separate groups. Select the title text placeholder, and copy and paste it. Move the copy to the bottom of the slide, where the apples were, and enter **How many do each of you get?** Select the first placeholder and give it an exit animation of Fade. Give the second placeholder an entrance animation of Fade.

- *Mac 2001/X/2004:* Mac versions do not support motion paths.

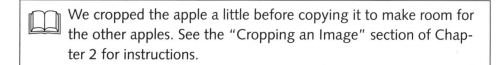 We cropped the apple a little before copying it to make room for the other apples. See the "Cropping an Image" section of Chapter 2 for instructions.

AutoShapes are also ideal for PowerPoint projects on polygons, from triangles to hexagons. Change their color, animate them, add some musical and/or WAV files.

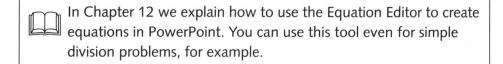 In Chapter 12 we explain how to use the Equation Editor to create equations in PowerPoint. You can use this tool even for simple division problems, for example.

Teaching Money and Percent Concepts

It is a good idea to use money to explain the concept of percent. It is worth mentioning that the word *cent* in Latin means one hundred. So, one cent means one part of one hundred. You may start your discussion using real or play money, and then continue your explanation using the images of cents, dimes, quarters, and dollar bills. One cent multiplied by one hundred will make a dollar, just as a dime taken ten times, or a quarter taken four times, will make a dollar. You'll find an abundance of pictures of coins and paper bills on the Internet that you can use in your project.

- *Windows 2000/2002/2003:* Click inside the table cell. On the Drawing toolbar, click the down arrow to the right of the Fill Color button and choose the desired color.

- *Windows 2007:* Click inside the table cell. On the Table Tools Design tab, click the down arrow to the right of the Shading button and choose the desired color.

- *Mac 2001/X/2004:* Click inside the table cell. On the Drawing toolbar, click the down arrow to the right of the Fill Color button and choose the desired color.

Another way of representing 100 percent is with a table containing ten rows and ten columns. Enter the numbers from one to one hundred in the cells.

You can also use this table to teach multiplication.

To represent 1 percent, select the cell with the digit 1. Then fill in that cell with a bright color that still allows the number to be seen clearly.

In the same way, you can display the idea of 10 percent, 50 percent, or any desired percent number. Before doing so, copy and paste the slide with the table as many times as you need for your project. On each copy, fill the cells to represent the desired percentage. For example, on the first slide you fill only one cell, representing 1 percent. On the next slide you may fill an entire row or column to represent 10 percent, and so on. You can also show that cells may not necessarily form groups, but be scattered to explain the basics of statistics—for example, you can fill twelve unconnected cells to show that 12 percent of humans are left-handed.

Showing Metric System Concepts

U.S. students in grades 2 through 5 have problems understanding the metric system of measurement. We offer the following project to help illustrate it.

Just as with the percent project, create a table with ten rows and ten columns. Explain that one-tenth of the line is one linear centimeter, show the proportion of the centimeter to the inch (one inch is 2.5 cm), and explain that one cubic centimeter of water is one gram (see Figure 11.5).

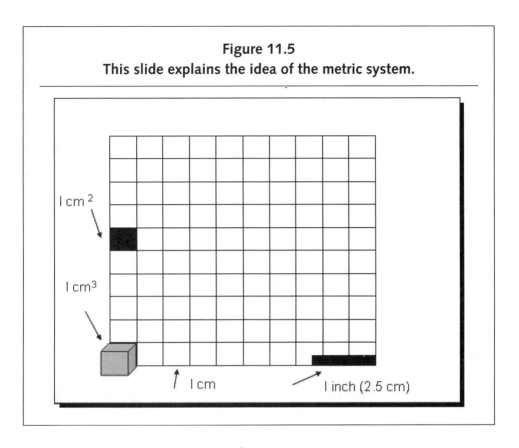

Figure 11.5
This slide explains the idea of the metric system.

Insert a Cube AutoShape (or Shape) in the Basic Shapes section to represent the cubic centimeter. Place it on one of the square centimeters. Fine-tune the placement using the arrow keys. To represent one inch on the one-centimeter select the Rectangle AutoShape, place it on the grid, and resize it so that its length is 2.5 centimeters. Fill with the black color.

Now you can talk about decimeters. Copy and paste the slide with centimeters; change "cm" to "dm." Indicate that the side of the square is 10 dm, which is 1 m or 100 cm. Insert the right brace at the side of the square, using the Right Brace AutoShape (or Shape) from the Basic Shapes section. Place it at the side of the square.

Insert a text box, and type **1 m** at the brace, as shown in Figure 11.6. Explain that one cubic decimeter is one thousand cubic centimeters. One cubic decimeter of water is one liter, or one thousand grams. It is also one kilogram.

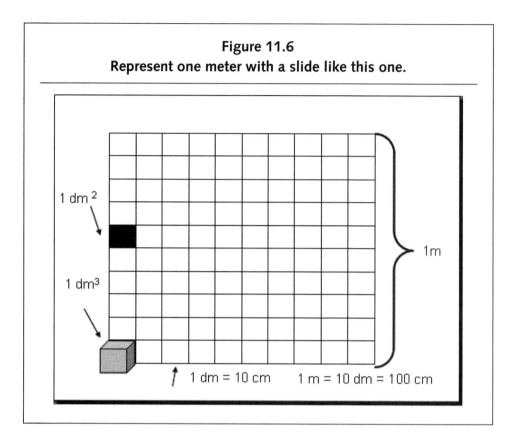

Figure 11.6
Represent one meter with a slide like this one.

1 dm^2

1 dm^3

1m

1 dm = 10 cm   1 m = 10 dm = 100 cm

For instructions on using text boxes, see "Inserting and Editing Text Boxes" in Chapter 2.

Finally, you can represent the cubic meter. Using the Rectangle AutoShape (Shape), draw a cube.

Insert a table with ten columns and ten rows to represent a hundred square decimeters (one thousand square centimeters). Adjust the grid in the side of the cube. You can fine-tune using the arrow keys. Place a brace by the side of the cube to indicate one meter (see Figure 11.7). Explain that one cubic meter is one thousand cubic decimeters or one hundred thousand cubic centimeters. As long as one cubic decimeter of water is one liter or one kilogram, explain that one thousand liters of water equals one thousand kilograms or one metric ton.

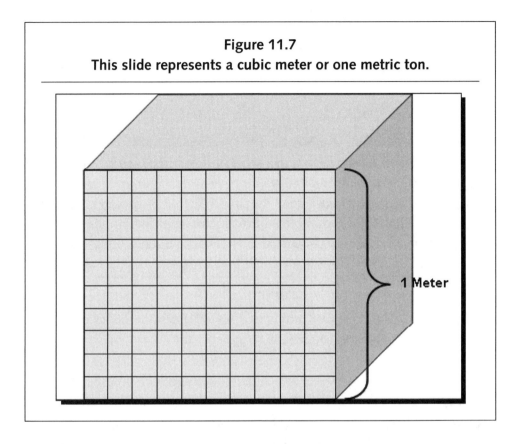

Figure 11.7
This slide represents a cubic meter or one metric ton.

1 Meter

Further explanations may include: one thousand meters equals one kilometer, one kilometer equals 1.6 miles, and so on.

As you can see, you can visually show many mathematical concepts in PowerPoint. With practice, you'll become an expert at using PowerPoint's tools to explain them.

SCIENCE

Students begin to study science in grades 2 to 5. At this stage it is very important to develop their interest in and curiosity about science, and PowerPoint offers great opportunities for that. It is in science that pictures, especially real-life photographs, play a really critical role. Combined with real nature sounds (birds chirping, sounds of water, sounds of the jungle, and so on), well-designed PowerPoint projects can create the "effect of presence." Here are some ideas for projects.

Life Cycle Projects

Life cycles of animals, such as butterflies, moths, bees, mosquitoes, frogs, and fish are easy to portray in PowerPoint. A great variety of pertinent material and great pictures are available on the Internet. You can also find animal sounds there.

 Use your favorite search engine to search on animal, insect, or nature and Wav. Save the sounds in a separate folder that you create for sounds, or in the folder where you have saved your presentation. If you use a special folder, copy the sound to your presentation's folder before inserting it. For more information on inserting sounds, see Chapter 3. You can use such sounds as background sounds—just make sure they aren't so loud that they drown you out!

If you want the sound to play throughout several slides or even the entire presentation, you can make the sound loop over and over.

HOW TO DO IT

- *Windows 2000/2002/2003:* Insert the sound into the slide. Click Automatically to the message, "How do you want the sound to start in the slide show?" Choose Slide Show ➢ Custom Animation. If you have other animations on the list, select the sound and click the Up Re-order arrow to put it at the top of the list. Choose With Previous from the Start drop-down list. From the sound's drop-down list, choose Effect Options. In the Stop Playing section of the Play Sound dialog box, choose the After option and enter as many slides as you need. Click OK. Now right-click the sound icon and choose Edit Sound Object to open the Sound Options dialog box, as shown in Figure 11.8. Check the Loop Until Stopped check box and click OK.

- *Windows 2007:* Insert the sound into the slide. Click Automatically to the message, "How do you want the sound to start in the slide show?" On the Animations tab, click Custom Animation. If you have other animations on the list, select the sound and click the Up Re-order arrow to put it at the top of the list. Choose With Previous from the Start drop-down list. From the sound's drop-down list, choose Effect Options. In the Stop Playing section of the Play Sound dialog box, choose the After option and enter as many slides as you need. Click OK. Now select the sound icon and click the Sound Tools Options tab. In the Sound Options group, check the Loop Until Stopped check box.

- *Mac 2001/X/2004:* Insert the sound into the slide. Click Automatically to the message, "How do you want the sound to start in the slide show?" Choose Slide Show ➤ Custom Animation. If you have other animations on the list, select the sound and click the Up Re-order arrow to put it at the top of the list. Choose With Previous from the Start drop-down list. From the sound's drop-down list, choose Effect Options. In the Stop Playing section of the Play Sound dialog box, choose the After option and enter as many slides as you need. Click OK. Now Ctrl-click the sound icon and choose Edit Sound Object to open the Sound Options dialog box, as shown in Figure 11.8. Check the Loop Until Stopped check box and click OK.

Figure 11.8
The Sound Options dialog box lets you loop a sound.

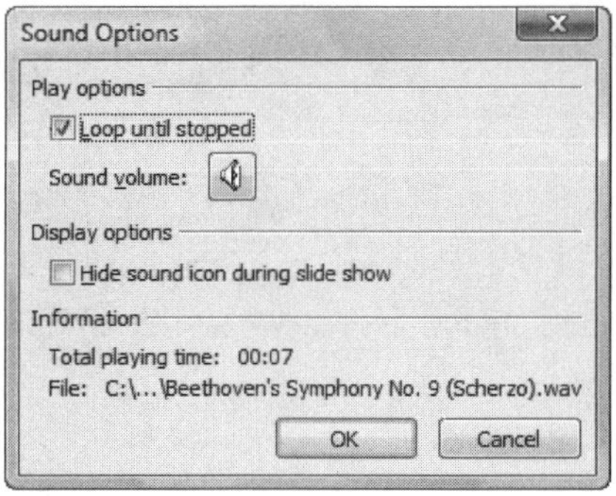

Animals and Their Habitats

Children love to see slide shows of animals and their habitats. For example, "Where do bears live?" is a great idea for a PowerPoint project. Other ideas are hibernating animals, baby animals, animals in danger (on the verge of extinction), and sea animals versus land animals (such as sea turtles and tortoises).

The list of animal projects you can create is endless. Whatever you choose, we offer the following recommendations:

- Use as many pictures as possible.
- Use as little text as possible.
- Use sounds, perhaps including some popular children's songs.
- Include pictures of baby animals, because children at this age tend to identify with baby animals.

The Water Cycle Revisited

One of the most popular projects during these grades is on the water cycle. Chapter 2 contains instructions for such a project, and in Chapter 3 (see "Adding a Sound or Music File") we showed you how to add a related sound.

In Chapter 2, we added a simple animation of arrows to demonstrate the water cycle, but if you're ambitious, you can create complex animations, like the one shown in Figure 11.9.

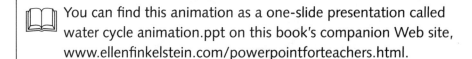

You can find this animation as a one-slide presentation called water cycle animation.ppt on this book's companion Web site, www.ellenfinkelstein.com/powerpointforteachers.html.

You can add an interactive chart of the water cycle, with clickable pictures representing different parts of the water cycle: precipitation, evaporation, and so on. We explained how to create clickable areas of a slide in Chapter 6.

Parts of a Cell

Use the idea of clickability to create an interactive picture of a cell: create a clickable picture of a plant or animal cell with hot spots on its parts. For example,

Figure 11.9
This complex animation of the water cycle includes precipitation, transpiration, runoff, and evaporation.

The water cycle

clicking on an organelle (mitochondrion, ribosome, and so on) might display the name of that organelle. Employ this PowerPoint activity both as an interactive exercise to learn and memorize the structure of the cell or as a quiz. In the former case students click on different parts of the cell and get feedback on the names of the parts; in the latter case they get assignments like "Click on an organelle" with the corresponding "Good job!" or "Try again!" feedback. Chapter 5 contains detailed instructions on how to create quizzes.

The Solar System

One of the most exciting and visually appealing PowerPoint projects at these grade levels is on the solar system. Use a black background. Pictures of planets and moons look especially gorgeous on a black background. You'll find many pictures of planets and moons on the Web, and most of them are shown against a black background. In case the background is light, if you have a Mac version, use the Lasso button on the Picture toolbar to carve the pictures from their background. If you have a PC version, you can crop the picture, and if some light background is left in the corners, cover these corners up with freeforms.

HOW TO DO IT

- *Windows 2000/2002/2003:* Select AutoShapes ➢ Lines ➢ Freeform. Trace around the light parts of the remaining picture background and connect the lines, so that the light area is completely surrounded. Double-click on the line and select the black color in the Fill section.

- *Windows 2007:* On the Insert tab, select Shapes ➢ Lines ➢ Freeform. Trace around the light parts of the remaining picture background and connect the lines, so that the light area is completely surrounded. Click on the line, click the Shape Fill button, and select the black color.

- *Mac 2001/X/2004:* Select AutoShapes ➢ Lines ➢ Freeform. Trace around the light parts of the remaining picture background and connect the lines, so that the light area is completely surrounded. Double-click on the line and select the black color in the Fill section.

Choose an interesting musical background for a project on the solar system—for example, the theme from Stanley Kubrick's film *2001: A Space Odyssey* (actually a piece by Richard Strauss titled *Also Sprach Zarathustra*). Search the Web for a midi file with this name. It is especially exciting to time the animation of the planets with the music: you can make the solar system zoom in slowly when the theme reaches its crescendo.

You can also add some stars to the black background. From the Stars and Banners group of AutoShapes (Shapes), choose the four-point star. Change the fill from its default color to white. Make it smaller. Copy and paste to make several stars. Treat the stars as a group to make more copies. Spread the stars on the window of the slide. Send them to the back of the order so that you can put the planets' pictures on top.

HOW TO DO IT

- *Windows 2000/2002/2003:* Right-click the picture and select Order ➢ Send to Back.

- *Windows 2007:* Right-click the picture and select Send to Back ➢ Send to Back.

- *Mac 2001/X/2004:* Ctrl-click the picture and select Order ➢ Send to Back.

Using Your Own Pictures and Video

PowerPoint science projects can use pictures and video clips taken in labs and in nature. You or your students photograph the details of the objects of study. Simple projects like "The Growth and Development of Tomatoes" can include pictures taken by you or students at all stages of the process. You can use the Callout group of AutoShapes (Shapes) to add labels to the photos. PowerPoint is an excellent medium through which to create projects using these pictures.

SOCIAL STUDIES

Social studies projects range from geography to history and include such topics as continents, nations of the world, cultures, wars, and historic events. As we already suggested, interactive maps can make such projects effective and fun. You can add a clickable map to any geography or history project. See Chapter 6 for details.

Another good idea is to create games based on the TV shows *Jeopardy* or *Who Wants to Be a Millionaire?* to review significant parts of the material covered. See Chapter 8 for instructions on how to create games in PowerPoint.

Field trip photographs, photographs of the local sites, and so on, provide great material for PowerPoint projects on social studies of the local community: the history of the city or town, great people of the community, community workers, and so on.

Students love to dress up in pilgrim and Indian costumes. You might take photos of the students and use PowerPoint to retell the story of the pilgrims. If parents haven't been invited to see the students in costume, print out books of the slides for the students to take home, or post the presentation on the school's Web site.

Again, we suggest using more pictures and less text. Audio files are a big plus—think about national anthems to accompany geography projects; use sounds of ancient music or wind in history projects.

SUMMARY

In this chapter we offered ideas for projects suitable for grades 2 to 5 in language arts, math, science, and social studies.

PowerPoint Projects for Grades 6 to 12

A s students move into middle and high school, their subjects become more diverse and complex, and so do their class activities, homework assignments, and projects. As children grow, their attention span lengthens. This suggests more sophisticated and larger projects. PowerPoint is not only a medium for class projects and activities but also a tool for individual projects. In many schools, PowerPoint begins to oust paper-based or trifold projects for science or social studies fairs. More teachers devise assignments in PowerPoint and post them with online delivery systems like EdLine, Blackboard, or Moodle, or use the school's own Web site.

PowerPoint projects can include short five- to eight-minute demonstrations to introduce new material as well as large gamelike projects to review vast material. PowerPoint can replace the chalkboard in explaining math problems or chemical reactions. It's an excellent means to create projects on art and literature, music, and social studies. This chapter offers some specific suggestions for you to use.

LIBRARY

With PowerPoint you can offer "book talks," which introduce books to students, as well as presentations on using the library and on library science.

Book Talks

School librarians may use PowerPoint to supplement book talks and introduce new books to students. For example, they can create a PowerPoint presentation on the book, using pictures, text, and in some cases, voice-recorded messages or music. To enhance student interest in a particular book or subject, they can run such presentations on the library's televisions. A PC to TV converter, such as Averkey (aver.com/ppd/averkey550.html) allows users to connect a computer to a television or a number of televisions. You loop the presentation, so that the project continues to play over and over until you hit Escape. Choose Slide Show ➤ Set Up Show. (In PowerPoint 2007, click the Slide Show tab and click Set Up Slide Show.) Check the Loop Continuously until 'Esc' check box and click OK.

You can also show the project with a set time for each slide, so that it advances from slide to slide automatically. Students who come to the library to study or exchange books can view these PowerPoint shows.

HOW TO DO IT

- *Windows 2000/2002/2003:* Choose Slide Show ➤ Slide Transition. In the Advance Slide section, check Automatically After and enter a number of seconds in the text box.

- *Windows 2007:* Click the Animations tab. In the Advance Slide section, check Automatically After and enter a number of seconds in the text box.

- *Mac 2001/X/2004:* Choose Slide Show ➤ Slide Transition. In the Advance Slide section, check Automatically After and enter a number of seconds in the text box.

In all versions, choose Apply to All (or Apply to All Slides) if you want the same time duration for all the slides; select Apply if you want the time duration for this particular slide only.

Pictures of the book covers can be obtained on the Web from sites that sell the books (www.barnesandnoble.com, www.booksamillion.com, www.amazon.com, and others). Book covers or pictures from books may also be scanned to enhance PowerPoint book talks. Add catchy little phrases on each slide to grab the students' attention, as well as the call number of the book. A show like this can include several books, normally of the same genre.

Book Reference System

An excellent PowerPoint library science project is an introduction to the book reference system. The project can be broken into separate presentations. A short quiz (review) after each show, as we explain in Chapter 5, is extremely helpful.

Start with genres. The presentation would thus describe genres, their distinctions, and what role they play in the reference system. Further presentations may include the Dewey decimal system and the main properties of a book (publisher, title, author, illustrator, table of contents, chapters, subchapters, and so on).

Another project idea is to teach students how to use dictionaries, both online dictionaries and traditional dictionaries. Again, a short review at the end helps students retain the material, especially if it includes some funny pictures and sounds. For example, a quiz could contain multiple-choice questions on which reference source would be most appropriate for a particular subject: dictionaries (of various types), thesauruses, almanacs, atlases, encyclopedias, and so on. A little competition can make such a quiz even more fun.

LITERATURE

PowerPoint projects on literature have a lot in common with those in library science. In fact, it's a great idea to offer joint projects that cover both subjects and involve both the teacher and the librarian. Such projects may examine genres of literature, styles, stylistic devices, literary elements, vocabulary development, and so on.

You can also create PowerPoint projects on great writers, poets, literary movements, and literary works. Describing the contemporary historical, political, or cultural setting makes presentations on writers, poets, and literary works more engaging. For example, a project on John Steinbeck's *Grapes of Wrath* could include a description of the Great Depression, some facts and figures about this time, and pictures, photographs, and music from that era. A project on Shakespeare could incorporate pictures of Stratford-upon-Avon, other pictures from that time, graphics, and music ("Green Sleeves" is one possibility). You can select some interesting backgrounds or create your own (see Chapter 2 for details). You can even use specific fonts to enhance the flavor of the time, Storybook being one of many possibilities.

 As we have already suggested, PowerPoint class games provide excellent opportunities to refresh students' memories about large portions of covered material. PowerPoint class games can also help prepare students for tests.

Literary and stylistic devices are great topics for PowerPoint projects: they can cover flashback, metaphor, foreshadowing, symbolism, metonymy, contrast, comparison, analogy, and more. Provide examples of the devices and explain their meanings, then offer samples of the devices for students to recognize through multiple-choice or true-false quizzes or reviews.

PowerPoint is also a great tool for teaching grammar. Projects in which students contrast correct and incorrect grammatical usages with immediate feedback can be very effective ("do well" versus "do good," "should have done" versus "should have did," "shook" versus "shaked," and so on). Again, you may want to focus on typical mistakes ("Can I do this?" versus "May I do this?"). Double negatives, run-on sentences, and incorrect usage make great projects.

As students' vocabulary develops, it is important that they learn to choose the correct word. PowerPoint projects might contrast words like "discrete" and "discreet," "cue" and "queue," and "envy" and "ennui" in context. Of course, games that ask students about the meanings of the words are always fun.

HISTORY AND GEOGRAPHY

By the sixth grade students have some basic knowledge of history and geography. Such PowerPoint projects as "Cradles of Civilization," "The Great Silk Road," or "The Crusades" combine both history and geography and refer students to a specific place and time. A good PowerPoint presentation on ancient Egypt, Rome, or Greece can produce a profound and long-lasting impression. We've seen students mesmerized by such historic characters as Cleopatra, Julius Caesar, and Spartacus.

Of course, it takes time, effort, taste, and persistence to create a good PowerPoint project on any of these topics. However, it is important to think about the effect of the project, which can be much greater than that of a simple lecture or a chapter in the textbook. Students at this level already begin to understand that you have done the project for them, and they appreciate your work. Remember, you can always reuse the project next semester or year, and you can always improve it and relate it to the present—discuss the influence of the Roman government on the structure and functions of the U.S. government, for example. This is the beauty of PowerPoint.

Literally tons of material are available on the Web for such projects. Any search will bring multiple pictures and other information. As we already suggested, you can also scan pictures from books and journals and use them in your PowerPoint projects.

Some specific project suggestions are as follows:

- *"From Hunting to Cattle Breeding and Agriculture."* This project explains how humans developed from hunter-gatherers to cattle breeders and plant growers. Use pictures of cavemen, prehistoric hunting tools, varieties of animals that were later domesticated (goats, sheep, boars, antelopes, chickens), ancient tools used to till the soil, stone and bronze axes, baskets and pots to store seeds, and so on. It is also important to describe the geographical aspects of this development (fertile soils, presence of water, favorable climate, and so on).

- *"The History of Money: From Barter to Credit Cards."* The project describes the origin of money, its development from gold and other precious metals to paper-based money and eventually to plastic (credit and debit cards). You can draw a parallel between the level of the development of a society and the level of monetary transactions. Abundant pictures of money, coins, and other related items are available on the Web.

- *"The History of Writing."* This project describes how the ancient civilizations developed the idea of recording and storing information using signs and characters. It is very interesting for students to learn the differences between hieroglyphs and letters, the relationship between a character and a word, a notion, or an idea it denotes. The project may not be able to cover all the ancient and modern alphabets and sign systems used in writing, but it should certainly offer students insights into the development of civilizations and cultures.

- *Major ancient civilizations.* Present projects on Egyptian, Greek, Roman, Indian, Chinese, and other cultures.

- *The history of major religions.* Discuss Christianity, Hinduism, Buddhism, or Islam. These projects should offer insights into the origins and influences of the major religions, and highlight their common values.

- *European history.* Examine medieval times, the Renaissance, the Reformation, the Industrial Revolution, and more. Unlike the projects on prehistoric and ancient times, these can include music from the era played in the background.

We already described how to create an interactive geographic map in Chapter 6. Using the same techniques you can create great projects on the geography of the United States and other countries. Because the geographic and political composition of the United States is quite complex, you may want to create such projects on regions rather than the entire country: New England, the first thirteen states, the southeastern states, the Gulf states, the Midwest, and so on. You can always put such projects on your Web site or EdLine to help your students review for a test. You may also want to include names of the capitals of the states, their populations, the year they became a state, and other information.

An endless list of topics could be effectively presented in the form of a PowerPoint project. It is up to your discretion and imagination to identify such topics and translate them into the language of PowerPoint. We recommend that you stick to the golden rule that we have already suggested: be stingy with words and generous with pictures.

CIVICS

We recommend projects on the structure of the U.S. government, both state and federal, their relations and subordination, the purposes of the governments, and their relationship to the Constitution. Such projects involve diagrams and flowcharts. You may want to use AutoShapes (called Shapes in PowerPoint 2007) to describe the relationships and connections between the elements of the government and its branches. See Figure 12.1 for an example.

Projects on citizenship may include the history of immigration, rights and responsibilities of a U.S. citizen, and so on.

SCIENCE

We've already described a project on the solar system for the younger grades (see Chapter 11). A more detailed and sophisticated project includes more data, more

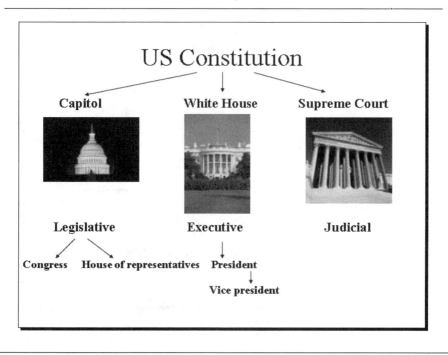

Figure 12.1
Use arrows and other AutoShapes (Shapes) to represent structures and relationships in civics.

pictures of planets and moons, and more facts and figures. Now that students have greater math skills, they can compare the mass of the planets and their distances from the sun. You may want to include physical and chemical data on gravity, magnetic fields, and composition of gases on the planets.

 From a purely aesthetic point of view, we suggest including some classical background music. Great pieces of the musical giants Bach, Mozart, or Beethoven can only accentuate the grandeur and cosmic beauty of the universe. Even in midi format, such works as "Air on a G String" by Bach or the first movement of Symphony Number 40 by Mozart amplify the impression of the majesty of the images.

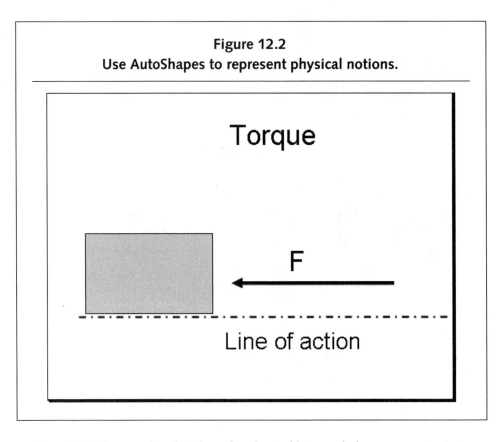

Figure 12.2
Use AutoShapes to represent physical notions.

Torque

F

Line of action

PowerPoint is a good tool to describe physical laws and phenomena. Projects on physics may include measurement, vectors, motion, force, torque, Newton's laws, work, energy, and power. It's a good idea to represent some physical notions with lines, arrows, and other basic shapes. It is also important to animate these shapes to make them more visually convincing. For example, you can animate the shapes denoting torque and applied force, as shown in Figure 12.2.

We explained the principles of animation in Chapter 2. For this animation, we wanted the box, the letter F, and the arrow to crawl in from the left. To select all three objects, we dragged across all three items to enclose them in a selection box. Then we added the Crawl In animation and set its direction to From Left. We used the Very Slow speed. Then we set the Start setting to With Previous so all three items moved simultaneously.

Earth science or geology projects can employ the same techniques we described in Chapter 6 for interactive maps. Different kinds of rocks and layers of Earth's crust can be represented in the form of interactive clickable pictures.

Biology and life science provide particularly wonderful opportunities for PowerPoint projects. Teachers can use a plethora of pictures and natural sounds to develop projects on all kinds of plants and animals, living environments, habitats, evolution, adaptation, endangered species, symbiosis, life cycles, reproduction, and so on. The list of projects, once again, is endless. We made many suggestions in Chapter 11; you just need to adapt the level of content for older children.

By employing nonlinearity, as we explained in Chapter 7, you can create problem-based activities. A nonlinear presentation on the taxonomy of animals and plants, for example, will increase understanding and retention, providing better and deeper understanding of the categories and subcategories. Problem-based activities include games, quizzes, and interactive maps and pictures.

You may want to create clickable graphics (described in Chapter 6) in biology and life science for complex structures with multiple elements, such as the intestines, plant and animal cells, the structure of the human heart, and the parts of a flower.

The project will allow for clicking on various elements of these complex structures, such as the nucleus, to identify them. They can also provide the corresponding positive or negative feedback.

Sometimes it is difficult to find a picture of a cell or intestines without labels and lines or arrows. If the picture is taken from the Internet, the words and lines are a part of the picture and you cannot simply erase them without changing the picture. Editing a picture with a picture editor may be tedious and even unsuccessful. Instead, to cover up existing labels and arrows, use a technique that is similar to creating hot spots, as described in Chapter 6.

1. Use the Freeform shape to trace around the labels and arrows. Once you complete tracing around a label or arrow and close the line, an AutoShape (Shape) forms.

2. Double-click on the line of the AutoShape (or right-click/Ctrl-click and choose Format Shape) to open the Format AutoShape dialog box.

3. Set the fill to white or the color of the background.

4. Set the line to No Line.

The AutoShape will cover the undesirable label or arrow. You can also edit pictures in picture editors like Adobe Photoshop or Corel Paint Shop Pro.

MATH

Math in middle and high school employs different formulas, special symbols, and equations. Although you can use PowerPoint's standard text to create equations, you'll soon find yourself very frustrated. Instead, use Microsoft Equation 3.0.

 Unfortunately, Equation 3.0 is not always installed by default. To tell if you have it, choose Insert ≻ Object. (In PowerPoint 2007, choose Object on the Insert tab.) In the Insert Object dialog box, you should see an item called Microsoft Equation 3.0. If you don't, you need to install it. To do so, you will need administrative rights to your computer to do Office updates. Also, if Office was originally installed from a CD, you will need access to that CD. You may need to check with your school's technology coordinator.

HOW TO DO IT

- *Windows:* Insert the Windows CD into your CD-ROM drive. Choose Start ≻ Control Panel. In the Control Panel, double-click Add or Remove Programs (in Classic View) or Programs and Features (in Windows Vista). From the list of programs, choose Microsoft Office. Click Change. Choose Add or Remove Features and click Next or Continue. At this point, you may need to choose Advanced Customization of Applications and click Update. From the list of Office components, double-click Office Tools. Right-click Equation Editor and choose Run from My Computer. Then click Update to install Equation 3.0.

- *Mac:* For version 2004, insert the Office CD into your CD-ROM drive. On the desktop double-click the Microsoft Office 2004 icon. In the Setup window, double-click Office Setup Assistant. Follow Steps 1 through 4. For Step 5 (Installation), for Select the Installation, click the location of your current installation of Office. For Select the Type of Installation You Want, choose Custom. From the list of Office components, click the Office Tools arrow and choose Equation Editor. Click Install. (*Note:* For Office 2001/X, insert the Office CD and find the Value Pack Installer in the Value Pack folder. Double-click the Value Pack Installation application. Choose Equation Editor and click Install or Continue. When done, click Quit.)

To open Equation 3.0, choose Insert Object, choose Microsoft Equation 3.0, and click OK. (In PowerPoint 2007, choose Object on the Insert tab.) Equation 3.0 opens, as shown in Figure 12.3.

Each button contains a category of symbols or templates for creating equations. Hover the cursor over a button to see a "tooltip" describing the category. Click the button to display a gallery of options. Sometimes you just click a symbol to insert it. For items like square roots or powers, you click a template and then enter letters or numbers in the box that appears. Try out the various options as well as the menu items to learn more about this program.

Figure 12.3
You can create complex equations with Equation 3.0.

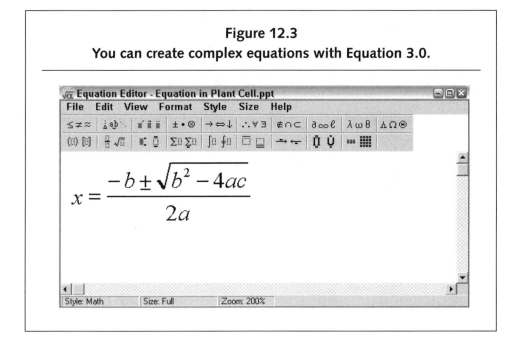

To return to Microsoft PowerPoint, on the File menu in Equation Editor click Exit and Return to *Presentation*. You will now see the equation on your slide. You can move it or resize it like an image.

 In Chapter 16, we describe a program called MathType, which offers more options for creating equations.

PowerPoint projects on geometry require the use of AutoShapes (Shapes). Again, AutoShapes provide excellent tools for such projects. For example, take a project on the area of triangles. To prove that a triangle has half of the area of a rectangle of the same height and length, you need to draw two equal triangles and place them so that they form a rectangle. Follow these steps:

1. Choose Right Triangle from the Basic Shapes category of AutoShapes/Shapes. Click on the slide to insert the triangle.

2. Adjust the triangle's size and position as desired. You may also want to change its outline and color.

3. With the triangle selected, copy and paste it. You now have two identical triangles, as shown in Figure 12.4.

4. Drag the second triangle's green dot to turn the second triangle upside down.

5. Use the arrow keys to fine-tune positioning the second triangle to the side of the first one to form a rectangle, as shown in Figure 12.5.

6. Use the same technique to form a rectangle from two isosceles or equilateral triangles. Once you have positioned the triangles to form a rectangle, use the Line tool from AutoShapes (Shapes) to draw a perpendicular line from the top of the first triangle to its bottom, and another perpendicular from the upper corner down to the extended bottom line of the first triangle.

7. To make the extension of the bottom line and both perpendicular lines dashed, double-click on the lines to open the Format AutoShape dialog box. From the Dashed drop-down list, choose one of the dashed line types. The result is shown in Figure 12.6.

Figure 12.4
Two identical triangles with a green dot.

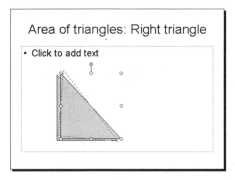

Area of triangles: Right triangle

• Click to add text

Figure 12.5
Two triangles form a rectangle.

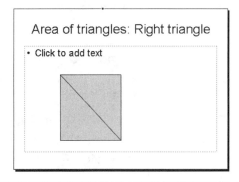

Area of triangles: Right triangle

• Click to add text

Figure 12.6
Use two isosceles triangles to form a rectangle to show the theorem of area of triangles.

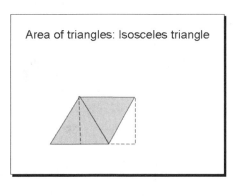

Area of triangles: Isosceles triangle

Employ similar techniques to display the theorems of area of a circle, volume of a can or a pyramid, and so on.

 See Chapter 16 for more information on using PowerPoint for geometry, including 3-D shapes.

ART AND MUSIC

There is no doubt that art projects can be enhanced with the PowerPoint medium. In our experience many PowerPoint projects on the arts have been appealing, informative, and designed with great taste.

Regular topics include works of an individual artist or sculptor, or on schools and movements. Among such topics are "Claude Monet and Edward Manet," "French Impressionists," "Leonardo the Artist," "Cubism," and so on. Reduce the text to names, titles, and years. Use the PowerPoint pointer option to bring attention to particular parts of the painting instead of using the regular cursor.

 See Chapter 4 to refresh your knowledge of the Pointer Options feature.

You may want to enhance your project with appropriate music. The art of the Renaissance looks so much better with the music of Bach, Mozart, or Scarlatti playing in the background. Impressionism calls for Debussy, Wagner, Ravel, and other such period musicians.

Just as music serves as a great background for projects on the arts, paintings and beautiful images provide vibrant backgrounds for projects on music. For example, Bach's *Badinerie* sounds exquisite against images of butterflies hovering over a sunlit meadow; Grieg's *In the Hall of the Mountain King* almost certainly requires images of a dark and somber mountain gorge. It is easy to create a clickable link or links to the slides with the music you wish to play. Follow these steps:

1. Create a hot spot or spots on the slide. For example, on the Menu slide on Tchaikovsky, write "Listen to *October*."

2. Hyperlink it to a slide with the *October* file inserted as a sound file.

3. Set the music file's Start value in the Custom Animation task pane or dialog box to Start with Previous. (If the slide contains other animation, place the audio file first in order by selecting it and click the Up Re-Order arrow.)

4. Insert an appropriate picture to accentuate the mood of the music.

5. Create a hyperlink back to the menu slide.

 Chapter 16 describes some art projects aimed at the college level. Many of these ideas are also appropriate for middle and high school students.

INTERDISCIPLINARY PROJECTS

More and more teachers attempt to employ interdisciplinary methods of teaching. One project thus covers several subjects—for example, a project on water can include information about physics (physical properties of water), math (amounts of water on the Earth), biology (the importance of water for animals, plants, and humans), social studies (the historic significance of water, water pollution), art and music (water in art and music), or literature and language arts (water in poetry and literature). Of course, such projects may require coordination among several teachers, which is not always easy to do. Still, interdisciplinary projects help students integrate their knowledge from different subjects; they help develop deeper and wider understanding of subjects and connect the subjects to real life.

PowerPoint is an excellent tool for such projects, because it combines all media, is user-friendly, and is powerful. We suggest that interdisciplinary PowerPoint projects become regular assignments for students. In Chapters 14 and 15 we will talk about how to teach PowerPoint to students.

SUMMARY

In this chapter we offered some ideas for PowerPoint projects in the middle and high schools as well as some tips on how to make these projects more interesting and effective.

We discussed ideas and techniques for library projects as well as literature, history and geography, civics, science and math, and art and music projects. We ended with a few words about creating interdisciplinary projects.

Online Resources for Teachers Using PowerPoint

This book can't begin to cover everything you might want to know about PowerPoint, so we've collected numerous resources on the Internet, where you can find more techniques, presentations, guidelines, games, and tips—all especially for teachers.

Some sites are general resources and they often contain links to other sites. Some specialize in games. A number of sites come from school districts that have pooled presentations their teachers have created. Some of these offer hundreds of presentations that you can download.

We've collected some articles on PowerPoint and education. These articles will help you round out your understanding of how PowerPoint can be effective as a teaching tool. Some excellent sites offer guidelines and rubrics for the best use of PowerPoint.

Many of the Web sites fit into more than one category, so be sure to read through the entire chapter to find what you need.

Don't forget our own companion Web site for this book—www.ellenfinkelstein. com/powerpointforteachers.html. There you'll find sample presentations, contributions by teachers like you, Internet resources, and more. In fact, so that you don't have to type all the Internet addresses in this chapter, you can find this entire chapter at the companion Web site, with live links—all you have to do is click.

As you go through this chapter, remember that Web sites can change or disappear. We checked all the URLs while writing this book, but as time passes, some may no longer be valid. Just try another resource.

POWERPOINT AND EDUCATION RESOURCES

We aren't the only ones who think PowerPoint and teachers are a perfect match, or that teachers need more information on how to use PowerPoint effectively in the classroom. A number of sites are either devoted to the topic or contain excellent resources.

We might as well start with Microsoft itself, which offers resources especially for teachers. At www.microsoft.com/education/tutorials.mspx, you can find a homepage for tutorials for teachers on all Microsoft products. There, you can choose your version of Microsoft Office. Another page, How-To Articles from Microsoft, at www.microsoft.com/education/howto.mspx, includes four articles especially meant for educators. Click the More link for over a dozen additional articles.

Perhaps the oldest list of PowerPoint resources is Tracy Marks's site at www.geocities.com/~webwinds/classes/powerpt.htm. This site hasn't been updated for a while but is still referred to often by teachers.

The Learning Light e-Learning Centre has a library page that includes a long list of resources for PowerPoint at www.e-learningcentre.co.uk/eclipse/Resources/usingms.htm#powerpoint.

Using PowerPoint in the Classroom at www.saskschools.ca/~qvss/technology/powerpoint_module.htm is a project of the Qu'Appelle Valley School Division in Regina, Saskatchewan, Canada. This resource has several pages that include a list of ways to use PowerPoint (informational presentations, procedure and how-to presentations, interactive presentations, and so on), and a step-by-step workbook. There are some excellent sample presentations, including some created by students. Note that these were saved in HTML format and you'll need to use the Internet Explorer browser to view them.

Alice Christy's Using PowerPoint in the Classroom, at www.west.asu.edu/achristie/powerpoint, is a list of links to articles, tips, and tutorials. The professor also offers her own PowerPoint presentation on the value of using PowerPoint in the classroom.

Internet4Classrooms' PowerPoint page, at www.internet4classrooms.com/on-line_powerpoint.htm, offers tutorials, project ideas for the classroom (vocabulary review, spelling activities), and eighteen presentations on various topics that you can download. There are tutorials on various PowerPoint features and presentations that show the use of these features. The site also has links to lots of PowerPoint games.

Indezine.com is one of the premier PowerPoint Web sites and it contains an article, "PowerPoint and Education," at www.indezine.com/products/power-point/ppedu.html. The end of this article contains a good set of links to further resources. Continue to peruse this site for its many other PowerPoint resources and tips. It's run by Geetesh Bajaj, a PowerPoint Most Valuable Professional (MVP), a Microsoft honorary designation.

SPOTLIGHT: PPT4T TEACHERS

PPT4Teachers, at www.ppt4teachers.com, sounds like it's our Web site, but it's been around longer than our book. The site is very well-rounded, so you can come back again and again to find something new. These are the main features:

- *Tips from numerous other sites, including from one of the authors of this book*
- *Two lengthy lists of useful software, hardware, and add-ons that work with PowerPoint or is otherwise useful for teachers*
- *An excellent assortment of tests, games, and rubrics*
- *Links to other sites*
- *Some free education-related backgrounds that you can use in your presentations*
- *More detailed reviews of some of the software*
- *A list of books on PowerPoint*
- *Some podcasts (MP3 sound files) on using PowerPoint in the classroom*
- *An excellent e-mail newsletter for which you can sign up*

We think that you'll find this site useful in your quest to make the best use of PowerPoint.

GAMES

We discuss games in Chapter 8, but you may want more resources for two reasons:

- You can find other types of games on some of the Web sites we list.
- You can find completed games that you can use without any work on your part.

Parade of Games in PowerPoint is an extensive set of games developed by faculty at the University of Wisconsin at Whitewater. Go to facstaff.uww.edu/jonesd/ games/index.html in Internet Explorer (the site doesn't work in Firefox) and choose one of the games on the right. In each case, you can download a sample game and a template. Buzz-Word Bingo, Flash Cards, Scavenger Hunt, and Trivia are just a few of the games available.

The University of Minnesota Center for Teaching and Learning has a site called Active Learning with PowerPoint. One of the topics, "Using PowerPoint to Play Educational Games," does an excellent job explaining some of the most popular game types and how they work in PowerPoint. Go to www1.umn.edu/ohr/teach-learn/tutorials/powerpoint/games.html. For an excellent list of resources, go to www1.umn.edu/ohr/teachlearn/tutorials/powerpoint/resources.html.

Homemade PowerPoint games is actually a project to collect PowerPoint games made by teachers and students. You can contribute your own. There's a collection (database) of games that you can download, as well as templates for your own games. Go to it.coe.uga.edu/wwild/pptgames.

SPOTLIGHT: POWERPOINT HEAVEN

Shawn Toh's PowerPoint Heaven, shown in Figure 13.1, provides PowerPoint movies, samples, games, animations, and animation tutorials. Some of the animation examples are awe-inspiring. The homepage is at pptheaven.mvps. org. Find the games at pptheaven.mvps.org/animations.html#Games. For the animation tutorials, go to pptheaven.mvps.org/tutorials.html. Toh is a Power-Point Most Valuable Professional.

Figure 13.1
PowerPoint Heaven is an excellent source for games and animations.

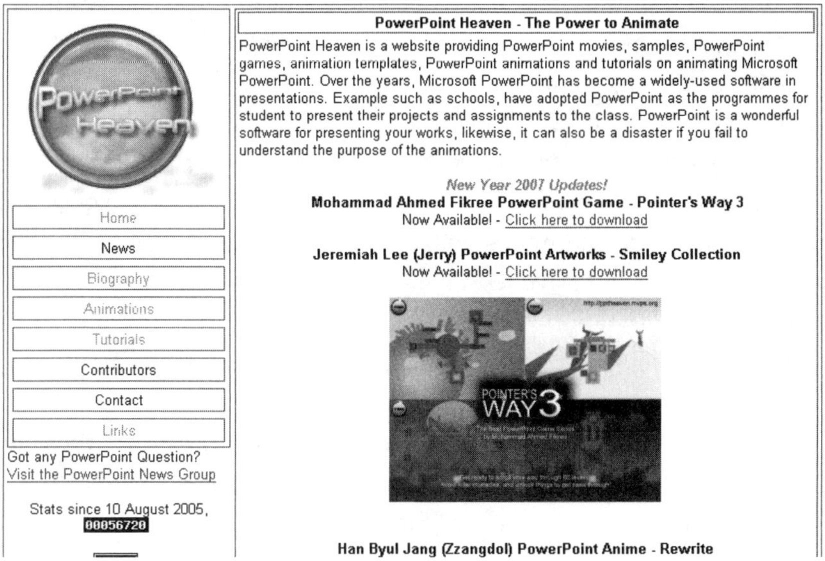

TJ's Ed Web, at www.webtj.net/hubbard/powerpoint.htm, offers a full set of PowerPoint projects for Spanish students, including some for special education students. Some are presentations, but many are *Jeopardy*-style quizzes.

You'll find several dozen *Jeopardy*-style quizzes in all disciplines for all ages at the Jeopardy Games page of the Elizabethtown, Kentucky, Hardin County Schools Web site. Go to www.hardin.k12.ky.us/res_techn/countyjeopardygames.htm.

PowerPoint Games, from Jefferson County, Tennessee, at teach.fcps.net/trt14/Power%20Point%20Games/power_point_games.htm, offers more than two dozen games, of many types and in several subject areas.

Presentation Magic has an excellent assortment of games that you can purchase. They are quite elaborate and each set contains many games. At www.powerpointmagician.com/downloads.htm, look for the PowerPak for K–12 link. You can download demo versions for free to see if you like them.

DOWNLOADABLE PRESENTATIONS

Teachers often create PowerPoint presentations to accompany their lectures, and the research that goes into these presentations makes them valuable to other teachers. A number of sites have posted presentations that you can download and use. Of course, pay attention to the age-appropriateness of each presentation.

The Nebo school district in Spanish Fork, Utah, has posted hundreds of presentations at www.nebo.edu/misc/learning_resources/ppt in the areas of general use, elementary level, secondary level, and classroom spotlights (back-to-school-night presentations, for example). You'll find presentations for social studies, science, math, history, reading, language arts, business, art, health—even home economics! This is an extensive resource.

Pete's Power Point Station, at www.pppst.com/index.html, contains presentations that you can download for social studies, language arts, science, and math. We didn't count, but this site also seems to have several hundred presentations. For example, if you click on social studies, then ancient history, then ancient India, you'll find fifteen presentations on the history of ancient India alone. Each topic likewise offers many options. See Figure 13.2.

Figure 13.2
Pete's Power Point Station.

Tennessee's Jefferson County school district has an extensive site of Power-Point presentations that you can download. The quality varies because these were created by many teachers. They cover all age levels. Some are informational, others are games. The main page is at jc-schools.net/ppt.html. Here are some discipline-specific pages:

- *Performing and visual arts:* jc-schools.net/PPTs-art.html
- *Language arts:* jc-schools.net/PPTs-la.html
- *Library:* jc-schools.net/PPTs-library.html
- *Math:* jc-schools.net/PPTs-math.html
- *Science:* jc-schools.net/PPTs-science.html
- *Social studies:* jc-schools.net/PPTs-socst.html

From the same school district, at teach.fcps.net/trt14, you can find even more PowerPoint resources for teachers.

ARTICLES

If you're interested in the more academic side of PowerPoint and education, you may want to read some articles. You may also want some ammunition to convince your school district to support the use of technology in the classroom. Either way, here are some resources that you'll find helpful.

Education World is a general educator Web site and it contains an article, "PowerPoint: Creating Classroom Presentations," at www.educationworld.com/ a_tech/tech/tech013.shtml. It includes guidelines for teachers, ideas for student projects, and a downloadable tutorial created in—what else?—PowerPoint.

The Tech Learning Web site has an article, "PowerPoint as an Interactive Multimedia Lesson," at www.techlearning.com/showArticle.jhtml?articleID=22101388. It explains how to use hyperlinks to create a quiz, just as we described in Chapter 5. The article further explains how to use the concept so that students can create their own PowerPoint quizzes. They come up with the questions, narrate the questions and answers, and the teacher puts all of them together into one presentation.

The University of Minnesota Center for Teaching and Learning has a site called Active Learning with PowerPoint at www1.umn.edu/ohr/teachlearn/tutorials/powerpoint/lecturing.html. This is a series of lectures (you can watch them in video format, too) about how to best use PowerPoint in an educational setting.

Jamie McKenzie has written an excellent article, "Scoring Power Points," at www.fno.org/sept00/powerpoints.html, about the requirements for creating meaningful PowerPoint presentations rather than meaningless ones (which he calls *PowerPointlessness*). This article runs the gamut from preparation, to content, to delivery.

An interesting article on PowerPoint accessibility at www.webaim.org/techniques/powerpoint explains how to make PowerPoint accessible to people who use screen readers (because of visual disability).

You may enjoy this article on the Kent County *Daily Times* Web site, "PowerPoint in the Classroom." After discussions in the school district that would require all fifth graders to be able to give a PowerPoint presentation, a librarian decided to go above and beyond that and inspire her second graders to do so. The project was a success and you can read about it at www.zwire.com/site/news.cfm?newsid=14551354&BRD=1718&PAG=461&dept_id=74409&rfi=6.

Teachers Improving Learning with Technology, at tilttv.blogspot.com, is a blog that is not solely about PowerPoint but often covers it. It's all about using technology in the classroom and you'll find lots of other interesting concepts as well.

While directed toward college teachers, the *Chronicle of Higher Education*'s article, "The Scholarly Lecture: How to Stand and Deliver," at chronicle.com/free/v50/i14/14b01501.htm, will be useful to many high school teachers as well.

TIPS AND TUTORIALS

Everyone can always use more help with PowerPoint. Although a book can provide more depth and be a useful reference, sometimes you just want some quick answers. Luckily, almost any site with PowerPoint content will offer useful material.

The Microsoft in Education site, at http://www.microsoft.com/education/tutorials.mspx, offers a couple of free tutorials for teachers on PowerPoint. You can download the tutorials.

SPOTLIGHT: ACTDEN'S POWERPOINT IN THE CLASSROOM

ActDen's PowerPoint in the Classroom (see Figure 13.3) is the cutest tutorial you'll ever see on PowerPoint. This is a great one to recommend to your students because of the humor. Go to www.actden.com/pp and follow Sue Special and Jim Jingle as they discuss how you can use PowerPoint's features easily.

About.com's Presentation Software page, at presentationsoft.about.com/od/classrooms, has tips for making classroom presentations and lesson plans. There are some great ideas for ways to integrate technology into the classroom, such as making a family tree, developing story writing and storytelling skills, and more. You'll also find links to games and tutorials. This site has a newsletter that you can sign up for. See Figure 13.4.

Figure 13.3
Learning PowerPoint is fun and funny at ActDen's site.

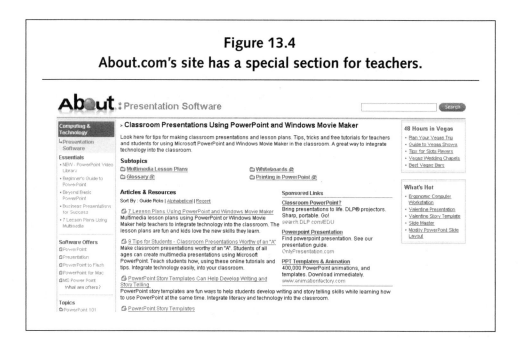

Figure 13.4
About.com's site has a special section for teachers.

Here's a site especially for science teachers: Science PowerPoint Tips and Tutorials. This blog, at visiscience.com/blog, is meant for teachers of older students. The site sells a tool that creates science slides, but it offers general advice for using PowerPoint's tools in the area of science.

The PowerPoint FAQ, at www.pptfaq.com, is the place to go if you ever have a thorny technical question about how to do something in PowerPoint, or if something just won't work right. This huge list of questions and answers was developed over several years by Steve Rindsberg, a PowerPoint MVP.

For quick and authoritative questions to your questions, go to the PowerPoint discussion group. This site is sponsored by Microsoft and you can ask your questions there, at www.microsoft.com/office/community/en-us/default.mspx?dg=microsoft.public.powerpoint&lang=en&cr=US.

SPOTLIGHT: ELLEN FINKELSTEIN

EllenFinkelstein.com, the site of one of the authors of this book, specializes in PowerPoint tips at www.ellenfinkelstein.com/powerpoint_tip.html. (See Figure 13.5.) You'll find them organized into three groups:

- *Content: Writing and organizing*
- *Design and graphics*
- *Delivery*

   You can also sign up for the free, monthly PowerPoint Tips Newsletter.

GUIDELINES AND RUBRICS

Sometimes your concern is not how to do it, but how to do it right. For this reason, guidelines on using PowerPoint are always helpful. In the educational field, rubrics help teachers grade the quality of PowerPoint presentations from a broad perspective and you can use the rubrics as guidelines for your own presentations as well.

   You can find three guides for using PowerPoint in the classroom (or perhaps not using it) from the Center for Teaching and Learning at Connecticut College at ctl.conncoll.edu/ppt/pdfs.html.

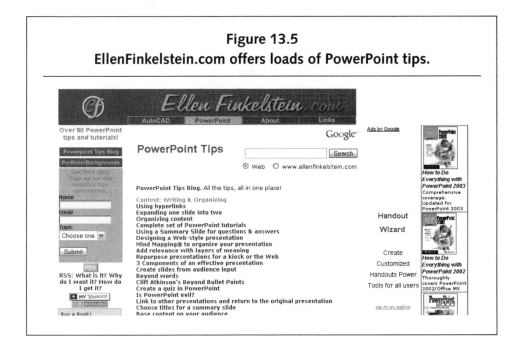

Figure 13.5
EllenFinkelstein.com offers loads of PowerPoint tips.

The Claremont McKenna College Teaching Resource Center's Web page on Evaluating Student PowerPoint presentations at www.cgu.edu/pages/762.asp provides a rubric you can use to evaluate students' presentations (or your own).

The University of Wisconsin has a complete rubric for evaluating PowerPoint presentations at www.uwstout.edu/soe/profdev/pptrubric.html.

Here's a rubric from the Art Teacher Connection: www.artteacherconnection.com/pages/powerpointrubric.htm.

This rubric, from North Carolina State University, is meant to help students to check their PowerPoint presentations before they hand them in. Go to www.ncsu.edu/midlink/mm2002.checklist.kids.htm.

SUMMARY

You could spend days going through all these resources, so don't become overwhelmed. With a few clicks here and there, you'll soon find a few favorite sites that suit your needs and perhaps come back to them whenever you need more assistance.

You may have noticed that many of the sites in this chapter are school district sites. You may want to organize the collection of PowerPoint presentations, projects, and games on your own district's site and make them available to other teachers.

PART FOUR

Teaching PowerPoint to Students

Chapter 14: Teaching PowerPoint in Elementary School
Chapter 15: Teaching PowerPoint in Middle and High School
Chapter 16: Teaching and Using PowerPoint at the College Level

This part of the book is intended for teachers of computer literacy and those enthusiastic teachers who want to develop computer-literate students.

Teaching PowerPoint in Elementary School

This chapter discusses how to teach PowerPoint to elementary school children, primarily those in grades 3 to 5, and includes ideas for projects the students can do while they're learning.

POWERPOINT AND KIDS

Is it too early to start teaching PowerPoint and other computer applications in elementary school? Let us ask another question: When is it too early?

Children today were born in the age of technology and computers. In contrast, many of their teachers were not exposed to computer technology at all as children and many more had little experience working with computers when they were in elementary school. If you feel that teaching PowerPoint in elementary school is too early, think about how an elementary school student can help you figure out the functions of your new cell phone. Think about the computer games children play before they learn to read, and about elementary school students playing computer games online with someone on the opposite side of the globe. Although we do not support the obsession with computer games that some children go through, we can certainly testify that modern elementary school children are completely prepared for PowerPoint.

Of course, not all elementary schools teach computer literacy. In our experience, PowerPoint activities in elementary school should not be regarded as teaching computer literacy. They should just be part of regular classwork with the children's regular teacher explaining how to perform certain tasks. This requires at least two conditions: a decent computer lab or an adequate number of computers in a regular classroom and an enthusiastic teacher.

Yes, children should learn how to copy and paste pictures using paper and scissors before they learn how to copy and paste pictures in PowerPoint. Yes, they should know all the letters and learn how to write before they type on a computer. And yes, they should know how to use watercolors, paints, and crayons before they learn how to edit pictures using a computer program. Then, why do we encourage PowerPoint for children in the elementary school? Here are our reasons.

- *PowerPoint is one of the most user-friendly programs around.* It combines sound, images, animation, and text. PowerPoint can become not only a tool of teaching but a tool of learning. It is not a regular tool, like books, pens, or paints. Rather, it is a tool that combines all of the above. Children can learn as a natural thing that paper, pencils, and crayons are not the only means to create projects. Projects are supposed to help children learn the world; actually, projects represent small pieces of the world. According to Vygotsky (1978), children construct their knowledge using learning tools, and computer applications are extremely powerful tools of such construction.

- *Honing computer skills at an early age is becoming increasingly important.* By the time today's elementary school children graduate from high school, computer technology will have made large steps forward, so the earlier children develop computer skills, the better.

- *Using PowerPoint develops the idea that you can make things happen and make them happen the way you want them to happen.* In other words, children begin to understand that by using computers they can program events and processes. This develops logical thinking.

- *PowerPoint may be the best introduction to computer technology.* PowerPoint is extremely helpful in developing problem-solving skills and higher-order thinking.

Here are some suggestions for elementary teachers on teaching PowerPoint.

Physical Arrangement of Computers

If you have computers in your classroom, as is common in many schools today, line them up along the walls so that you can see what is happening on the monitors. This way you can always help, make suggestions, and approach each student with ease. Swivel chairs are a great idea, so that your students can see your explanations on the large screen and easily turn back to their computers. Arrange computers in the same fashion in the computer lab, if you have one.

The first sessions will be the hardest, but as children get used to the procedures, things will settle down.

Learning PowerPoint, Working on Projects

Have your children write a brief story—about the three little pigs and the wolf using only pictures, for example—and then get them to retell the story. Make the pictures available for them by placing them on the desktop of their computers. Explain how to insert the pictures in the presentation. Later such projects can include sounds, music, and animation. You'll be amazed at how easily and quickly children pick up computer operations and memorize them.

Do not emphasize that you are "working with PowerPoint"; simply mention it. The focus of the work should be on creating a story, or a project, not on learning PowerPoint. Your students should have their own folders with their projects, and we recommend that you have the backup copies.

Working with PowerPoint should not take up too much of their regular classroom work—thirty to forty-five minutes a day one to two times a week will suffice in the beginning. By the fifth grade, projects become more sophisticated and the time spent on the projects increases accordingly. Remember, when working on PowerPoint projects your students should work on their content subjects rather than on their PowerPoint skills. PowerPoint is just a great medium in which students learn by creating something, and this is the best way to learn (Woolfolk, 2005).

More Pictures, Fewer Words

As we've mentioned many times, PowerPoint's strongest suit is its great capacity for presenting and editing images. Take advantage of this feature. Besides, elementary school students are not quite ready to use a lot of text in a PowerPoint project. Using too much text with PowerPoint can discourage students from undertaking further projects in PowerPoint or other programs. Elementary students especially enjoy working with animated pictures.

Animation Is Fun!

Animation is one of PowerPoint's advantages. Animated pictures are fun, but animation of text, shapes, and other items is a more important feature. Teachers should not disregard animations created by children, even though they may sometimes be unnecessary and even tacky. By learning animation, children learn how to time items in PowerPoint. This skill can be translated into more complex skills when they eventually work with more sophisticated programs. Teachers should caution children against too much animation, but praise original works.

Working with different types of animation effects, their order, and additional features like timing and media options can develop students' spatial and logical thinking.

What They Can and Can't Do

It may be too early for elementary school students to do an Internet search for pictures. Although schools and school districts have reliable protection programs, still there are chances that students can get to an "unwelcome" site. Besides, an Internet search can take a long time. We highly recommend that teachers obtain all the pictures, music, audio, and other files and make them available for the students by placing them either on the computer desktops or the school's server.

Sometimes even small children create projects with questionable content. We worked with a third grader who used PowerPoint's animation to create a scene in which a squirrel was run over by a truck. Though very creative, this project was inappropriate. There is a fine line between encouraging creativity and permissiveness. Teachers should always be aware of what students do and how far they are drifting from the assigned projects.

Small Fingers, Large Imaginations

Students' imaginations and creativity can be simply endless, and PowerPoint is a great tool for developing creativity. Teachers can show how various functions and tools of PowerPoint work, and then give them an assignment. Some students will use PowerPoint in a most unique and unusual way. We learned from our students, including elementary students, almost as much as they learned from us—maybe more!

Not all students are equally creative and imaginative. Some will need help more often than others; some may not need any help at all. No matter, the teacher's priority should be on the content of the project, not its PowerPoint form. In some cases you can prompt children to add more fun (animation, sound, music), but only if they do not know how to do it. If they focus on the form rather than content, they may eventually lose interest in PowerPoint completely.

Let's say that you ask the students to create a project in arithmetic. Explain that they should pretend to be teachers teaching division and multiplication. The project they create using pictures of apples, flowers, teddy bears, and so on, will be for their fellow students. Of course, you will help some students create these projects, but many students will come up with original projects all on their own.

Start Simply

How to start? Chances are that many of your second, third, and fourth graders have already used a keyboard and e-mail. That they have used PowerPoint or edited pictures is less likely. In any case, we suggest that you tell them a little cute story while showing a PowerPoint project on the story with animation, sound, and other fun things. Then ask them if they liked the story. "Do you want to create a project like this?" you may ask next. This way you will get them interested in the program.

The next steps are described in the following sections.

Introduce text placeholders

Show students that they can write in the title and text placeholders and what the difference is between them. Let them type their names or some other simple information. Show how to make a font larger and smaller. Chances are this will take up your whole first lesson.

Show how to insert images

Working with images is a very important, if not the most important, part of Power-Point. Start with images from Clip Art. Have several interesting images saved from the Internet; place them on their desktops or in their folders. Explain the idea of folders and picture files using a paper folder and several pictures. Explain what computers and PowerPoint will do to show these pictures. Show them how to insert the pictures, make them larger and smaller, and show them in a slide show.

You may also want to show them how to work with AutoShapes: how to edit, fill with color, and change their sizes and shapes.

Teach them to save

Saving can often be a challenge. A typical mistake made by children (and many adults too) is this: "I saved it, but I don't remember where!" Again, use a paper folder and pictures to explain how to save files correctly. Explain the difference between Save and Save As. It is a good idea to suggest saving by using the shortcut Ctrl+S (⌘+S for Macs).

Kids love noise!

Do not be surprised if, once you explain how to use audio effects, your classroom is filled with the sounds of explosions, ricochets, screeching brakes, gunfire, and more. Some teachers remove speakers from their classrooms or labs to make their lives easier. Please don't do that. Kids love noise, and there is nothing wrong with

Figure 14.1
You can take screenshots of PowerPoint and insert them onto a slide.

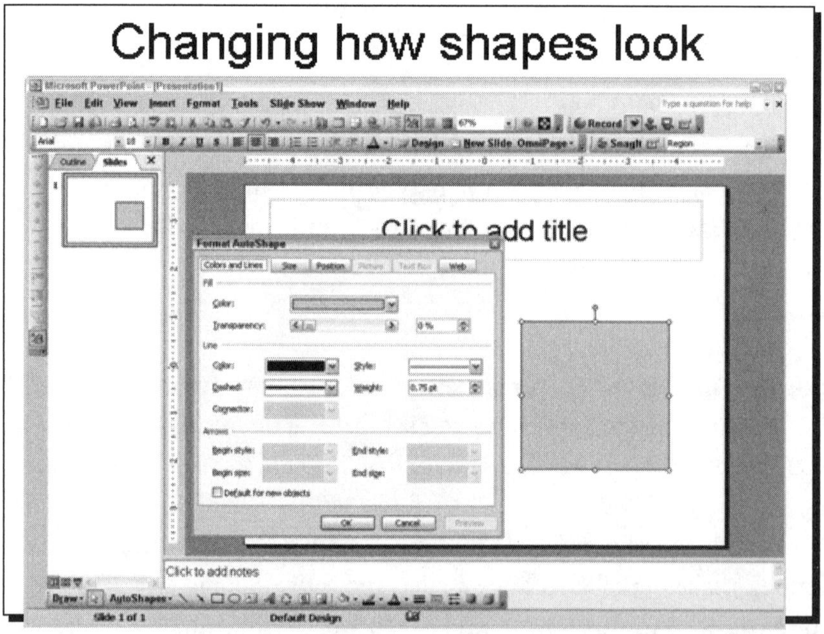

it. Teach them how to use sound appropriately—that is, to enhance the effect but not to distract.

Use PowerPoint as a chalkboard or SmartBoard

We already described in Chapter 4 how to use PowerPoint's Pointer Options feature. Use this feature to draw on the screen as you explain to your children how to use PowerPoint. In some cases you will need screenshots of PowerPoint, as shown in Figure 14.1.

HOW TO DO IT

Select the view for which you need to explain the desired features.

- *Windows:* Press the PrintScreen key on the upper row of keys. Open a new PowerPoint presentation or insert a new slide and select Paste. The picture of the screen will be pasted. Edit the picture to make it occupy the whole slide.
- *Mac:* Press ⌘+A+3 at the same time. If your sound is on, you will hear a camera clicking sound. The picture will be saved on the desktop. Insert a new slide or start a new presentation and insert the picture. Edit it to occupy the entire slide.

Teach your students how to use the PowerPoint Pointer Options feature. It will be important when they show their own projects.

Project ideas

As we've mentioned already, PowerPoint projects for elementary school kids should not be big or too complex. Simple activities with numbers, shapes, and pictures make good projects. For example, ask the students to get a green triangle or a red oval into their PowerPoint slide. Ask them to arrange three apples so that the smallest is on the left, and the largest is on the right. Older students can create slide shows like "My City" or "My State." Take a look at Chapters 10 and 11 for more ideas.

SUMMARY

Is PowerPoint in elementary school rewarding? To answer this question from the scientific point of view we would need to stage sophisticated and exhaustive longitudinal studies. But that is not the goal of this book. As educators, we feel strongly that students benefit from using PowerPoint.

Do you know who will provide you with the best answer to this question? Parents! Parents of elementary school children are particularly interested in their children's progress. They also understand very well the value of computer skills. If you collect your students' work and show it to your students' parents, you will see how excited and proud they are. You can also e-mail the projects to parents with comments and explanations. Your students' progress and their parents' recognition will be the greatest reward for your efforts to teach PowerPoint to your elementary school students.

Teaching PowerPoint in Middle and High School

I n this chapter we will talk about our experience teaching Power-Point to middle and high school students, and offer some suggestions.

Whereas in the elementary grades, the class teacher is usually the one who uses PowerPoint together with the students as a means of teaching and learning many different subjects, in middle and high school PowerPoint normally becomes a part of computer literacy or computer science classes.

This chapter is for computer literacy and computer science teachers, as well as for teachers of other subjects. As we stated several times already, PowerPoint should not be taught in isolation from other subjects as a computer application only. We highly recommend that computer literacy teachers work in close contact with other teachers and help students create projects using PowerPoint for these subjects, rather than for their own computer literacy or other computer classes. Likewise, subject teachers need to be aware of their students' PowerPoint skills to devise assignments and projects involving PowerPoint as a tool.

We do not suggest any particular activities or project ideas in this chapter; you will find them in other chapters. Every school has a different policy on the grade level at which PowerPoint starts being taught, and on how many hours and classes are assigned to the subject. Some schools do not teach PowerPoint to students at all, some cover it in middle school, and some in high school. We only want to share our experience with you in general terms, and we hope you find it useful.

> For a list of topics that cover the range of PowerPoint features, see Chapter 16.

PROJECT-BASED AND PROBLEM-BASED ACTIVITIES

Imagine you are at the science and social studies fair in one of your school's computer labs or canteen. Computer monitors run students' projects, with proud and slightly nervous students standing by. As a member of the team of judges, you approach one of the students. She introduces herself and begins her project, done in PowerPoint.

The project is on the life and achievements of Thomas Edison. The student displays the pictures and photographs of Edison and his famous inventions: telephone, electric bulb, phonograph, and others. She explains what physical phenomena and laws were applicable in each invention, and how important it was for the progress of technology and humankind in general. Some slides have sound imitating the first sound recordings, others have little video clips demonstrating the work of the first electric bulbs and telephones. The entire project is in black and white to underscore the flavor of the time. Only the last quarter of the show has bright colors; it tells us about how Edison's ideas are implemented nowadays. The student answers all your questions; you can see that she knows her subject well. Her teacher, who directed the project, later explains that the student will get credit in science, social studies, and computer literacy for her project.

After taking some notes, you approach another student. His project, also done in PowerPoint, is on economics. He shows pictures and little clips of new and used cars; he explains how different makes of cars hold their original value and how much their maintenance costs over the years. Graphs and charts show cars' depreciation and reliability ratings. Finally, the student ranks cars, trucks, and SUVs according to their value to a car dealer and suggests retail prices and profit margins for the twenty most popular used makes and models. Now you know what your next car will be!

This fair may not resemble those that you have attended. The authors of this book have arranged fairs like this, and so have many teachers across the United States. But many schools still display cardboard pieces with pictures pasted on them and some text written with a felt pen. Amazingly, most of the pictures these days are downloaded from the Internet, printed, cut out with scissors, and glued to the boards. In other words, these projects were computer-based until the point of creating the final product.

Unfortunately, this is the case in many schools. The great potential of computer applications for project-based and problem-based learning, and especially PowerPoint's potential, is not revealed sufficiently in middle and high school. Research clearly suggests that technology can enhance problem- and project-based learning considerably (Samsonov, Pedersen, and Hill, 2006). In fact, some research indicates that technology-using students outperform traditional students in problem- and project-based learning (Edutopia, 2001).

As we have already explained in the previous chapters, PowerPoint offers a lot of potential for helping students create great projects. A *good project* is the product of research, processing data, analyzing, synthesizing, and arranging the findings in an organized, compact, and visually appealing fashion. A *good PowerPoint project* is a product of research, processing data, analyzing, synthesizing, and arranging the findings in an organized, compact, and visually appealing fashion. Hmm, sounds similar! But the PowerPoint project combines different types of media and has links to the Internet, vastly increasing the overall knowledge resources. That's the difference.

PowerPoint's potential stretches far beyond school fair projects. What can be a better way to help students retain a vast chunk of material than creating a quiz or a *Who Wants to Be a Millionaire?*–type game with a multitude of questions? What could be a better way to learn political geography than to create an interactive map? While preparing a project of this kind, a student goes over the entire material. If students expect to present the project in class, they may be excited to include some fun stuff: thought-provoking questions, original feedback, funny audio effects. If the project is assigned to a team, the members will learn from one another both computer skills and the subject matter.

TEACHING PRESENTATION SKILLS

PowerPoint is a presentation tool. Most projects are created to be presented in class. Presentation skills are another important set of skills for students to learn. Remember, it is the presenter, not the presentation, and it is the person, not the presented file, that is important. We have encountered two extremes here: students either read the entire presentation, including the text on slides, or they just click through the presentation, expecting the viewers to follow. We discuss these extremes in Chapter 4.

One technique that works well is to get the students to critique each other's projects. Encourage positive criticism so that they start by appreciating the pluses and later suggest improvements when it comes to minuses. Organize a contest for the best projects and use a panel of judges from the class. Make sure that the judges evaluate not only the project but the presentation too. Introduce the rubric of requirements for particular types of projects before the students begin their work and stick to this rubric in the contest.

 Chapter 13 lists several online resources for PowerPoint rubrics.

ORGANIZING CONTENT

Emphasize to students the importance of quality, well-thought-out content. A big problem with PowerPoint is that students can dumb down content by reducing the entire topic to a few bullet points. Make sure that students understand that a presentation has to cover the topic in depth. Furthermore, the project should be devoted to one subject and not include irrelevant information.

Just as students are taught how to build a sentence, then a paragraph, and finally an entire paper, students must also be taught that oral presentations have a structure:

- Introduction to the topic
- Main theme, with points well developed
- Conclusion

Students who master the art of creating a well-organized oral presentation, using PowerPoint as a support, will find this skill useful throughout their careers.

INTRODUCING DESIGN PRINCIPLES

When you teach PowerPoint to middle or high school students, you should not limit yourself to explaining the directions and commands. PowerPoint projects must be informative but concise, visually appealing but not tacky, unpretentious but not primitive. Even adults have difficulty getting this right, but if you ask students to pay attention to the design as they learn, they'll be starting off on the right foot. The following are several suggestions.

Consistency versus Variety

Explain that a project should be consistent in both content and form. Font, font size and style, backgrounds, and background music, if any, should be the same or alike throughout the entire project. Using inappropriate sound effects and animations may detract from the project.

However, variety in images, colors, animations, and so on can be pluses—if they stay in the same style and serve the same purpose.

Layout Options

Layout options are important when working with pictures, tables, diagrams, graphs, and hyperlinks. Explain the different layouts. It is a good idea to show that most layouts are interchangeable, except for the blank layout. This will help your students organize their projects from the very beginning.

Objects can be placed anywhere on a slide. An excellent art lesson is in two-dimensional design, which is important when laying out a poster or a slide. Discuss symmetry and asymmetry and show students how to hand-draw several possible positions of objects, such as an image and text. Then ask them to choose the one they find most appealing and reproduce it on a slide.

Color

One of the common mistakes students make is to select the wrong colors for the font and the background. You may want to explain the importance of using contrasting colors for the font and the background and introduce the students to color schemes. See Chapters 2 and 3 for details.

Talk not only about color in terms of contrast for legibility but also about the psychological effects of color. Show them how the same presentation, first done in primary colors and then in muted, complementary colors, give very different impressions.

Animation

Animation is fun for elementary school kids, but in middle and especially high school, animation should only be used when it supports the theme of the project. You'll want to explain to your students that too much animation makes a project look childish. They should know, however, that animation can add some fun and even some content (especially with motion paths).

 See Chapter 11 for an explanation of how to create animation using motion paths.

Nonlinear versus Linear Approaches

Not all students in middle and even in high school understand the idea of categories and subcategories. Nonlinearity in PowerPoint helps develop this notion. Students need to understand that they can preprogram the show so that anyone can view or present it the way it was designed. Using hyperlinks rather than defaulted on-click advancing helps students develop their spatial thinking and prepares them for computer-based activities such as Web design and Web site construction. To make the concept of nonlinearity more understandable, compare a nonlinear presentation to a Web site.

A good way to teach students these concepts is to have them hand-draw (or create in PowerPoint) a flowchart of a nonlinear presentation. This is an excellent exercise in organization. PowerPoint's connectors are great tools for this task, as shown in Figure 15.1.

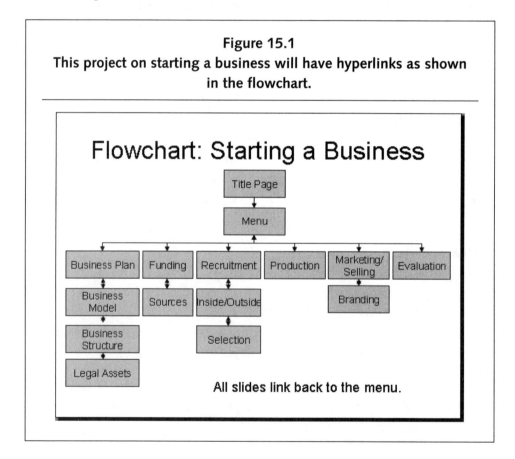

Figure 15.1
This project on starting a business will have hyperlinks as shown in the flowchart.

Interactivity

Presenting a good PowerPoint project to students is an effective teaching activity. Having students create and present their own PowerPoint projects on the topics they study is even more effective. The best way to learn is to learn by doing. The earlier section of this chapter gave some good examples; here we only want to suggest once again: encourage your students to design with PowerPoint.

COLLABORATING WITH PEERS

Again, we do not believe PowerPoint should be taught in isolation from other subjects, as a program only, using material that is unrelated to the subjects students are learning. If you teach PowerPoint as part of your computer-educating class, get in touch with the content area teachers. Some of them may have little knowledge of PowerPoint, if any. Talk to them; explain what kind of projects the students can create as part of that particular class's curriculum, and provide some samples. Work together with your peers to assign projects according to the curriculum. The students can work on the projects during your class and in a computer lab, as needed.

A project can include more than one subject. In this case you may want to work with more than one peer. Invite the peers to jointly develop the rubric for the projects and discuss the grading.

Organize school science and social studies fairs with projects in PowerPoint and other applications. Post the winning projects on the school's Web site.

Help students create electronic portfolios that include PowerPoint projects. Save good projects as examples for your future students.

ENCOURAGING CREATIVITY AND INTEREST IN COMPUTER SCIENCE

Our experience suggests that among your students you will find some who will strive to learn more than your curriculum offers. Although PowerPoint in general is a great introduction to computer science, Visual Basic for Applications (VBA) is yet another step forward. It is not for all students, but there will always be several enthusiastic, computer-loving children who are willing to study more challenging material. VBA is not easy, but even if you don't know it, you can learn it together with your enthusiastic students. The next class will be easier! Chapter 9 provides a simple VBA example for creating graded quizzes. Certain students will enjoy taking this code apart and creating their own graded quizzes.

PowerPoint is a good test for computer aptitude. In some cases, students who are not known for their great progress in other subjects actually find themselves in PowerPoint, which then triggers their interest in computers in general and to more challenging programs. It may eventually determine a choice of a career.

Sometimes it is rewarding to allow your students to go beyond the assigned tasks; in some cases even somewhat questionable practices with PowerPoint can lead to original solutions and discoveries. Be prepared for your students to teach you something that you never thought was possible in PowerPoint!

SUMMARY

In this chapter we offered recommendations on teaching PowerPoint to middle and high school students. Students' learning is problem-based and project-based when they work with PowerPoint. When teachers create good projects, it involves collaboration between teachers of different subjects. PowerPoint is also an excellent program to introduce students to computer science. When taught creatively, it can determine a career choice for some students.

Teaching and Using PowerPoint at the College Level

As you have seen, this book is targeted primarily at teachers in pre-kindergarten through twelfth grade, but we want to take a look at PowerPoint at the college level as well. Of course, college professors use PowerPoint extensively. They use it mostly to accompany lectures, but interactive projects have a place too.

We've heard about schools that require all fifth graders to know how to create a simple PowerPoint presentation. If that were true, all college freshmen would know how to use PowerPoint. But this is not so; although many do, others don't. Many colleges offer computer literacy classes that include PowerPoint in the curriculum. Some professors find that they need to provide quick lessons to their students so that they can get up to speed and complete their assignments.

In this chapter, we'll discuss some of the ways that both professors and students can use PowerPoint at the college level. We've selected a set of college-level disciplines, but our list isn't exhaustive. If we haven't covered your subject, this chapter will give you ideas that you can apply to it. The second part of the chapter provides some ideas for teaching PowerPoint.

 Look back at Chapter 4 for some best practices that apply to teachers at all levels.

ARTS AND HUMANITIES

Perhaps the archetype of a PowerPoint presentation in the humanities is the art lesson. Each slide shows a painting or sculpture, or work from another genre. As each piece is displayed, you discuss it and elicit comments from the students. Seeing the artwork on the big screen is much more satisfying than looking at it in a book! Figure 16.1 shows a sample slide.

Even in studio classes, such as ceramics or painting, PowerPoint can give the students a break from the clay or paint and show them examples of art from around the world, in various eras, and in multiple styles, to spur their creativity. Although projectors often alter the colors somewhat, you can still do a presentation on colors; the range of available colors is very wide.

One of the advantages of PowerPoint is that you can focus on a particular part of a picture, painting, or sculpture by cropping it and blowing it up on a separate

Figure 16.1
You can easily share art with the class as a whole when you put it into a PowerPoint presentation.

Contrast the style used for the humans and the animals

slide (if it does not blur the picture). If you have a choice of two versions of an image, the larger image will result in sharper enlargements. See Chapter 2 for details on resizing images.

Likewise, in any class where you want to discuss the wide range of possibilities, you can show photographs of:

- *Theater.* Show costumes and sets, as well as photos from plays.
- *Dance.* Show costumes, sets, photos, and choreography notation.
- *Music.* Display photos of instruments, old scores, and musical notation. Of course, you can also add music sound files.
- *Literature.* Include book covers, illustrations, old manuscripts, paintings of authors. If you're discussing storytelling or creative writing, use PowerPoint as a storyboarding tool.
- *Philosophy.* Diagrams (Euler, Venn, and others) are excellent ways to visually portray logical concepts. Placing philosophical statements for consideration on a slide allows the entire class to join in viewing them together.

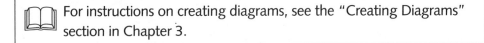 For instructions on creating diagrams, see the "Creating Diagrams" section in Chapter 3.

- *History and geography.* Paintings of historical events, portraits of important people, photos of daily life in the past, maps, old documents or newspapers work well.
- *Languages.* Show tables of verbs, parts of speech; show the text of complete conversations.

Language skills are particularly suited to games and quizzes or reviews, as we've already discussed. College students aren't much different from high school students in this regard and benefit from repetition, review, and competitive or collaborative challenges.

For all subjects, college-level instructors can create quizzes and reviews in the same ways we've discussed throughout this book. Of course, the questions will be harder. But there are other differences:

- *Make positive and negative feedback slides simple, rather than cute.* Eliminate the cartoon clip art and the sounds, unless you are completely sure they will work in a positive way.

- *Avoid bright, primary colors.* Use muted colors instead.

- *Avoid the impulse to simplify content.* You can use smaller font sizes when students are running the presentation on their own computers, and this way you can fit in more text.

When using PowerPoint to accompany your lectures, be sure not to offer slide after slide of bullets. Such presentations tend to put students to sleep, unless you're an extremely dynamic lecturer. Try to find ways to add images and to use the slide space more creatively. Diagrams are a good way to present processes and time lines.

The same suggestion is appropriate for students' projects. Students may deliver final presentations back-to-back at the end of the course during one or two sessions; it is hard to keep all the viewers focused. Adding images, animation, and especially quizzes at the end help maintain the audience's attention. Besides, it shows how deeply the students understood the material, and how creatively they can apply it.

SOCIAL SCIENCES

PowerPoint is essential for showing the graphs and research results that are so important to the science side of the social sciences. We explain how to create graphs in Chapter 3, in the "Create Graphs" section.

Some social science concepts are complex and sophisticated. The best way to present these ideas may be in full sentences, rather than bulleted points. Two-column layouts are good for making comparisons of opposing theories, for example. Tables are also useful, as shown in Figure 16.2. However, remember that you can only fit so much text on a PowerPoint slide; your job as a teacher is to bring out the details.

- *Psychology.* Show graphical results of experiments as well as photographs of the experimental environment. Diagrams, such as Maslow's Hierarchy of Human Needs, are often shown on PowerPoint slides. Other suggestions: Piaget versus Vygotsky, behaviorism versus constructivism, and so on.

Figure 16.2
Compare theories in a table.

Freud vs. Jung

Religion	Escape, fallacy	Place of safety, means of communication
Driving force	Sexuality	Desire to feel complete
Unconscious	Individual thoughts, images, experiences	Includes collective unconscious
Therapist's role	Expose repressed feelings in unconscious	Help recognize work of unconscious

- *Anthropology.* Photographs of other societies, including people, artifacts, houses, and clothing, are important.

- *Sociology.* Photographs of people in various countries, at various socioeconomic levels, of various races, religions, and so on, help students visualize sociological concepts. Use charts and graphs to support statistical and demographical data. See Chapter 3 to remind yourself how to create a chart and use it in PowerPoint.

- *Education.* You probably remember some PowerPoint presentations from your own courses in education. Procedural diagrams or even simple lists can show student teachers how to organize materials for a lesson or use step-by-step methods of classroom management. Two-column comparisons, tables, charts, and graphs are helpful for comparing theories of learning.

MATH

PowerPoint is an excellent tool for displaying equations and the systematic processes of mathematics. Whether you are showing equations or geometric shapes, PowerPoint is usually up to the task.

Photographs of real-world objects, whether natural or man-made, that portray mathematical concepts are excellent for relating mathematics to the world around us. For example, a photo of a pitched roof in construction is a good introduction to trigonometry.

Displaying Equations

You can use animation to display a sequence of equations one after the other, as we explained in Chapter 2. For complex equations, you may need to use Microsoft Equation Editor 3.0; see Chapter 12 for an explanation of this tool.

If you have a very long series of equations that can't fit on one slide and you want the students to see all of them at once, PowerPoint is limited. One option is to increase the size of the slide or turn it 90 degrees to portrait orientation. However, you'll need to check that your projector will display this properly. You may be able to rotate the text 90 degrees and turn the projector on its side for this slide to get the desired result, but this isn't very smooth unless you're doing it for the entire presentation.

SPOTLIGHT: MATHTYPE FOR COMPLEX EQUATIONS

For even more professional options, you can try MathType, a software package by Design Science. This package offers more fonts, easier access to symbols, and the ability to color part of an equation. You can download a free thirty-day trial version at www.dessci.com/en/products/mathtype/trial.asp. You can find a tutorial on using PowerPoint 2003 with MathType at www.dessci.com/en/support/mathtype/tutorials/mt_ppt/tutorial.htm. Figure 16.3 shows an example of a slide displaying complex equations created in MathType. Although you can't see it in the black-and-white figure, the equations use three different colors to help delineate various parts of the equations.

Figure 16.3
You can create complex equations using Microsoft Equation Editor 3.0 or Design Science MathType.

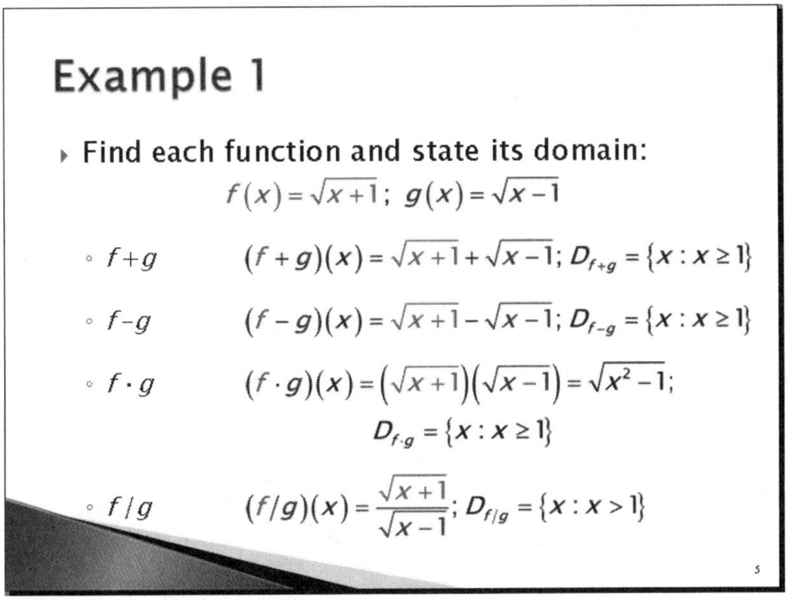

Example 1

▸ Find each function and state its domain:
$$f(x) = \sqrt{x+1}; \quad g(x) = \sqrt{x-1}$$

- $f+g$ $(f+g)(x) = \sqrt{x+1} + \sqrt{x-1}; \; D_{f+g} = \{x : x \geq 1\}$

- $f-g$ $(f-g)(x) = \sqrt{x+1} - \sqrt{x-1}; \; D_{f-g} = \{x : x \geq 1\}$

- $f \cdot g$ $(f \cdot g)(x) = \left(\sqrt{x+1}\right)\left(\sqrt{x-1}\right) = \sqrt{x^2 - 1};$
$$D_{f \cdot g} = \{x : x \geq 1\}$$

- f/g $(f/g)(x) = \dfrac{\sqrt{x+1}}{\sqrt{x-1}}; \; D_{f/g} = \{x : x > 1\}$

5

Note: Our thanks to Bob Mathews for the slides shown in Figures 16.3 and 16.4.

HOW TO DO IT

- *Windows 2000/2002/2003:* Choose File ➤ Page Setup to open the Page Setup dialog box. From the Slides Sized For drop-down list, choose one of the preset sizes or use the Width and Height text boxes to specify a custom size. In the Slides box of the Orientation section, choose Portrait. (The default is landscape, which is wider than it is long.) Click OK.

- *Windows 2007:* On the Design tab, click the Page Setup button in the Page Setup group to open the Page Setup dialog box. From the Slides Sized For drop-down list, choose one of the preset sizes or use the Width and Height text boxes to specify a custom size. In the

Slides box of the Orientation section, choose Portrait. (The default is landscape, which is wider than it is long.) Click OK.

- *Mac 2001/X/2004:* Choose File ➤ Page Setup to open the Page Setup dialog box. From the Slides Sized For drop-down list, choose one of the preset sizes or use the Width and Height text boxes to specify a custom size. In the Slides box of the Orientation section, choose Portrait. (The default is landscape, which is wider than it is long.) Click OK.

Diagrams can also make math concepts clearer. Figure 16.4 shows a diagrammatic portrayal of a composite function. You can find the two presentations shown in Figures 16.3 and 16.4 on the companion Web site at www.ellenfinkelstein.com/powerpointforteachers.html.

At the college level, you don't need to be afraid to use the Normal view of PowerPoint if you want to develop equations in real time, as you explain them. Students are mature enough to look past the software's user interface and focus on what you're doing. Although electronic whiteboards specialize in the capability of capturing and saving handwritten content, you may not have one available. In this case, PowerPoint can serve the same function. When you're done, you can save the presentation and make it available to students electronically.

 If the size of a page in Word suits you better, you can use Microsoft Word in the same way. .

Geometry

Of course, PowerPoint is excellent for geometry, as long as the shapes aren't too complex. PowerPoint comes with a good selection of AutoShapes (or Shapes), but they aren't oriented to geometry. However, PowerPoint 2007 has added the following shapes:

- Hexagon
- Septagon
- Octagon
- Decagon
- Dodecagon

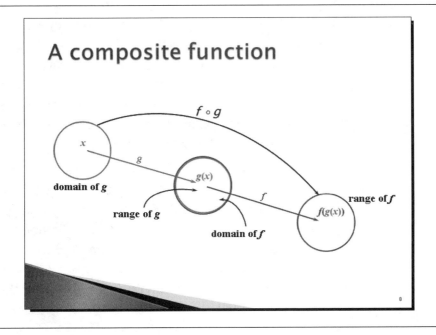

Figure 16.4
You can use PowerPoint's drawing features to graphically portray mathematical concepts.

The only three-dimensional shapes are a cylinder and a cube, but you can extrude any two-dimensional shape into three dimensions. Many people have no idea of the 3-D capabilities of PowerPoint.

HOW TO DO IT

- *Windows 2000/2002/2003:* Draw any AutoShape on a slide and resize it as desired. With the AutoShape selected, on the Drawing toolbar, click the 3-D Style button and choose one of the 3-D styles from the gallery. For many more options, click 3-D Settings to display the 3-D Settings toolbar, shown in Figure 16.5. Use the four Tilt buttons to change the angle of the object in 3-D space. Use the Depth button to change the depth (extrusion). Use the 3-D Color button to change the color of the sides of the shape.

- *Windows 2007:* Draw any shape on a slide and resize it as desired. With the shape selected, click the Format tab. In the Shape Styles group, click Shape Effects ➤ 3-D Rotation and choose one of the rotations. For many more options, click 3-D Rotation Options to display the 3-D Rotation pane of the Format Shape dialog box. You can make some precise changes to the rotation there. Then click the 3-D Format category. Use the Depth text box to change the depth (extrusion). Use the Color drop-down list in the Depth section to change the color of the sides of the shape.

- *Mac 2001/X/2004:* Draw any AutoShape on a slide and resize it as desired. With the AutoShape selected, on the Drawing toolbar, click the 3-D Style button and choose one of the 3-D styles from the gallery. For many more options, click 3-D Settings to display the 3-D Settings toolbar, shown in Figure 16.5. Use the four Tilt buttons to change the angle of the object in 3-D space. Use the Depth button to change the depth (extrusion). Use the 3-D Color button to change the color of the sides of the shape.

If you have some software that you use to create complex geometrical shapes, you can get those shapes into PowerPoint in a number of ways:

- *Save as an image.* Most drawing software allows you to save objects in JPG, GIF, PNG, or BMP format. You can then import the image file (as we explain in Chapter 2).

- *Copy and paste.* In many cases, you can select the object you drew, copy it to the Clipboard, and paste it directly onto a slide.

- *Take a screen capture.* You can take a screen capture. On the PC, press Alt+Print-Screen to capture the window. (Press PrintScreen to capture the entire screen.) On the Mac, press ⌘+Shift+4 to capture the window. (Press ⌘+Shift+3 to capture the entire screen.) Then paste onto a slide. You'll probably have to crop the image. (See "Cropping an Image" in Chapter 2.)

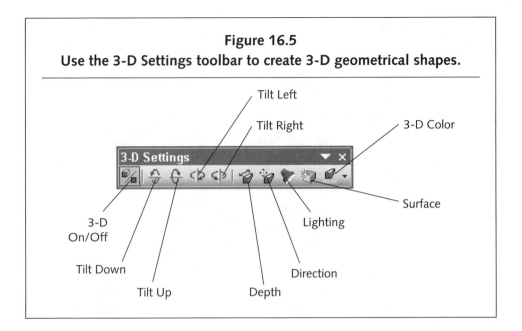

Figure 16.5
Use the 3-D Settings toolbar to create 3-D geometrical shapes.

SCIENCE

PowerPoint is a no-brainer for science, and it overtook the overhead projector a long time ago. Photos taken through a microscope are stunning, as the sampling in Figure 16.6 shows. Even line drawings of structures are most effective when shown large on the screen.

Graphs are used in all the sciences and you can use PowerPoint's graphing capabilities, as we described in Chapter 3. You can also import data or a graph from Microsoft Excel by copying and pasting.

In chemistry, equations and processes are easy to portray on slides. See the section on mathematics earlier in this chapter, as well as in Chapter 12, for more information on creating equations in PowerPoint. AutoShapes (Shapes) include some flowchart symbols that can be useful in chemistry, or you can draw your own.

In physics and astronomy as well, photographs and diagrams are easily added to a presentation. Photographs of galaxies are just as beautiful as photos of cells!

As we mentioned in the previous section on mathematics, if you want to write equations or other content as you discuss them, you can use PowerPoint's Normal view, then save the presentation and make it available to the students, perhaps by posting it on the course's Web site.

Figure 16.6
Photos of cells and other biological structures make beautiful and educational slides.

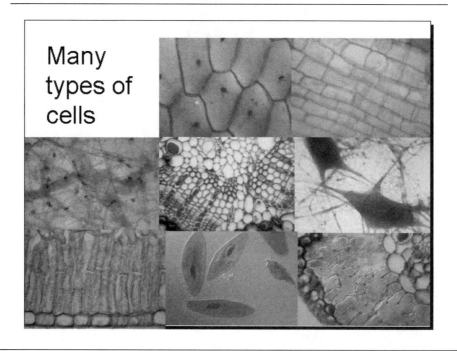

BUSINESS

As you probably know, PowerPoint is ubiquitous in the business world, and it's not far behind in college business departments. In fact, so many business lectures are done in PowerPoint that it isn't saved for special projects anymore. The challenge is to create presentations that are more than simply bulleted slides.

Your presentations should be examples for your students, so that when they go out into the business world, they too will create compelling presentations rather than boring ones. See the discussion of best practices in Chapter 4.

Here are some guidelines:

• When describing a process, the passage of time, or a procedure, turn the text into a diagram. PowerPoint 2007's SmartArt diagrams are especially useful. See "Creating Diagrams" in Chapter 3 for more information.

- For bar, line, and pie charts, use multiple colors but keep them streamlined to make them more meaningful (see again Chapter 3 for details).

- Use images to evoke concepts, and leave out the words, at least for one slide in each topic. For example, to introduce a discussion of recruiting in a human resource management course, show a photograph of a recruiter interviewing an applicant.

- If you use backgrounds at all, keep them subtle so they don't attract attention away from the content.

- Pay extra attention to the organization, logic, and flow of the content. Start with an overview, develop ideas sequentially, and end with a conclusion.

In addition to accompanying lectures, PowerPoint is an excellent choice for facilitating discussion. For example, in a class on business ethics, you could display the description of a business situation and then launch a discussion on what actions would be ethical or unethical.

You can write up a business case on a slide and use that as a springboard for a discussion as well. However, make sure that the text fits legibly on one slide. If not, don't use PowerPoint and use printed matter instead.

TEACHING POWERPOINT

By the time they reach college, almost all students have some computer literacy, so they pick up PowerPoint fairly quickly. The difference in teaching PowerPoint at the college level is that you should emphasize best practices and content organization.

The discussion here is designed for professors who need to quickly teach PowerPoint to students, not for those teaching an entire semester course, or even an entire unit, in PowerPoint. Of course, such a curriculum devoted to Power-Point would be much more detailed.

A tutorial exercise, such as the one we created in Chapter 2, is usually enough to get students started creating their own presentations. Here are the basic topics you need to cover:

- Considering the purpose of the presentation and the needs of the audience

- Creating an outline and collecting relevant images

- Opening PowerPoint and starting a new presentation
- Saving in various formats
- Creating a title slide
- Adding new slides
- Choosing and changing the slide layout
- Adding text in text placeholders
- Adding notes
- Using the Outline pane
- Changing views (Normal, Slide Sorter, and Slide Show)
- Moving through a presentation in Normal view
- Adding images
- Editing images
- Working with backgrounds and templates
- Adding AutoShapes (Shapes), including text boxes and WordArt
- Editing AutoShapes (Shapes)
- Moving, copying, and deleting slides
- Creating graphics and diagrams
- Adding hyperlinks
- Adding animation
- Adding sound, narration, and video
- Delivering a presentation

That's a long list of topics! You don't need to cover them in exactly that order. In fact, if you use a tutorial, the order will be determined by the process of creating the presentation.

For example, you can have the students create a simple presentation with just some text and one inserted image. They could then deliver that presentation. This process enables students to see the entire process very quickly. You can then go back and have students elaborate on their presentation, adding AutoShapes (Shapes), animation, sound, and so on.

This technique of starting with a simple presentation helps students who know nothing about PowerPoint get started quickly. Once your students are all functioning at a similar level, you can introduce more advanced features.

Emphasize to students that in learning to give presentations with PowerPoint they'll be learning skills that will be useful throughout their lives:

- Clearly presenting their ideas and conclusions to others
- Speaking in public
- Organizing main points
- Presenting various types of speeches—informational, motivational, or technical

Discuss the use of PowerPoint in students' majors; this will pique their interest. Then let students use PowerPoint according to their interests:

- *Let the artists be artistic.* Artists may spend hours creating one slide, using PowerPoint's drawing tools. Figure 16.7 shows an example. Actually, the student worked for days on this slide and ended up with an intimate knowledge of PowerPoint's graphical capabilities.
- *Let the writers write.* Writers may work for hours crafting their words.
- *Let the programmers program.* Computer science students will enjoy delving into the Visual Basic for Applications (VBA) programming language to make PowerPoint perform new tricks. We provide a very simple introduction to VBA in Chapter 9.
- *Let the businesspeople sell.* Business students will work on motivating their audience.
- *Let the performers perform.* Performers will turn the presentation into a theatrical event.

Allowing students to use PowerPoint in their own ways is just fine. Of course, you should have your own rubric for grading presentations and explain some best practices, but don't discourage the natural diversity that will arise. You'll see some marvelous presentations!

Figure 16.7
Artistic students will enjoy creating beautiful slides.

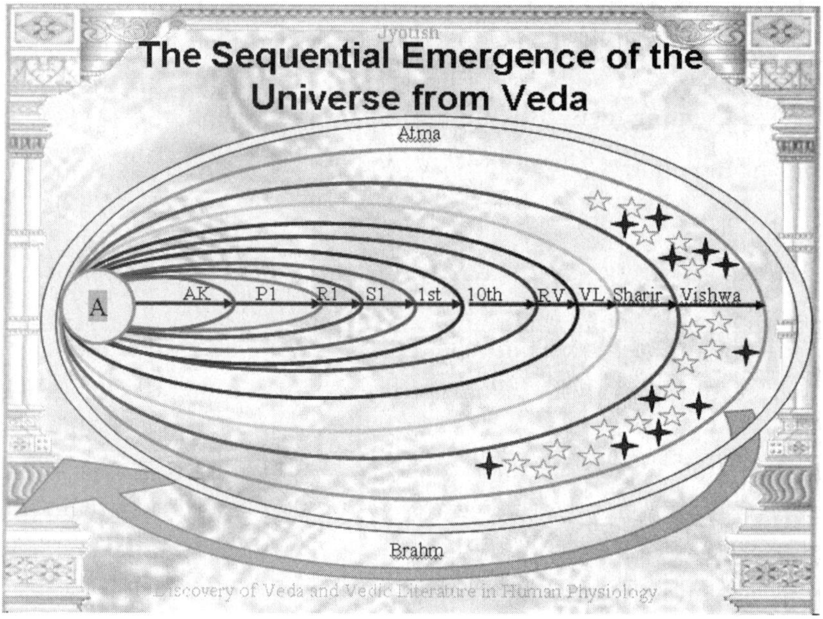

SUMMARY

In this chapter, we offered ideas for using PowerPoint in many college-level disciplines. We looked first at the arts and humanities, and then at social sciences, math, science, and business.

We concluded with a discussion of how to teach PowerPoint at the college level.

REFERENCES

Bartsch, R., and Cobern, K. "Effectiveness of PowerPoint Presentations in Lectures." *Computers & Education,* 2003, *41*, 77–86.

Carello, C. "Hi-Tech Presentations: Are They Powerful or Pointless?" *Teaching with Technology Today,* 2002, *9*(3). Retrieved June 1, 2007, from http://www.uwsa.edu/ttt/articles/carello.htm.

Crispen, P. D. "Now That I Know PowerPoint, How Can I Use It to TEACH?" Presentation at the NECC conference, Feb. 2006. Retrieved June 1, 2007, from http://64.233.167.104/search?q=cache:znQ0YgmZiiwJ:www.kemst.hi.is/vefur/sidur/powerpoint/how_do_i_use_powerpoint_to_teach.ppt+%E2%80%9CNow+That+I+Know+PowerPoint,+How+Can+I+Use+It+to+TEACH%3F%E2%80%9D&hl=en&ct=clnk&cd=3&gl=us.

Edutopia. *Project-Based Learning Research.* Edutopia, 2001. Retrieved May 28, 2007, from http://www.edutopia.org/project-based-learning-research.

Finkelstein, E. "PowerPoint Principles for Education." *Presentations,* 2005. Retrieved June 1, 2007, from http://www.presentations.com/msg/search/article_display.jsp?vnu_content_id=1001179164.

Frey, B., and Birnbaum, D. J. *Learners' Perceptions of the Value of PowerPoint in Lectures,* 2002. ERIC Document Reproduction Service: ED467192.

Levy, Y. *The Effects of Background Music on Learning: A Review of Recent Literature,* 1986. Retrieved June 1, 2007, from http://edweb.sdsu.edu/Courses/Ed690DR/Examples/LitRev/Levy.htm.

Marcovitz, D. *Powerful PowerPoint for Educators: Using Visual Basic for Applications to Make PowerPoint Interactive.* Westport, Conn.: Libraries Unlimited, 2004.

Mathews, B. Algebra of Functions.ppt and Rational Functions Quiz.ppt.

Mayer, R. E. *Multimedia Learning.* New York: Cambridge University Press, 2001.

Roblyer, M., and Edwards, J. *Integrating Educational Technology into Teaching* (2nd ed.). Upper Saddle River, N.J.: Prentice Hall, 2000.

Samsonov, P., Pedersen, S., and Hill, C. "Using Problem-Based Learning Software with At-Risk Students: A Case Study." *Computers in the Schools,* 2006, *23*(1/2), 111–124.

Savan. "The Effect of Background Music on Learning, Psychology of Music." *Psychology of Music,* 1999, *27*(2), 138–146.

Vygotsky, L. S. *Mind and Society: The Development of Higher Mental Processes.* Cambridge, Mass.: Harvard University Press, 1978.

Woolfolk, A. *Educational Psychology* (9th ed.). Boston: Pearson, Allyn & Bacon, 2005.

Research on Multimedia and Learning

Research on multimedia and learning helps a teacher understand how to use any multimedia program, including PowerPoint, so that students learn the most. When looking at the research, it's good to pay attention to the source, because some of the research was done by companies looking to sell projectors and software. Also, some research is quite old, used a small number of subjects, or was done on college students. In the end, although it's hard to find rock-solid results, a number of conclusions are clear.

In this appendix our aim isn't to discuss theories of learning; that could take many more books. The research is fairly clear that children learn and remember more when they're actively involved in the learning process (Woolfolk, 2005). For this reason, this book emphasizes interactive PowerPoint projects that create a dialog between the student and the subject matter.

RICHARD E. MAYER'S MULTIMEDIA RESEARCH

Perhaps the most prolific and cited researcher is Richard E. Mayer, professor of psychology at the University of California, Santa Barbara. He has written eighteen books and more than 250 articles and chapters that focus on multimedia learning. His book *Multimedia Learning* (2001) examines a series of experiments on various types of multimedia lessons and the results in terms of both retention (how much students remembered) and transfer (how well they could apply the knowledge).

 Richard Mayer's work did not deal with young children. He tested older students' results in learning simple lessons like how lightning is created.

The result is a set of seven principles that you can easily apply to your PowerPoint presentations and projects:

1. *Multimedia Principle.* Learning was better from words and images together than from just words. In other words, adding relevant images aids learning.

2. *Spatial Contiguity Principle.* Students learned better when related words and images were near rather than distant from each other. For example, putting text on one slide and a corresponding image on the next slide would not be as effective as putting them on the same slide.

3. *Temporal Contiguity Principle.* Students learned better when related words and images were presented at the same time rather than one after the other. For PowerPoint, this is very similar to the previous principle.

4. *Coherence Principle.* Learning was better when extraneous text, images, and sounds were excluded. This very important principle acts as a restraint to the concept of adding images and sounds. Only relevant images and sounds are aids to learning. Pretty music or images have the opposite effect.

 It should be noted that there is a significant amount of research suggesting that pleasant, especially classical, background music enhances learning. For example, Savan, in "The Effect of Background Music on Learning, Psychology of Music," found that beautiful background music produced a favorable effect on learning, especially in children with disabilities (1999). Yiftach Levy, professor of psychology at San Diego University states, "Some amount of background music may in fact be helpful in the learning process, both in a structured school setting and under self-directed homework conditions" (1986).

5. *Modality Principle.* Students learned better from animation and narration than from animation and on-screen text. Mayer explained that this result comes because people can handle visual and aural input together better than two visual inputs. In a presentation, therefore, you might use animation and explain the concepts verbally, omitting any text.

6. *Redundancy Principle.* Students learned better from animation and narration than from the combination of animation, narration, and on-screen text. This principle relates to the previous one—combining animation and on-screen text duplicated the visual input.

7. *Individual Differences Principle.* Students with little knowledge of a subject learned less with poorly designed instructions than students who knew more about it. The conclusion is that you need to consider students with less background in the lesson's material and make sure that a PowerPoint presentation meets their needs.

These principles can help you design a presentation, especially if you plan to test the students on the results and want them to retain and understand the maximum content. They are specific enough to help you figure out where and when to use pictures, and what kind, yet allow you lots of leeway.

OTHER RELEVANT RESEARCH

Most research on the effectiveness of PowerPoint specifically has been done with undergraduate students. For example, Bartsch and Cobern, in "Effectiveness of PowerPoint Presentations in Lectures" (2003), found that students preferred PowerPoint to overhead transparencies. In a result similar to that of Richard Mayer, they found that students recalled and recognized less of a lecture when pictures were not relevant.

Frey and Birnbaum, in "Learners' Perceptions of the Value of PowerPoint in Lectures" (2002), asked 160 undergraduate students what they thought about the value of PowerPoint in lectures and found that students felt that it had a positive effect, helping them take notes and study for exams.

Carello (2002) did a controlled study comparing PowerPoint with overheads and found no difference in students' grades. You can find this study at www.uwsa.edu/ttt/articles/carello.htm. The author concluded:

Even though the PowerPoint presentations did not improve learning by the student audience and student presentation scores were equal using both PowerPoint and overheads, I feel that learning to develop PowerPoint presentations is a valuable skill. Students can now use PowerPoint for future presentations and in the job market. In addition, I found students to be more creative in developing their project, and they performed additional research on their topics on the Internet in order to find relevant images to use in their presentations. My students reported to me that they enjoyed preparing these presentations more than the overhead presentations. I firmly believe that students embrace learning more when they enjoy the process. In the future, I will encourage students to use PowerPoint for their presentations.

Patrick Douglas Crispen, faculty training and support coordinator for California State University, Long Beach, sent us a PowerPoint presentation called, "Now That I Know PowerPoint, How Can I Use It to TEACH?" In this presentation, he brings out principles based on the available research and includes an excellent bibliography. He also discusses note-taking and legibility.

 Find Patrick Crispen's presentation on this book's companion Web site at www.ellenfinkelstein.com/powerpointforteachers.

CONCLUSIONS

As you can see, how you design a PowerPoint presentation will affect the learning outcome. We discussed best practices in Chapter 4 to help you get the best results.

In truth, there is little research on the value of PowerPoint in the K–12 environment. You may need to do your own research to see what types of presentations and projects work.

Other research, which we don't cover here, was done in a business context. That research was directed toward the effectiveness of PowerPoint presentations in motivating an audience to make a decision, such as to buy a product or service. We felt that this research was not appropriate in the field of education. In fact, as we explained in the beginning of this book, a good part of the reason why we wrote the book is that there is so little information on PowerPoint available specifically for teachers.

What is your goal when you create a presentation or project? Do you want your students to remember and understand the maximum? In that case, don't add extraneous sounds and unrelated images to a minimum.

It's pretty clear what we mean by extraneous sound—music throughout the presentation or sound effects that are not necessary to make the point. In contrast, if you're discussing insects, you could have a slide that says, "This is what a cricket sounds like," add the sound of a cricket, and discuss how crickets make that sound—and why.

Unrelated images are harder to ferret out. According to the research, even general images that are not necessary are distracting. For example, in a lesson on the water cycle, a picture of fish in the ocean is not necessary for understanding the water cycle; therefore, it's irrelevant.

A lot depends on your goal. For older students, if the presentation or project is the main medium for delivering lesson content, and you want students to remember and understand it, all pictures and sounds should further the content. They shouldn't compete with it or be there for the sake of aesthetics.

However, your goal may be different:

- You may want to present a new unit and pique the students' interest in the topic. In this case, you're actually trying to excite the students to learn and will present the serious content later.

- You may want to use music, for example, to enhance the aesthetic effect of images.

- You may want to make the learning fun, rather than serious. This works for content that is repeated many times, such as multiplication tables. We all know that it's important to make learning fun!

- You may be working with young students and feel that they need the extra stimulation of sound and color.

It may be true that a straightforward presentation with narration and images will result in higher test scores than one with bells and whistles, but as teachers you've probably discovered that you need to elaborate. A balance of the two approaches may work best in your classroom. Some students may respond best to bright colors and sounds; others may not. An initial presentation may be different than a review. So you need to judge what type of teaching tool is necessary in each situation.

Your style as a teacher is also a consideration. Naturally, your PowerPoint projects will reflect your style and background. Whatever works well for you in all your teaching will work well when you use PowerPoint. Therefore, don't rush to use all the available extreme effects in PowerPoint if you usually teach in a low-key manner.

PowerPoint offers many opportunities for you to customize lessons for a situation or for a specific student. No other program makes this process easier. We hope that this book has provided you with the tools you need to find many solutions that will enhance the education of your students.

What's on the Companion Web Site

We're pleased to provide a companion Web site to *PowerPoint for Teachers: Dynamic Presentations and Interactive Classroom Projects.* You'll find it at www.ellenfinkelstein.com/powerpointforteachers.html. This site provides you with many PowerPoint presentations that we discuss in the book, and additional content that we think you'll find useful.

PRESENTATIONS AND OTHER DOWNLOADS

Most of the content on the companion Web site consists of presentations and supplementary files. Here's what you'll find:

- *Chapter 2:* The site offers the Water Cycle presentation.
- *Chapter 3:* The site includes the Water Cycle with Thunder presentation, as updated by the instructions in Chapter 3.
- *Chapter 5:* Find the Water Cycle Review quiz that we describe in Chapter 5.
- *Chapter 6:* The Map of Europe presentation is a clickable map that we built. We also have an image of a world map that you can use, in case you can't find one.
- *Chapter 7:* Find the Animal Categories presentation, a menu-based project on animals.

- *Chapter 8:* Find samples of each of the games that we cover.

- *Chapter 9:* Find the graded quiz, called Math Quiz, here, both with and without the VBA code. We also created a Ten-Question Math Quiz presentation that you can use as a template to create your own ten-question quiz with four possible answers for each question.

- *Chapter 10:* Download the Our Zoo Trip presentation and an image of a butterfly for the animation project.

- *Chapter 11:* We created an elaborate animation—Water Cycle Animation—that you can download.

- *Chapter 13:* The entire chapter is available for download, with live links, so that you can click the links instead of typing them.

- *Chapter 16:* A former teacher submitted two algebra presentations and gave us permission to make them available. One is a straight presentation with great graphics; the other is a quiz.

RESOURCES

Teachers are always looking for clip art and photos to add to their PowerPoint projects, so the companion Web site includes a list of online resources where you can find images that are not copyrighted.

Sounds and music are often hard to find, so we've included a list of sites that contains the resources as well. Finally, we've scoured the Web for a few videos that you can add to your presentations.

ADD YOUR OWN RESOURCES

Have you found a great resource that isn't on the PowerPoint for Teachers Web site? Tell us about it! On the page, you'll find a button that will lead you to a forum where you can tell us about a great resource for teachers. We'll check it out and add it to the site if we agree.

INDEX

A

About.com, Presentation Software page, 273–274

ActDen's PowerPoint in the Classroom, 273

Action button, 160; Custom option, 187

Action Settings dialog box, 133–134, 140, 186–189, 208; Run Macro option, 208

Active Learning with PowerPoint site (University of Minnesota Center for Teaching and Learning), 268, 272

Add Objects Section, Formatting palette, 33

Adobe Acrobat (PDF) files, saving notes/handouts as, 119

Adobe Photoshop, 257

Advance Slide section, Animations tab, 250

Age-appropriateness, 105–106

Amazon.com, 250

Ancient civilizations projects (grades 6 to 12), 253

Animal Categories.ppt, 154

Animals and their habitats project (grades 2 to 5), 244

Animate dialog box, 96

Animation, 10, 141; adding, 71–73; dialog box, 72–74, 96; effects, 107–108, in elementary school PowerPoint projects, 282; and math projects, 219–223; and middle/high school students, 291; object, 72, 73–75; science projects (grades 6 to 12), 256; slide transitions, 72, 75; tab, 72, 75, 96, 132, 134, 164, 219, 221, 223, 242–243, 250; text, 72–73

Anthropology projects, 299

Art and music projects (grades 6 to 12), 262–263

Art Teacher Connection rubric, 276

Articles, online resources for teachers, 271–272

Artists, and slide creation, 309–311

Arts and humanities projects, at the college level, 296–298

Audio feedback, adding to interactive maps, 150

AutoShapes (Shapes), 50, 130, 135, 147–149, 223, 247, 254, 260, 303–304, 306; dialog box, 55–56, 59; and math projects, 223–225

.avi (video format), 99

B

Background dialog box, 57–58, 64, 66–69, 104–105

Background graphics, removing from a slide, 56–58

Background music, adding, 95–97

Backgrounds, 103–104, 307; adding, 62–69; creating for an individual slide, 64–69; gradient, 65–67; picture, 67–69; solid, 64–65; template, choosing, 63

Badinerie (Bach), 262

Bajaj, Geetesh, 267

Bar charts, 86; colors in, 307

barnesandnoble.com, 250

Best practices, 103–121; age-appropriateness, 105–106; animation effects, 107–108; backgrounds, 103–104; bullets, 109–112; color schemes, 106–107; context, importance of, 113–114; electronic access, providing, 119; handouts/notes, printing, 118–119; maximizing learning, 116–120; note taking, using Power-Point to help students with, 116–118; sounds, 108–109; special effects, 106–109; text, 112–113

Blackboard (online delivery system), 249

Blacking out the screen, 78

Blank Presentation option, 26

BMP (.bmp), 85

Body parts project (pre-K to grade 1), 226

Book reference system project (grades 6 to 12), 251

Book talks, 250–251

Booksamillion.com, 250

Boolean variables, defined, 195

Brightness button, 47

Brightness, changing, 46–47

Bulleted List Slide, 36

Bullets, 109–112; tab, 107, 112

Bullets and Numbering dialog box, 111–112

Business projects (college level), 306–307

Buzz-Word Bingo (game), 268

C

Carello, C., 315

Cell parts project (grades 2 to 5), 245

Center for Teaching and Learning at Connecticut College, PowerPoint guides at, 275

Chalkboard, PowerPoint as, 285

Charts, 62; creating, 86

Check for Updates option, 185

Choose Insert ➢ Picture ➢ From File, 43

Choose With Previous, Start drop-down list, 243

Civics projects (grades 6 to 12), 254

Claremont McKenna College Teaching Resource Center (Web site), rubric to evaluate presentations, 276

Class games, 167–181, *See also* Games; *Jeopardy* (PowerPoint version), 179–181, 247; memorization games, 167–173; spelling games, 173–176; *Who Wants to Be a Millionaire?* (PowerPoint version), 176–179, 247

Class question-and-answer game, 11

Click to Add Notes option, Notes pane, 31–32

Click to Add Title placeholder, 144, 146, 151

Clickable maps, 17

Clickable menu, with hyperlinks, 11

Clip art, inserting, 44–45, 81

Clip Art gallery, 13, 24, 44, 100; dialog box, 45

Clip Art icon, 45

Clip Art on Office Online link, 24–25
Clip Gallery task pane, 94–95
Clipboard, 209–210
Coherence principle, 314
College level, 295–310; arts and humanities, 296–298; business, 306–307; math, 300–305; science, 305–306; social sciences, 298–299; teaching PowerPoint at, 295–310
College presentations, and PowerPoint, 20
Color dialog box, 107
Color schemes, 106–107; dialog box, 106–108
Coloring, changing, 46–47
Colors and Lines tab, Format AutoShape dialog box, 137–138
Colors dialog box, 64, 107, 177
Community workers project (pre-K to grade 1), 227
Companion Web site, 5, 25, 319–320; presentations/downloads, 319; resources, 320
Compress Graphic Files check box, 49
Compress Pictures button, Picture toolbar, 49
Compressing images, 49–50
Computer science, encouraging creativity/ interest, 293–294
Constructivist approach, 10
Content placeholder, 31
Context, importance of, 113–116
Contrast, changing, 46–47
Conventions, 4–5
Corel Paint Shop Pro, 257
Crispen, Patrick Douglas, 103–104, 119, 316
Crop button, Picture toolbar, 48
Cropping images, 47–48

Custom Animation task pane/dialog box, 72–73, 96, 219–223, 243
Custom tab, 107

D
Default layout, 30
Delete key, 57
Demote button, 39
Demoting text, 38
Depth button, 303–304
Design principles: animation, 291; color, use of, 291; consistency vs. variety, 290–291; interactivity, 293; introducing, 290–293; layout options, 291; nonlinear vs. linear approaches, 292
Design tab, 107, 301; Background dialog box, 58, 64, 67, 69; ribbon, 89
Design Template dialog box, 63
Design Templates tab, 63
Developer tab, 190
Diagrams, 62, 297, 298; creating, 89–92; Diagram Gallery, 90; Diagram Style Gallery, 91; inserting, 89–91; options, 92
Dictionary use project (grades 6 to 12), 251
Digital camera, gathering pictures/media using, 25
Digital photographs, 85, 101
Directions/order project (pre-K to grade 1), 227
Disable All Macros with Notification option, 190–191
Distribute Horizontally/Distribute Vertically options, 158
Domestic/wild animals project (pre-K to grade 1), 226
Downloadable presentations, 270–271
Drawing toolbar, 59–60, 62, 135–136, 147, 156, 158–159, 231–232, 238, 303–304; PowerPoint, 28
Drawing Tools Format tab, 159

E

Economics project, 290

EdLine (online delivery system), 251

Education projects, 301

Education World Web site, 273

"Effect of Background Music on Learning, Psychology of Music" (Savin), 316

"Effectiveness of PowerPoint Presentations in Lectures" (Bartsch/Cobern), 317

Effects tab, 96, 219, 220

Elementary school: animation, 284; audio effects, 286–287; images, inserting, 285; imagination/creativity development, 284–285; physical arrangement of computers, 282–283; pictures, use of, 283; PowerPoint as a chalkboard or smartboard, 287; project content, 284; project ideas, 287; saving a child's work, 286; teaching PowerPoint in, 281–288; text placeholders, introducing, 285; working on PowerPoint projects, 283

EllenFinkelstein.com, 276–277

Entrance tab, 220, 221

Equations, displaying, 302–304

European history project (grades 6 to 12), 256

F

File Extensions check box, 84

File Name text box, 33–34

Filename extensions, 84

Files of Type drop-down list, 41

Fill Color button, 240–241

Fills, formatting, 55–56

First presentation, 23–80; lesson plan, creating, 24; media, gathering, 24–25; outlining your talk, 24; starting a new presentation, 26–33; storyboard, 24

Five senses project (pre-K to grade 1), 226

Flash Cards game, 270

Folder Options dialog box, 84

Folders, creating, 34

Font Color drop-down list, 60–61

Font dialog box, 169

Font Size drop-down list, 60–61, 232

Fonts, 4

Food project (pre-K to grade 1), 226

Format AutoShape dialog box, 55–56, 58–59, 137, 232, 259, 262

Format Background dialog box, 69

Format Data Series dialog box, 89

Format Picture dialog box, 50

Format Shape dialog box, 138, 306

Format tab, 50, 55, 91, 137–138, 158, 232, 306; Drawing tools, 159; Picture Styles group, 49; ribbon, 45

Format tab, Picture Styles group, 49

Formatting palette, 37, 61; Add Objects Section, 33

Formatting toolbar, 60

Fractions projects (grades 2 to 5), 230–240

Freeform, 147, 249

From Hunting to Cattle Breeding and Agriculture project (grades 6 to 12), 255

G

Games, 120, 268–269, See also Class games; grades 2 to 5 project, 250; homemade, 270; and language skills, 299; online resources for teachers, 270–271; PowerPoint Heaven (Toh), 270; teaching with, 17

Geography projects (grades 6 to 12), 252–256; project suggestions, 253–254

Geography review: appropriate picture map, selecting, 143–150; audio/narration, adding, 150; copying/pasting slide, 144–145; creating,

143–150; hot (clickable) spot, 146–150; negative feedback slides, creating, 145–146; question slides, creating, 145–146; tips for more fun, 150–151

Geometry projects: college level, 302–305; grades 6 to 12, 260

GetStarted section of code, 195–196

GIF (.gif), 85

Good PowerPoint project, defined, 291

Google, searching for images using, 86

Graded tests, 11; calculating/displaying results, 202–206; code, adding, 190; creating, 183–212; first answer to first question, 198–200; macros, assigning to buttons, 207–209; multiple-choice test, creating, 186–189; negative feedback, 197; positive feedback, 197; PowerPoint and programming, 183–185; printing the results, 207; questions/answers, 201–202, 210–211; quiz with more than two answer choices, creating, 209–210; second answer to first question, 200–201; starting over, 207; student's name, getting, 197; testing, 209; Visual Basic Editor (VBA), opening, 190

Grades 2 to 5 projects, 229–250; language arts, 229–230; math, 230–243; science, 243–249; social studies, 250

Grades 6 to 12 projects, 251–266; art and music, 263–266; civics, 256; cross-curriculum, 266; history and geography, 254–256; interdisciplinary projects, 266; library/library science, 251–253; literature, 253–254; math, 260–263; science, 256–259

Gradient background, 65–67

Gradient tab, 66–67

Graphs, 62; creating, 86; editing, 88–89; inserting, 87–88

Grayscale, 47

Grouping the text box, 158

Guidelines for PowerPoint, 277–278

H

Handouts/notes, printing, 118–119

Hide Background Graphics check box, 58

High school, 19–20; computer science, encouraging creativity/interest in, 295–296; content organization, 292; design principles, introducing, 292–295; peer collaboration, 295; presentation skills, teaching, 291–292; teaching PowerPoint in, 289–296

High security setting, 190

Higher-order skills, development of, 282

History of Money: From Barter to Credit Cards project (grades 6 to 12), 255

History of Writing project (grades 6 to 12), 255

History projects (grades 6 to 12), 254–256; project suggestions, 255–256

"Home slide," 154

Home tab, 31, 33, 36, 92, 112

Homemade PowerPoint games, 270

Hot (clickable) spot, 146–150, 262; creating for the wrong area, 149; drawing, 146; linking to positive feedback, 147–149

Hyperlink to Slide dialog box, 133, 140

Hyperlinks: adding, 159–166; of slides, process for, 159–160; to the Web, creating, 164–166

I

Icons, 4

Image Control button, 47

Image files, 84–85; inserting, 43–44; types of, 85

Images: adding, 42–50; clip art, inserting, 44–45; coloring/contrast/brightness,

Images (continued)

changing, 46–47; compressing, 49–50; copying/pasting, 85; cropping, 47–48; digital photographs, 85, 101; editing, 45–46; finding on the WWW, 86; graphs, creating, 86; image files, inserting, 43–44; inserting, 285; scanning, 85; sources for inserting, 85–86; using, 84–92; using to invoke concepts, 307

In the Hall of the Mountain King (Grieg), 262

Indenting code, 196

Indezine.com, 267

Individual differences principles, 315

Initialize section of code, 196

Insert Chart dialog box, 87

Insert Clip Art dialog box/task pane, 144

Insert Diagram or Organization Chart button, 62

Insert Hyperlink dialog box, 129–130, 147, 164, 165

Insert Object dialog box, 258

Insert Picture from File icon, 43

Insert tab, 43, 45, 50, 54, 58, 60, 91, 92, 100, 129, 133, 135–136, 140, 144, 147, 151, 156, 160, 163, 223, 232

Insert Table dialog box, 179

Insert Text Box option, 60

Integer variables, defined, 194

Interactive activities, 10–11

Interactive maps, 11, 143–151; geography review, creating, 143–150

Interactive project, example of, 12

Interactive quizzes, 84

Interactive reviews, 125–151; forward link, creating, 139–141; "Good job!" slide, 139–141; important points, choosing, 125–128; interactivity, 128–142; multiple-choice answers,

writing, 126–128; options for more fun, 141–142; question writing, 126; "Try Again!" response, 128–130

Interactivity, 128–142, 293

Interdisciplinary projects, 227–228

Internet: finding images on, 86; as media source, 25; and multimedia files, 101

Internet4Classrooms' PowerPoint page, 267

J

Jeopardy Games page (Elizabethtown, Kentucky, Hardin County Schools Web site), 269

jeopardy-like.ppt, 181

Jeopardy (PowerPoint version), 179–181, 247; playing with teams, 180; steps in creating, 179–180; template for, 181

Jingle, Jim, 272

JPEG (.jpg, .jpeg), 85

L

Language arts projects (grades 2 to 5), 229–230

Language arts projects (pre-K to grade 1), 215–216

Language skills: and games/quizzes, 297

Layout: choosing, 30–31; options, 291

Layout tab, 89

"Learners' Perceptions of the Value of PowerPoint in Lectures" (Frey/ Birnbaum), 315

Learning: maximizing, 116–120; research on, 313–318

Learning Light e-Learning Centre, 266

Lesson plan, creating, 24

Levy, Yiftach, 314

Library/library science projects (grades 6 to 12), 249–251; book reference system, 251; book talks, 250–251

Life cycle projects (grades 2 to 5), 242–243

Line charts, 86; colors in, 307

Linear, one-way presentation, 10

Linear PowerPoint presentation, 15

Linearity vs. nonlinearity, 15–17

Link Narrations In check box, 99

Literature projects (grades 6 to 12), 251–252; grammar, 252; literary and stylistic devices, 252

Living/nonliving objects project (pre-K to grade 1), 226

Loop Until Stopped check box, 96, 242–243

M

Macro-enabled presentation, 189

Macros: assigning to buttons, 207–209; defined, 184, 207; for quiz buttons (table), 208

Major religions history projects (grades 6 to 12), 254

Map of Europe.ppt, 151

Maps of states/U.S. project (pre-K to grade 1), 227

Marcovitz, David, 183

Master Slide view, 211

Math problems/quizzes, 20

Math projects (college level), 300–305; equations, displaying, 300–302; geometry, 302–305; MathType, 300

Math projects (grades 2 to 5), 230–241; fractions, 230–237; metric system concepts, 238–241; money/percent concepts, 237–238

Math projects (grades 6 to 12), 258–261; geometry, 260; Microsoft Equation 3.0, installing, 258

Math projects (pre-K to grade 1), 216–225; animation, 217, 219–223; AutoShapes, 223–225; collecting images for, 218–219

Math Quiz-No VBA.ppt, 185

Math Quiz.ppt, 185, 192, 193, 330

Mathews, Bob, 301

MathType (Design Science), 260, 300

Mayer, Richard, 314, 315; multimedia research, 313–316

McKenzie, James, 272

Media, gathering, 24–25

Medium security setting, 191

Memorization Game.ppt, 173

Memorization games, 167–173; slide with complete text, creating, 168; slide with less text, creating, 168–173

Menu-based projects, 153–166; hyperlinks, 159–160; menu slide, 156–159; nonlinear presentations, 153–154; sections, creating, 154–156

Menu slide, 156–159; linking to sections, 163–164

Menus, 28; PowerPoint, 28

Metric system projects (grades 2 to 5), 238–241

Microphone, for narration, 98

Microsoft Clip Art and Media homepage, 24, 95, 100

Microsoft Clip Art gallery, *See* Clip Art gallery

Microsoft Clip Art page, 99; PowerPoint resources, 266

Microsoft Equation 3.0, 258–259; installing, 258; returning to PowerPoint from, 260

Microsoft in Education site tutorials, 272

Microsoft Office Clip Organizer, 93

Microsoft Office Online Clip Art page, 94–95

Microsoft Office Word dialog box, 117, 119

Middle school, 19–20; computer science, encouraging creativity/interest in,

Middle school *(continued)* 293–294; content organization, 290; design principles, introducing, 290–293; peer collaboration, 293; presentation skills, teaching, 289–290; teaching PowerPoint in, 287–294

Modality principle, 315

Money/percent projects (grades 2 to 5), 237–238

Moodle (online delivery system), 249

More Brightness or Less Brightness button, 47

More Contrast or Less Contrast button, 47

Movie window, adjusting size of, 99

.mpeg (video format), 99

Multimedia, 81–101; adding to learning, 82–83; background music, 95–97; concept visualization, 82; content, 101; creativity/thinking, sparking, 82; data visualization, 82; defined, 81–82; diagrams, 89–92; examples, showing, 83; graphs, 86–89; images, using, 84–92; metaphors, 83; mood, creating, 83; music file, 93–95; music/sounds, adding to fun with, 82; narration, 98–99; processes, showing, 82; research on, 313–318; resources, 100–101; sounds, 93–95; using effectively, 82–84; video, 99–100; words, drawing attention to, 83

Multimedia Learning (Mayer), 313–315

Multimedia principle, 314

Multimedia Settings tab, 96

Multiple-choice answers, writing, 126–128

Multiple-choice quizzes, 11, 16; sample of, 13

Multiple-choice test: cover slide, 186–188; creating, 186–189; finishing the presentation, 189; first question slide, 188; fourth slide, 189; third slide, 189

Music file, adding, 92–96

N

Narration: adding, 97–99; adding to interactive maps, 150; microphone, 98

Nebo school district (Spanish Fork, Utah), downloadable presentations, 269

Negative feedback, 125; example of, 13

New Presentation dialog box, 63

New presentations, *See also* Presentations; New Slide button, 36

New Slide dialog box, 26, 29, 33

Nonlinear PowerPoint presentations, 16, 153–154

Normal view, 27–28

North Carolina State University rubric, 276

Note taking, using PowerPoint to help students, 116–118

Notes, 4; adding to a slide, 31–32; printing, 118–119

Notes Below Slides option, 119

Notes Next to Slides option, 119

Notes pane, 28; Normal view, 28

"Now That I Know PowerPoint, How Can I Use It to TEACH?" (Crispen), 316

O

Object animation, 72; adding, 73–75

Objectivist (nonconstructivist) methods, 10

Omit Background Graphics option, Master check box, 58

On Mouse Click check box, 164

Online resources for teachers, 265–276; articles, 271–272; downloadable presentations, 270–271; games, 268–269; guidelines/rubrics, 275–276; PowerPoint and education resources, 266–267; tips/tutorials, 272–275

Open dialog box, 41
Order and Timing tab, 219
Our Zoo Trip.ppt, 216
Outline: entering in PowerPoint, 37–40;
     importing, 40–41
Outline tab, 28, 30, 37–40, 42, 44, 79, 104,
     118
Outlines, formatting, 55–56
Outlining toolbar, 39
Outlining your talk, 24

P
Page Setup dialog box, 301–302
Patterns tab, 89
Peer collaboration, 293
Pete's Power Point Station, 269
Photographs, digital, 85, 101
PICT, 85
Picture background, 67–69
Picture Styles feature, 49
Picture tab, 68, 69
Picture toolbar, 47–48
Picture Tools Format tab, 159
Pie charts, 86; colors in, 307
Pie Slice shape, 233
Pilgrim project (grades 2 to 5), 247
Plant parts project (pre-K to grade 1), 225
Play Sound dialog box, 96–97, 242–243
Play Using Animation order check box,
     96–97
PNG (.png), 85
Positive feedback, 11; example of, 9, 14
Powerful PowerPoint for Educators: Using
     Visual Basic for Applications to Make
     PowerPoint Interactive (Marcovitz),
     183
PowerPoint: animation capabilities, 10; as
     a chalkboard or SmartBoard, 285; and
     the constructivist approach, 10;
     creating projects using, 123–212;
     drawing toolbar, 28; effective teaching
and, 9; entering an outline in, 37–40;
     first presentation, 23–80; flexibility of,
     9; incorporating in your teaching, 9;
     interdisciplinary projects, 227–228;
     menus, 28; and multimedia, 81–101;
     online resources for teachers using,
     265–276; power of, 10; problem- and
     project-based activities, creation of,
     10–11; and programming, 183–185;
     repetition, value of, 12–13; ribbon, 28;
     starting, 26; and storytelling skills
     development, 230; as support for
     instruction, 11–19; teaching at college
     level, 295–310; teaching in elementary
     school, 279–286; teaching in middle
     and high school, 287–294; teaching to
     students, 277–310; 3-D capabilities of,
     303–304; toolbars, 28; user-
     friendliness of, 280; versatility of,
     10–11; when not to use, 20–21
PowerPoint accessibility (article), 272
"PowerPoint as an Interactive Multimedia
     Lesson" (Tech Learning Web site
     article), 271
PowerPoint dialog box, 26, 63
PowerPoint discussion group (Web site),
     274
PowerPoint FAQ (www.pptfaq.com), 274
PowerPoint for Teachers Web site, 319
PowerPoint Games (Jefferson County,
     Tennessee), 269
PowerPoint Heaven (Toh), 268–269
"PowerPoint in the Classroom" (article),
     272
PowerPoint Macro-Enabled Presentation
     option, 189
PowerPoint presentations (Jefferson
     County, Tennessee), 271
PowerPoint projects: for grades 2 to 5,
     229–248; for grades 6 to 12, 249–263; for
     pre-kindergarten to grade 1, 211–228

PowerPoint show, 79

PPT4Teachers, 267

Pre-kindergarten to grade 1 projects, 211–228; language arts, 215–216; math, 216–225; oral instructions, 215; science, 225–226; social studies, 227

Preferences dialog box, 49

Prekindergarten/kindergarten, 19

Presentation Magic (PowerPak for K–12), 269

Presentation skills, teaching, 289–290

Presentations: animation, adding, 71–73; backgrounds, adding, 62–69; charts, 62; context, importance of, 114–115; diagrams, 62; images, adding, 42–50; inserting a slide using the default layout, 29–30; moving around, 41–42; navigation method, 115; Normal view, 27–28; shapes, 50–62; slide, adding, 28; slide shows, 76–79; text, adding, 36–37; title slide, creating, 28–29; viewed as a class, 115; viewed individually, 115–116; you as, 120

Previous Slide button, 42

Print dialog box, 118, 118–119

Print What drop-down list, 118

PrintablePage procedure, 205

PrintablePage section, 211

PrintResults macro, 205

PrintResults procedure, 207

PrintResults section, 211

Problem-based learning: encouraging, 17–19; as modern schools' priority, 20; and PowerPoint, 285

Problem-solving skills, development of, 20, 280

Procedure, defined, 195

Programming, and PowerPoint, 183–185

Project Gallery dialog box (Mac), 26

Project-based learning, and PowerPoint, 285

Psychology projects, 298

Q

Question-and-answer game, 11

Quick Access toolbar, 69

Quizzes, 11, 16–17; and language skills, 297

R

Record Narration dialog box, 98–99

Redundancy principle, 315

Remedial work, and PowerPoint, 20

Repetition, value of, 12–13

Resize Placeholder/Shape to Fit Text check box, 211

Retention, assessing, 17

Reviews, 11, 16

Ribbon, 28, 45; PowerPoint, 28

Rindsberg, Steve, 274

Rubrics, 275–276

Run Macro option, Action Settings dialog box, 208

S

Save As dialog box, 33–35

Save As Type box, 34

Save button, Standard toolbar, 33–34

Save Image As, 42, 144

Scavenger Hunt game, 268

"Scholarly Lecture, The: How to Stand and Deliver" (*Chronicle of Higher Education* article), 272

School fair projects, 288–289, 293

Science and social studies fair, 288–289, 293

Science PowerPoint Tips and Tutorials (blog), 274

Science projects (college level), 305–306

Science projects (grades 2 to 5), 241–247; animals/habitats, 244; cells, 244–245; life cycles, 242–243; solar system, 245–247; using pictures/video, 247; water cycle, 244

Science projects (grades 6 to 12), 254–257; animation, 256; biology and life science, 257; clickable graphics, creating, 257; earth science and geology, 256–257; Freeform shape, 257; physical laws/phenomena, 256

Science projects (pre-K to grade 1), 225–226

"Scoring Power Points" (McKenzie), 272

Sections: linking menu slide to, 163–164; linking to the menu, 160–161

Security settings, checking, 190–191

Select Picture dialog box, 45

Select Place in Document dialog box, 130–131, 136, 148

Select to Animate dialog box, 96

Send To Microsoft Office Word dialog box, 119

Set Microphone Level option, Record Narration·dialog box, 99

Shape Effects button, Format tab, 55

Shapes, 50–62; aligning, 58–59; background graphics, removing from a slide, 56–58; editing, 55; fills, formatting, 55–56; formatting, 55; inserting, 50–51; outlines, formatting, 55–56; resizing, 58–59; slide master, using, 52–54

Shapes button, 160; Insert tab, 147

Shapes (PowerPoint 2007), 254, See also AutoShapes

Size and Position dialog box, 58

Size tab, 59

Slide: adding, 28; with a specified layout, inserting, 32–33

Slide Layout task pane, 31, 33, 36, 155

Slide master, 57; using, 52–54

Slide Master tab, 67, 69, 105

Slide pane, Normal view, 27

Slide Show Slide Transition option, 164

Slide Show tab, 98

Slide Show view, 95, 99, 149, 185

Slide shows, 76–79; navigating through slides, 78–79; projectors, 76; saving your project as a PowerPoint show, 79; Slide Show view, 77–79

Slide Sorter button, 70

Slide Sorter view, 141, 159; moving, 69–70

Slide Transition dialog box, 75, 131–132, 134, 164; testing, 166

Slide transitions, adding, 72, 75

Slides: copying/pasting, 71; creating navigation between, 161–162; deleting, 71; dragging a slide to new position, 70–71; moving, 69–70; navigating through, 78–79; pasting Home button to, 161

Slides tab, 66–69, 69, 104; Normal view, 28

SmartArt diagrams (PowerPoint 2007), 62, 91, 306

SmartArt Graphic dialog box, 91

SmartArt Styles group, Design tab, 91

SmartBoard, PowerPoint as, 285

Social sciences projects (college level), 298–299

Social studies projects: grades 2 to 5, 247; pre-K to grade 1, 227

Sociology projects, 299

Solar system project (grades 2 to 5), 245–247

Solid background, 64–65

Sound effects, adding, 141–142

Sound Options dialog box, 96, 243–244

Sound Settings tab, 96

Sound Tools Options tab, 96, 243

Sounds, 108–109; adding, 92–95

Spatial contiguity principle, 314

Special effects, 106–109

Special, Sue, 272

Spelling Game.ppt, 176

Spelling games, 173–176, *See also* Class games; Games; positive feedback slide, 174–175; slide with wrongly spelled word, creating, 173–174

Standard tab, 107; Colors dialog box, 177

StartAgain macro, 205

Stop Playing section, Play Sound dialog box, 243–244

Storyboard, 24

Storytelling skills development, and PowerPoint, 230

String variables, defined, 194

Student art/recordings, and multimedia, 101

Symbols, 4

T

Table Tools Design tab, 238

Tables, 298–299

Teachers Improving Learning with Technology (blog), 272

Tech Learning Web site, 271

Temporal contiguity principle, 314

10-Question Math Quiz.ppt, 211

Text: adding, 36–37; demoting, 38; using wisely, 112–113

Text animation, adding, 72–73

Text-based vs. picture-based presentations, 13

Text Box button, 156

Text Box tab, 166, 211

Text boxes, inserting/editing, 59–61

Textures tab, 54, 55

Theme colors, 106

Thomas Edison project, 288

3-D capabilities, PowerPoint, 304

3-D Rotation options, 304

3-D Settings toolbar, 304

TIFF (.tif, .tiff), 85

Tilt buttons, 303–304

Tips, 4

Title and Content layout, 36, 57, 155, 156, 179

Title master, 57

Title Only layout, 156, 189, 231

Title slide, creating, 28

TJ's Ed Web, 269

Toh, Shawn, 268

Toolbars, 28; PowerPoint, 28

Tracy Marks's Web site, 266

Transition Speed drop-down list, 75

Transparency slider, 55, 138

Transportation project (pre-K to grade 1), 227

Trivia game, 268

Trust Center Settings button, 190–191

"Try Again!" slide, 128–130; back link, creating, 132; button, adding, 132–134; copying/pasting, 142; invisible clickable button, inserting, 134–135

Tutorials, online resources for teachers, 272–275

U

Ungraded reviews, creating, 17

Using PowerPoint in the Classroom project (Alice Christy), 266

Using PowerPoint in the Classroom project (Regina, Saskatchewan, school district), 266

V

Variables, 194–195

Video, 99–100; formats, 99; inserting, 99; movie window, adjusting size of, 99

View tab, 52, 70, 84, 105, 112

Visual Basic Editor, 209–210; GetStarted section of code, 195–196; Initialize section of code, 196; introductory section of code, 194–195; pasting in code, 192–193; understanding the code, 193

Visual Basic for Applications (VBA), 184, 293–294, 310; benefits of, 184; opening the VBA window, 190–192; and reusable code, 185

W

Warnings, 4

Water cycle animation.ppt, 244

Water Cycle presentation, 50; completed diagram, 61; title slide, creating, 28–29

Water cycle project (grades 2 to 5), 244

Water Cycle Review.ppt, 141

Watermark option, 47

Weather patterns project (pre-K to grade 1), 226

Who Wants to Be a Millionaire? (Power-Point version), 176–179, 247; fifty-fifty-choice, 178; music, adding, 178; steps in creating, 176–178; template for, 177, 179

whowantstobeamillionaire-like.ppt, 179

WMF (.wmf), 85

.wmv (video format), 99